Swedish Vo
in the Russo
Winter War, 1

Swedish Volunteers in the Russo-Finnish Winter War, 1939–1940

MARTINA SPRAGUE

McFarland & Company, Inc., Publishers
Jefferson, North Carolina, and London

LIBRARY OF CONGRESS CATALOGUING-IN-PUBLICATION DATA

Sprague, Martina.
Swedish volunteers in the Russo-Finnish Winter War, 1939-1940 / Martina Sprague.
p. cm.
Includes bibliographical references and index.

ISBN 978-0-7864-3981-2
softcover : 50# alkaline paper ♾

1. Russo-Finnish War, 1939–1940— Participation, Swedish. 2. Russo-Finnish War, 1939–1940— Political aspects. 3. Russo-Finnish War, 1939–1940— Diplomatic history. 4. Sweden — Foreign relations — Soviet Union. 5. Soviet Union — Foreign relations — Sweden. 6. Sweden — Foreign relations — Finland. 7. Finland — Foreign relations — Sweden. 8. Sweden. Armén — History — Russo-Finnish War, 1939–1940. 9. Finland. Maavoimat — History — Russo-Finnish War, 1939–1940. 10. Soviet Union. Raboche-Krest'ianskaia Krasnaia Armiia — History — Russo-Finnish War, 1939–1940. I. Title.
DL1105.F672S87 2010
948.9703'2 — dc22 2010025540

British Library cataloguing data are available

Front cover: F19 flight squadron pilots and ground personnel preparing an aircraft for takeoff (Krigsarkivet, Svenska Frivilligkåren, Kriget 1939–1940); inset, Finland's Frihetskors, Cross of Liberty 4th class (Krigsarkivet, Finlandskommitten, 1939–1940)

Manufactured in the United States of America

McFarland & Company, Inc., Publishers
Box 611, Jefferson, North Carolina 28640
www.mcfarlandpub.com

To Lars-Erik (Lasse) Jokela,
Friend and Finn

Table of Contents

Military and Political Figures (by Country)

Sweden

Beckhammar, Hugo (Major, Chief for F19 Flight Squadron)
Douglas, Archibald (Commander of the Northern Army Corps)
Dyrssen, Magnus (Commander Combat Group I)
Ehrensvärd, Carl August (Vice Admiral, Commander)
Ekström, Martin (Commander Combat Group III)
Günther, Christian (Minister of Foreign Affairs from December 13, 1939)
Hansson, Per Albin (Prime Minister)
Linder, Ernst (General, Chief for the Volunteer Corps)
Sandler, Rickard (Minister of Foreign Affairs until December 13, 1939)
Sköld, Per Edvin (Minister of Defense)
Tamm, Viking (Commander Combat Group II)

Finland

Cajander, Aimo Kaarlo (Prime Minister until December 1, 1939)
Erkko, Eljas (Minister of Foreign Affairs until December 1, 1939)
Kallio, Kyösti (President)
Mannerheim, Carl Gustaf (Commander-in-Chief of the Armed Forces)
Niukkanen, Juho (Minister of Defense)
Ryti, Risto (Finnish Statesman, Prime Minister from December 1, 1939)
Söderhjelm, Johan Otto (Minister of Justice)
Tanner, Väinö Alfred (Minister of Foreign Affairs from December 1, 1939)
Yrjö-Koskinen, Aarno (Finnish Minister in Moscow)

The Soviet Union

Khrushchev, Nikita (Secretary of the Moscow Regional Committee)
Kollontay, Alexandra (Stalin's Envoy in Stockholm)
Kuusinen, Otto Vilhelm (Former Leader of the Finnish Communist Party)
Meretskov, Kirill (Commander-in-Chief of Leningrad Military District)
Molotov, Vyacheslav (Minister of Foreign Affairs)
Stalin, Joseph (Leader of the Soviet Union)

Germany

Blücher, Wipert von (German Minister in Finland)
Goebbels, Josef (Minister of Propaganda)
Hitler, Adolf (Reichskanzler)
Ribbentrop, Joachim von (Minister of Foreign Affairs)

The Western Allies

Chamberlain, Neville (Prime Minister of Great Britain)
Churchill, Winston (British Statesman, later Prime Minister)
Daladier, Édouard (Prime Minister of France)
Ganeval, Jean (Colonel, France)
Ling, C .G. (British Military Attaché in Finland)

Introduction

Finland's heroic struggle to preserve independence and defend its territories, citizens, and culture against the Russian superpower to the east has been acknowledged many times, as have the bravery and resourcefulness of the Finnish troops in the 105-day conflict termed the Russo-Finnish Winter War of 1939–40 (hereafter shortened to the Winter War). But the story of the more than 8,000 Swedish volunteers who fought for Finland's cause is largely unexplored outside the borders of Sweden. The difficulty of the political situation of neutral Sweden, sandwiched between Nazi Germany and the "Russian Bear," resulted in that country having to walk a diplomatic tightrope when determining if and how it would support Finland's cause. Plans for a Swedish volunteer force were laid several months prior to the Soviet Union's invasion of Finland on November 30, 1939. The day of the attack when the Red Army violated Finland's borders and the Soviet air force bombed Helsinki, volunteer recruitment centers opened within Sweden.

Sweden's goal in coming to the aid of Finland was two-fold: to preserve Finland as a buffer against Russia — if Finland fell, Sweden believed it would be next — and to preserve the tradition and camaraderie that existed between the Swedes and the Finns. But problems developed. Although the Swedish and Finnish soldiers were united in purpose, they had never trained under common command and did not speak the same language.[1] Part of the Swedish volunteer force had received no military training at all, and only a small part had been trained in winter operations. Many of the soldiers, particularly those from southern Sweden, had never fired a weapon or stood on a pair of skis.[2] The Swedish volunteers also lacked adequate supplies of weapons, ammunition, and clothing and faced several other difficulties such as frost injuries and influenza.

Of even greater importance than the problems the individual soldiers suffered on the battlefield was the extraordinarily complex political situation that developed with respect to Swedish neutrality in World War II (or noncombatant status in the case of the Winter War).[3] Germany's invasion of Poland and England's and France's declaration of war against Germany were not a threat to neutrality per se. Sweden's geographical location by the Baltic Sea, however, and the access to numerous ports had made the country disputed territory for most of its history. Sweden's natural resources of iron ore proved essential to Hitler's weapons industry and became a hotly debated issue between the Western Allies and Germany, with Sweden in focus, throughout the war. Moreover, the Soviet invasion of Finland, which at first appeared an isolated incident not directly tied to the hostilities in the rest of Europe, came to upset the delicate balance of power in the region and mandated that Sweden act as mediator for peace. Of utmost importance was that the Russo-Finnish conflict be kept separate from the greater war between Germany and the Allies. Had peace not come when it did roughly a hundred days after the first shots were fired, an Allied invasion of Sweden would have been probable and would have turned the country into a primary World War II battleground.

The Winter War was not the first war in which Sweden had come to the assistance of a foreign nation. Although Sweden's last "official" war took place in 1814 — when the king to be, Karl XIV Johan (Jean-Baptiste Bernadotte, a marshal under Napoleon who had been imported from France to be crown prince of Sweden and repair Sweden's weak leadership), invaded Norway in an almost bloodless conflict that resulted in three dead and fifteen injured Swedish soldiers, and forced Norway into union with Sweden — and despite Sweden's neutrality declaration in both world wars, Swedish citizens had participated in foreign wars and humanitarian missions on several continents from the nineteenth century to present day, often fighting for the ideal of helping an oppressed people attain social and political equality.[4] These wars ranged from Denmark's conflicts with the German states in the mid-nineteenth century to the Anglo-Boer War in the early twentieth century when a small number of Swedish volunteers fought on the side of the Boer Republics (an even smaller number was engaged on the British side as well). In the twentieth century, Swedish volunteers joined the Swedish Brigade and served in the Finnish Civil War of 1918 (also called Finland's War of Independence) on the side of the "white" nationalists against the "red" communists. Swedish volunteers fought in the Spanish Civil War of 1936–39 in the struggle against Francisco Franco's forces who were supported by Adolf Hitler and Benito Mussolini. After the conclusion of the Russo-Finnish Winter War, which is the focus of this book, Swedish volunteers served in the Finnish Continuation War of 1941–44, and in the German Waffen-SS in the anti–Bolshevik campaign in the Soviet Union. The number of Swedish volunteers in most of these wars was relatively low, totaling in the hundreds (the Continuation War employed approximately 1,700 volunteers in the Finnish Army).[5] Only in the Winter War did the number of volunteers reach an amazing 8,260, with several thousand more applicants desiring to serve but never seeing battle.[6]

At the start of the war, the Swedish government considered it unsuitable to publicly announce its intention to support the volunteers who went to Finland to fight. Earlier that year, Germany and the Soviet Union had entered into a treaty of nonaggression — the *Nichtangriffspakt*— for the purpose of preventing or at least delaying hostilities toward one another. A key issue of this pact was the mutual promise to come to each other's assistance should either country come under attack by a third party. Sweden thus feared that if the volunteer corps became public knowledge, Germany would enter the war in defense of the Soviet Union. Some historians have argued that Sweden was overly worried about a German retaliation and that it was not in Hitler's best interest to allow the Soviet Union to conquer Finland and establish itself so close to the Swedish iron ore mines. It is possible that Hitler was in favor of a long conflict between the Soviets and the Finns because it would have prevented Stalin from focusing on the Balkans.[7] Although the Western Allies offered to send help to Finland, Sweden denied these troops passage through northern Sweden because it would violate Swedish neutrality and jeopardize relations with Germany. Concerns also lingered that the Allies might occupy the mines in northern Sweden and halt the exports of iron ore to Germany. Such an event would certainly trigger a German retaliation.[8] If Sweden were pulled into the war, there would be very unhappy consequences for all of Scandinavia. A recurring question was thus the extent to which Sweden should exercise neutrality. Restraint was necessary in order to assume a strictly defensive role in the war. At the same time, the Swedes believed that they had an obligation to come to the assistance of the other Nordic countries, including Finland, with material and voluntary manpower.

The first volunteers arrived in Finland around the turn of the year. Although the volunteer corps was initially forbidden to advertise in the newspapers, a few weeks into the war the government allowed the recruitment centers to advertise on public transport. Meanwhile, more recruitment centers opened in Sweden, working feverishly until 8,260 volunteers out of 12,705 applicants stood ready to support Finland's cause. The Swedish volunteer force became the largest assembly of volunteers in any modern war.[9] In addition to the troops fighting at the Salla front in northern Finland, approximately two hundred men served in the artillery in Vasa in the western part of Finland. Another few hundred served in the air defense of Turku (see also Åbo), in the coastal defense of the Pellinki Islands east of Helsinki, and in a small fighter and bomber squadron in northern Finland. Several hundred doctors and nurses (and veterinarians for the horses) volunteered at military and civilian hospitals, and in field hospitals established by the Swedish Red Cross.[10]

Despite Sweden's enormous efforts to support Finland, the role of the Swedish volunteers has been mentioned only in passing in history books about World War II. If Sweden is mentioned at all, it is generally with focus on the questionable and much debated neutrality breach toward the end of the war when Sweden allowed German troops on leave to transit through Swedish territory. Moreover, Russian and Finnish history is often overshadowed by the attention afforded the German soldier in written sources detailing the World War II experience. Sweden's role in the Winter War may therefore seem even less significant when viewed against the backdrop of twentieth century war history. The purpose of this book is to fill that gap by examining the trials and tribulations of the Swedish volunteer force in the Russo-Finnish Winter War of 1939–40, a conflict that stretched across the desolate and difficult terrain of the thirteen hundred kilometer long border between Finland and the Soviet Union, much of which consisted of marshes and forests with few and poorly maintained roads. The book will bring attention to the unusually large number of volunteers, unequalled in any other military volunteer mission, who in defense of Western democracy offered their lives for Finland's cause on the ground and in the air.

Although the focus of the book is the Swedish volunteer force in Finland, history and politics cannot be studied in isolation. In order to provide a more complete picture of the complex situation that became World War II, some overlap with respect to Finnish and Soviet combat operations is necessary, as is a study of Soviet, German, and Allied political interactions with Sweden and Finland. A secondary aim of the book is thus to dissect the political situation that neutral Sweden, a country of relative obscurity, had to juggle in order to further its most cherished values of social equality and economic security in a time that demanded military buildup and political involvement on the world scene. The role that the Winter War played in the early stages of World War II helped shape many of the decisions made by Germany's Reichskanzler Adolf Hitler, and makes the study of the political and social conditions on the Scandinavian peninsula particularly crucial to understanding the development of the conflict between Germany and the Western Allies, and Hitler's subsequent invasion of the Soviet Union.

The purpose of the book is to offer a new perspective on the Winter War by approaching it from the viewpoint of neutral Sweden. The book is divided into five chapters. Chapter 1 examines the political background of the Winter War and the events that preceded the conflict, the Soviet Union's request for territory, and the first shots fired at Mainila on the Karelian Isthmus. It provides an assessment of the Soviet Union's strategic plan, Finland's defensive measures, and Sweden's reaction to the war. Chapter 2 brings to light the extraordinary efforts Sweden made to send material assistance to Finland. It discusses recruitment propaganda, volunteer arrival and training in Torneå by the Finnish-Swedish border at the top of the Gulf of Bothnia, and the difficulties the volunteers encountered during the ski march to the front. Chapter 3 covers combat operations on the ground and in the air, including the setbacks the volunteers suffered due to weather and terrain in subsequent battles against the Red Army. This chapter also analyzes the tactics of the primary belligerents: the Finnish and Soviet armies. Chapter 4 examines the role of Sweden as a mediator for peace, the threat of invasion by the Western Allies, and the possibility that the war would be brought to the Scandinavian peninsula. It discusses the political struggles that led to the armistice on March 13, 1940, and the concessions Finland had to make as a result of the hard-won peace. It covers the final bloody exchange and the general sentiment of the soldiers once they learned that peace had been negotiated. Chapter 5 provides an analysis of the Finnish, Soviet, and Swedish armies; their accomplishments and losses, and their strengths and weaknesses. It makes an assessment of the conditions experienced by the volunteers taken captive in Soviet prison camps. This chapter also discusses the social and political forces that motivated the Swedish leadership to promote neutrality and avoid official military engagement in the war.

For her research, the author has relied on a large quantity of primary source material from Sweden including political documents, telegrams and other correspondence, and accounts of individual experiences such as memoirs, diaries, and military logs detailing the day-to-day activities of the war. A number of secondary sources including books, articles, and documentaries have also been enlisted in order to provide a balanced perspective that is as void as possible of the author's personal biases. The author is indebted to Bo Lundström, Per Clason, and Bertil Olofsson at the War Archives in Stockholm, Sweden for help in answering questions, locating documents, and providing most of the photos that appear in this book.

1

Political Background of the Winter War

A Brief Swedish and Finnish History

Sweden's role in the Russo-Finnish Winter War and the people's motivation for lending Finland support can be understood best if one acquires some basic insight into the shared histories of the two countries. At the conclusion of the Thirty Years' War, 1618–48, all of Finland belonged to Sweden. The Great Northern War and the 1708–09 Battle of Poltava, considered Sweden's greatest military catastrophe — where more than half of Sweden's forces were annihilated in a single battle in the Ukraine by the Russian troops of Peter the Great — were instrumental in ending Sweden's role as a great power and consequently leading to Sweden having to surrender several of its possessions east of the Baltic. In 1809, during continued conflicts with the great enemy to the east, Sweden lost Finland to Russia. This was an emotional loss that the population of Sweden never quite did get over. The peace treaty, signed between the Kingdom of Sweden and the Emperor of Russia on September 17, 1809, mentioned several points of historical value. Article IV might be of particular interest. In brief, it stated that His Majesty the King of Sweden and any successors to the Swedish throne promised to forego for the benefit of the Emperor of Russia and any successors to the Russian Empire for all future days the Finnish territories which the Emperor of Russia had conquered during the war, including the inhabitants, cities, harbors, fortifications, villages, and islands of these territories. Instrumental to this agreement was the surrender of the valuable Åland Islands located in the Baltic Sea approximately halfway between Sweden and Finland. The King of Sweden further promised that neither he nor his successors would engage in a future attempt to repossess the forfeited territories. According to Article V, the new border would stretch along the Åland Islands to Torneå at the top of the Gulf of Bothnia. Since

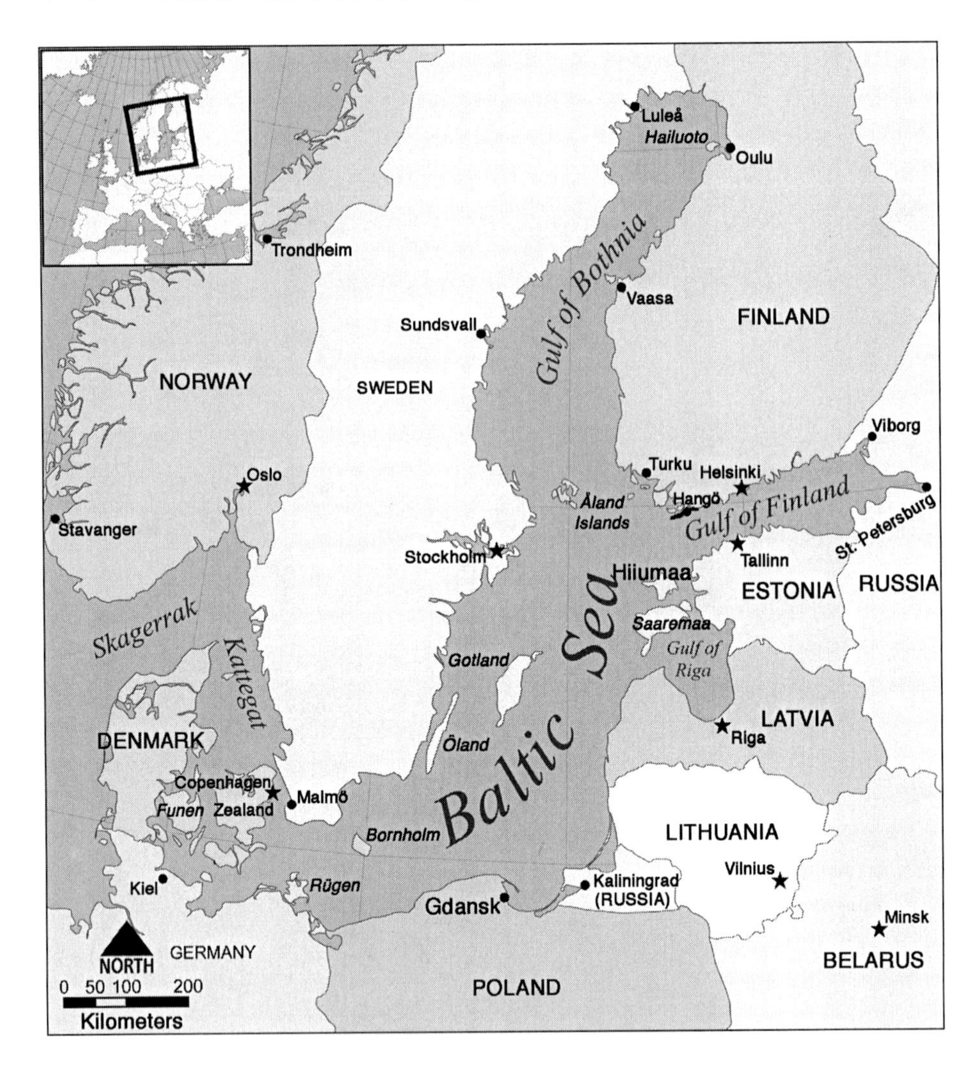

The Scandinavian peninsula by the Baltic Sea. Note Sweden's long coastline. The country's strategic location has been envied by outside powers for hundreds of years, and has resulted in Sweden's involvement in numerous conflicts particularly with Russia for most of its history (source: Norman Einstein; slightly revised).

both Sweden and Finland have large archipelagos along their coastlines, it was further decided that the islands closest to the coast of Finland should befall to Russia and those closest to the coast of Sweden should remain with Sweden. Article X declared that any Finns residing in Sweden at the time and any Swedes residing in Finland should be given the option of returning to their respective fatherlands.[1]

The people of Finland continued to display loyalty toward the Swedish king after the treaty was signed, which prompted Tsar Alexander I to make Finland a Grand Duchy of Russia. Finland could then retain its own laws, language, administration, and constitution. The compromise was not without political ambition, however. Not only did it permit Finland to become relatively prosperous through exports, particularly timber, to Western Europe, it permitted the country to remain a good trade partner with Russia.[2] The tsar also hoped that Finland's beneficial geographical location would act as a barrier to foreign aggression directed at St. Petersburg, the Russian capital and center of power.[3] Since its establishment, St. Petersburg had controlled the land bridge between Russia and Finland across the Karelian Isthmus. Helsinki, just across the Gulf of Finland, had been a rival city to St. Petersburg for three hundred years. In 1917, St. Petersburg became "the heart of [the] revolution" that destroyed tsarist Russia. The city was renamed Leningrad in 1924 in honor of the first leader of the Soviet Union.[4]

Russia's march toward superpower status had started to worry the Swedish leadership immediately after the traumatic loss of Finland in 1809. When Sweden imported French Marshal Jean-Baptiste Bernadotte as a suitable successor to the throne a year later, it was in the hope that the Marshal would help Sweden get back on its feet. (Bernadotte ascended the throne in 1818, after serving as crown prince for a number of years.) But the new crown prince would not hear of any attempts at restoring the old boundaries of the Swedish empire and set his sights instead on Norway. Bernadotte's decision had profound consequences for the future of the country. Although Sweden may well have had the military capacity and leadership in the French Marshal to snatch Finland from Russia, it would likely have resulted in continued conflicts with the great enemy. By foregoing this option, the people of Sweden could live in relative peace for several generations. Bernadotte's successor Oscar I continued to worry about Russian expansion and reintroduced the idea of retaking Finland, this time with the assistance of the Western powers, and bringing the country into the already existing Swedish-Norwegian union. A driving force behind the king's ambitions was the fear that Russia might want to fortify the Åland Islands, which were strategically located in the Baltic Sea.[5] The national identity of these islands and the responsibility for their defense in case of war would be debated for the next hundred years. In the end, the idea of a joint Swedish and Finnish defense of the islands fell on deaf ears.

Finland was treated relatively well as a Russian state and protectorate. With the industrial explosion of the mid to late nineteenth century, things began to change. Timber from the forests became much sought after on the world market. People left their farms and moved to the cities, and farmers could no longer profit as before from cultivating the earth. Better and more efficient tools and machinery led to a decreased need for manual labor on the farms. These changes propagated pessimistic attitudes among the population, who became receptive to social reform. Labor parties began to gain a foothold in Finland and appeared worrisome to Russia's leadership, particularly since much of the activity took place so close to the Russian capital.[6] As the nineteenth century drew to a close, Russia became critical of the higher quality life and the many privileges the Finns enjoyed, and entertained the thought of creating a greater unified Russia. When the hated Nikolai Bobrikov, who was appointed by Tsar Nicholas II as the Governor-General of Finland in 1898, began a campaign for the "russification" of Finland, large numbers of Finns resisted the oppressive measures that demanded subordination to the Russian Empire and refused to report for military service. Loyalty to the tsar declined further as Russia was defeated by Japan in the Russo-Japanese War of 1904–05.[7]

With the outbreak of World War I, Russian troops poured in great numbers into Finland, causing fear in the populace that Russia would attempt to completely annihilate Finnish autonomy. The political unrest led to conflicts between socialist and non-socialist forces. At the completion of the Russian Revolution and the collapse of the Russian monarchy in 1917, many Finns considered a rebellion leading to Finland's permanent independence from the country that would become the Soviet Union the only viable option.[8] After six hundred years of Swedish domination and one hundred years of Russian rule, the time was ripe for action, particularly since World War I had taken a heavy toll on the Russians and weakened their ability to launch a strong counterforce.

Ensuring the country a political standing that would afford the citizens prosperity in the long run required competent military leadership, however. Thus, Finland started to look toward Germany for assistance with training of military professionals. Hundreds of Finns passed through neutral Sweden via ship or railway to seek education as noncommissioned and commissioned officers in Germany. Germany, who was still engaged in war with Russia, responded positively to the opportunity to train the Finnish troops.[9] The nearly two thousand Finnish volunteers who received military training in Germany in preparation for the War of Independence, however, were seldom mentioned in military circles in Helsinki.[10]

Why was Germany willing to lend Finland a helping hand? Although Finland was grateful for the assistance, the core German motives were likely self-serving. The new political situation that developed as Germany engaged in offensive action against the Baltic states and occupied Estonia also demanded a hand in Finland's future. Should a new eastern front be established and the Western Allies manage to land troops in Murmansk, the results would be catastrophic for Germany. Finland constituted an important strategic location. By assisting Finland on its road to independence, Germany would ensure a weaker Russia. Germany's ability to exert pressure and control the spread of hostile forces from Russia through intervention in Finland was thus of prime political importance.[11] When civil war broke out in Finland not much later, Germany would transport weapons and ammunition to "white" Finland via Swedish territory.[12]

Finland's strife to establish a European-style parliamentary democracy did not come without setbacks, however. "In 1918, [as] Finnish communists supported by the Soviet Union attempted to overthrow that government ... [the] Finnish aristocrat Baron Carl Gustaf Mannerheim, a former general in Russia's imperial army," was chosen to lead Finland in the struggle for independence.[13] Upon accepting the position as Supreme Commander, Mannerheim declined armed intervention from Germany or Sweden, although he welcomed volunteers and material assistance. He defended his position by emphasizing how "a nation's liberation, if it is to have lasting effect, must come by the people's own efforts, trials, and blood."[14] He meant that a state's sovereignty could be guarded only if the citizens were united and ready to defend their culture and ideals. Without unity an army could not be strong, and only a people confident in their beliefs could meet future trials successfully. The security and honor of the nation and the welfare of the people had now become Finland's primary aspirations.[15] Mannerheim's ideals would have profound meaning twenty years later when Finland's renewed conflicts with the Soviet Union demanded extraordinary unity, morale, and fighting spirit.

The people of Sweden, who had still not managed to heal their emotional scars from the catastrophic loss of Finland a hundred years earlier, followed the struggle with interest and launched an intensive propaganda campaign on behalf of the "whites," or the Finnish nationalists who favored an independent Finland. (The opposing force, the "reds" or the communists, was leaning toward a Finland that was integrated as part of Russia.) Sweden exported large amounts of material resources to Finland including humanitarian necessities such as medicine, tents, and blankets in addition to weapons, which the government had officially placed a ban on shipping but which nevertheless made their way to Finland.[16] Sweden also organized a volunteer force called the Swedish Brigade consisting of approximately 1100 volunteers, 94 officers, and 500 other commanders, and whose members fought on behalf of the "whites" and served as mediators in the civil war.[17] Opinions varied and not all Swedes sympathized with the "whites," however. Many Swedes viewed the war as an internal conflict in which Sweden ought not to get involved, but the Swedish people at large supported Finland's struggle for independence.[18] The idea of chasing the communists back behind their own lines seemed even more attractive when viewed in light of the fact that Finland had been a legitimate territory of Sweden for much of its history. The Swedish government proceeded cautiously in order to avoid violating the neutrality laws, and made it clear that any request for official military help would be denied. Releasing Finland from Russia's grip seemed the ethical thing to do. Yet, Sweden's neutrality must be protected at all cost. Sweden's political leadership had spent decades improving the welfare of the country and citizens, and could not afford to get pulled into the hostilities that were brewing between the Great Powers.[19]

After a few months of intense fighting, the "white army" emerged victorious. Finland had finally managed to shake off the Russian yoke and take its place as a free and independent nation in the Western world. Russia recognized Finland's independence in 1920 through the Treaty of Dorpat. The Petsamo area in the north and the Karelian Isthmus, the land bridge between Finland and Russia including the city of Viborg, would now be part of Finland, as would the Åland Islands, although the fate of these islands and their defense in case of war would continue to be debated.[20] Once Finland realized independence its population became largely homogenous, with 96 percent of the people adhering to the Lutheran religion and 11 percent still speaking Swedish as their primary language. Swedish was thus recognized as an official minority language in Finland, although even this minority felt that they were culturally closer to the Finns than to the Swedes.[21]

Finnish culture proved unique because Finland had for centuries been controlled by Sweden or Russia. The result of a new and independent Finland was a population that was leaning a bit toward the west and a bit toward the east. Still, "[t]he dominant characteristics of Finnish culture, society, and political tradition associated the country with Scandinavia."[22] In 1938, at the twentieth anniversary of Finland's independence, the people were no longer politically split. The atmosphere in Finland proved strongly anti–Russian and anti-communist. Russia and Finland thus came to harbor mutual suspicions toward one another. Although Finland feared that Russia might try to force communism on the Finns, Russia feared that Finland, on account of its Scandinavian traditions, might allow a strong foreign power to use the country as a "springboard for an assault on Russia."[23] Russia continued to hold the opinion that Finland, because of its past history and geographical location, ought to lean more toward the Soviet Union than toward the Western world with respect to foreign policy.[24]

As has been demonstrated through this brief survey of Swedish and

Finnish history, Finland's political and cultural orientation toward Western democracy and Sweden's interests in Finland had sprung largely from the past experiences of the two countries. Without examining the complexity of the political situation at the outbreak of World War II and the subsequent Soviet invasion of Finland, however, including the ability of the Swedish government to act as a counterforce to the people's sentiments and desire to officially stand on Finland's side and contribute with armed force, one's view of Sweden's role in the war would be largely incomplete. Was it more important to do what the common man perceived as ethically correct and send military help to Finland, or act on less emotional grounds and ensure that Sweden would not get dragged into the war or become a battleground for Germany and the Western Allies? These questions and their consequences will be examined in greater detail throughout the book.

The Geographical Location Problem

Finland's geographical location proved to be part of the problem that led to the Russo-Finnish Winter War. Leningrad with approximately five million inhabitants proved more populous than the whole country of Finland, and Finland's border with Russia was located only some forty kilometers west of the big city.[25] As tension in Europe grew, Soviet Leader Joseph Stalin realized that the security of the Soviet Union depended on the strength of Leningrad, which housed 30–35 percent of the state's defense industry.[26] Whoever controlled the city also controlled the passage of troops between Finland and Russia across the Karelian Isthmus, and the seafaring traffic from the Baltic Sea via the Gulf of Finland and Lake Ladoga. Even if Finland with its small population posed no direct threat to the Soviet Union, the Karelian Isthmus became subject of controversy because it could be used by a hostile power to launch a threat against Leningrad. From Sweden's viewpoint, the fact that Finland bordered the Gulf of Bothnia in the north and the Gulf of Finland in the south proved problematic and could open Soviet access not only to Sweden but to the whole Scandinavian peninsula. During the military buildup in Europe in the 1930s, Sweden could sense a potential threat coming from the east and thus cooperated with Finland regarding reconnaissance missions against the Soviet Union. A hostile power occupying the demilitarized Åland Islands, for example, could aim its weapons at Stockholm, the Swedish capital, and at Turku, the first capital and oldest city in Finland, and thus remain a continuous worry. In case of war, both Germany and the Soviet Union would likely attempt to occupy the islands in their strife for control of the Baltic Sea.[27]

Political discussions prior to the outbreak of war revealed at least four possibilities that could endanger Swedish sovereignty: A Soviet attack against Finland through the Karelian Isthmus, spreading to the city of Viborg and on to Helsinki; a Soviet attack against Sweden from the Baltic Sea against the coastline of Stockholm-Norrköping; a Soviet attack against Sweden across the Finnish-Swedish border in the north for the purpose of conquering northern Sweden; or a German attack against Skåne in the southern part of Sweden.[28] Sweden was not overly concerned with Germany, however. History had confirmed that the Soviet Union was the traditional and most formidable enemy of both Sweden and Finland, and Sweden must be vigilant of aggression from the east. Although leaving Finland to fend for herself in case of a Russian invasion would likely have a negative influence on the beneficial relationship that Sweden enjoyed with Finland, as the political situation developed in Europe it became evident that Sweden's geographical location, its long coastline and access to numerous ports, and its richness in natural resources were factors that must guide the decisions of the Swedish government.

Simultaneously, the Soviet Union worried about the military buildup in the west. A pact of nonaggression between the Soviets and the Finns, signed in 1932 and reaffirmed in 1934 for a period of ten years, stipulated:

> The High Contracting Parties mutually guarantee the inviolability of the frontiers existing between the Republic of Finland and the Union of Socialist Soviet Republics, as fixed by the Treaty of Peace concluded at Dorpat on October 14, 1920, which shall remain the firm foundation of their relations, and reciprocally undertake to refrain from any act of aggression directed against each other. Any act of violence attacking the integrity and inviolability of the territory or the political independence of the other High Contracting Party shall be regarded as an act of aggression, even if it is committed without declaration of war and avoids warlike manifestations.[29]

The treaty, meant to strengthen the relations between the two countries, nevertheless failed to convince Stalin that he was safe from a threat via the way of Finland.

The situation worsened with a changing regime in Germany. Although hostilities toward Sweden had earlier been viewed as possible only if coming from the east, it was now fully possible that a threat to Swedish sovereignty could come also from the west. If Sweden failed to step forward and defend Finland against Soviet aggression, Finland would possibly look at an alliance with Germany, particularly since Germany had assisted Finland in its War of Independence.[30] Sweden would then be sandwiched between Germany and Germany-friendly Finland, and would be left with little bargaining power if demands were placed on its territory or natural resources.

The Nonaggression Treaty Between Germany and the Soviet Union

Germany invaded Poland on September 1, 1939 and thus lighted the fuse that triggered World War II. England and France declared war on Germany two days later.[31] The *Nichtangriffspakt*, a treaty of nonaggression signed in August 1939 between Germany's Minister of Foreign Affairs, Joachim von Ribbentrop, and the Soviet Union's Minister of Foreign Affairs, Vyacheslav Molotov, further complicated the situation. The most controversial part of the pact was the "secret protocol," or statements that determined how Germany and the Soviet Union were to divide Eastern Europe, with "territorial and political rearrangement in the areas belonging to the Baltic states (Finland, Estonia, Latvia, Lithuania)," and "territorial and political rearrangement of the areas belonging to the Polish state."[32] The Molotov-Ribbentrop pact, as it came to be called, contributed to Finland's decision to reaffirm its position of neutrality in a potential war; however, this was before Finland knew how the Baltic states were to be divided.[33]

Preserving the independence of the Baltic states, particularly Estonia by the southern coast of the Gulf of Finland, was of utmost importance to the future security of Finland. The secret protocol of the pact ran contrary to this concern and thus shifted the balance of power in Europe by giving Stalin free hands in the region.[34] Poland was to be partitioned with the western part befalling Germany and the eastern part the Soviet Union in an effort, it was said, to promote peace between the countries and strengthen the neutrality agreement of 1926; the so-called Berlin Treaty, which was the forerunner to the Molotov-Ribbentrop pact.[35] But the division of the Baltic states would unlikely be the extent of Hitler's and Stalin's actions. Sweden speculated that once the Soviet Union had reached a certain degree of success in Finland, Germany would strive to establish a strong presence in the Baltic Sea and occupy the Åland Islands, thereby securing the Swedish exports of iron ore.[36]

Despite the seemingly friendly signing of the pact, little secret was made of the fact that there was no love lost between Germany and the Soviet Union. In 1938, Nikita Khrushchev, the secretary of the Moscow Regional Committee, had been tasked with building a new Communist Party in Ukraine since the old Party had been destroyed in the purges. The central idea was to "russify" Ukraine by ensuring that people opposed to Soviet communism would not hold positions of power in the Party. This exercise involved the elimination of everyone in favor of German fascists.[37] Khrushchev, who was with Stalin when the nonaggression pact was signed, pointed out that Hitler had clearly stated his visions in *Mein Kampf* and believed that war between the Soviet

Union and Germany was inevitable. Hitler "spelled out the aggressive designs he had on the world and the misanthropic philosophy which motivated him," Khrushchev noted. "He set as his sworn duty the annihilation of Communism and the storming of its citadel, the Soviet Union.... *Mein Kampf* didn't say anything about peaceful coexistence with us.... [I]t wasn't a change of heart that moved Hitler to send Ribbentrop to Moscow on the twenty-third of August, 1939."[38]

Hitler might have hoped that the Soviet Union would ally with Germany in the early stages of the war to prevent Britain from interfering in the conflict. But since neither Hitler nor Stalin attached much weight to a signature on a piece of paper, what advantage did they hope to gain by entering into the pact? To Hitler, it ensured his successful invasion of Poland without fear of retribution from the Soviet Union. The day after Russia breached the Finnish border, Josef Goebbels, the German minister of propaganda, would tell his diary that the more instability the world experienced, the better it would be for Germany.[39] To Stalin, it was likely a part of his grander scheme of "russifying" all of Europe, including Germany. Hitler's invasion of Poland would inevitably draw a response from England and France. Once the war had been under way for some time and Hitler had worn his forces thin, Stalin could enter the conflict at a date of his choosing. A war in Europe would ultimately facilitate Stalin's expansionist visions. Without the pact, however, Hitler would not dare to attack Poland, would fail to draw retaliation from Britain and France, and would thus retain much of his strength. These factors combined would make a Soviet offensive in the area less workable.[40]

Stalin's speech to the Politburo (Central Committee of the Communist Party) on August 19, 1939, is further evidence that he desired to start a war in Europe. The speech, which focused on the benefits he could gain through the Molotov-Ribbentrop pact, emphasized how Europe would be "subjected to serious upheavals and disorder" the moment England and France intervened. "In this case," Stalin explained, "we will have a great opportunity to stay out of the conflict, and we could plan the opportune time for us to enter the war." History had demonstrated that the communist movement lacked the strength to seize power without a major war. A long war was desirable in order that England and France would be exhausted by the time they defeated Germany, and would no longer remain a threat to the Soviet Union. When this happened, Stalin could send his Red Army into Europe. Once he had "russified" Germany, it would only be a matter of time before the Red Army would move into France. But what would be the consequence should Hitler prove victorious in his battles with England and France? Stalin meant that the war would likely weaken the German army, anyway, to the point that

Hitler would be unable to stand against the communist movement in an occupied France. A revolution would be unavoidable and would create an opportunity for Russia to come to the aid of France, all for Stalin's gain. A world revolution aiding Stalin's political ambitions would then be just around the corner.[41]

Although Stalin, Molotov, and Khrushchev believed that the pact would delay Hitler's planned war in the east and enable the Soviet Union to build strength to exercise its interests in Poland and the Baltic states, Hitler had his own vision of how the war would proceed. The day before Ribbentrop signed the pact, Hitler commented to his generals that he and Stalin were the only world leaders with enough foresight to properly prepare for the future, which was why they would now "shake hands" and celebrate the newly established "border" between Germany and the Soviet Union. Hitler considered this division of territory only temporary, however, while he exercised his powers in Poland and Lithuania unhindered and without fear of interference from the Soviet Union. When Stalin died, as he certainly would soon since he was in poor health, the Soviet Union would fall under Hitler's command.[42] Hitler likely thought that he had made a fool of Stalin and the Soviet leadership by signing the nonaggression pact. He could now conquer one nation at a time and alone decide when it was suitable to pursue the Soviet Union.[43]

Meanwhile, eager to secure his borders, Stalin battled with how to deal with Finland. Leningrad was within firing range of the Finnish-Soviet border on the Karelian Isthmus. Although the Scandinavian-leaning Finnish government was viewed as a political threat to Marxist-Leninist ideology, it was unreasonable to suggest that little Finland with its three and a half million people posed a significant threat to Leningrad. Any political analyst could detect Stalin's true desires: To control Finland in order to increase his sphere of influence in Europe in light of the many uncertainties the future held. A powerful enemy could gain access to Finnish territory and use it as a staging ground for an offensive against the mighty Soviet city. Control of some islands in the Gulf of Finland would also be necessary in order to ensure Soviet access to the waters beyond the Gulf and the rest of Europe.

Sweden and Finland watched with dismay as the Soviet Union forced Estonia, Latvia, and Lithuania under its control. The Baltic states had only minimal time to consider in earnest the agreement that was handed them and, although they had evaded direct warfare, they no longer existed as sovereign states. The annexation of the Baltic states was important to Soviet defense strategy. Stalin now had a "wide coastal frontier" that would prevent the Allies or Germany from using these territories to block his forces or launch an offensive against Russia.[44] But the Finns faced an impending crisis. Remembering how Germany had actively supported them in the War of Independence twenty years earlier, as late as October 1939, the Finnish leadership expressed optimism that Hitler would intervene in this conflict, too, and prevent harm from reaching the Finnish people.[45] But the truth of the matter was that the Molotov-Ribbentrop pact precluded the Finns from counting on protection from Germany against a Soviet invasion. From Sweden's viewpoint, the pact dissolved the previous balance of power and jeopardized Sweden's position by the Baltic Sea. Hostilities could now come to Swedish territory by the way of Germany or Russia.[46] A worst-case scenario would lead to Sweden, this small country with a population of just under six and a half million people and with a long-standing tradition of neutrality, having to fight a two-front war.

Soviet Demands on Finnish Territory

Finland's expanding ties to the Western powers created further unrest and worry among the Soviet leadership. That Russia had lost Finland in the War of Independence had become an irritant and constant threat to Russian security. At the height of World War I, when Russia was weakened by internal problems, agreeing to Finland's independence was the right thing to do. Now, twenty years later, Russia's war machine had regained strength and the present situation was deemed inadequate. As tension increased and the international situation worsened, access to Finnish territories became of primary strategic concern to Stalin. If hostile forces entered the Gulf of Finland or advanced toward the Finnish city of Viborg located roughly a hundred kilometers from Leningrad, there was little hope of neutral Finland coming to the aid of the Soviet Union. In order to avoid such a catastrophe, and since he could not move Leningrad, Stalin suggested that the border between the countries be moved and Finland trade the eastern part of the Karelian Isthmus less than five kilometers from Leningrad in return for certain areas in East Karelia and the promise that the Soviet Union would no longer oppose the fortification of the Åland Islands, with the exception that no country, including Sweden, would participate in building and manning the fortifications. When confronted on the issue of why it was necessary to move the border further from Leningrad, Stalin replied that it was the same reason that made it necessary "to move the Polish frontier farther from Berlin."[47]

Stalin also desired to establish an air force base on Hogland, an island in the Gulf of Finland. The Finns considered the Soviet request to lease this island along with several others for a period of thirty years unacceptable, and denied the request. Additionally, Stalin asked that Finland give him access to suitable harbors, primarily Hangö (see also Hanko Cape), a peninsula on the southernmost tip of Finland, for the purpose of blockading enemy access through the Gulf to Leningrad, and that all Finnish fortifications on the Karelian Isthmus be destroyed.[48] Although these demands may have been reasonable from a Soviet perspective, the fear was that Stalin would continue asking for even greater concessions until all of Finland would fall under Russian dominion, or at least until Finland had been severely weakened and could no longer mount an effective defense.[49] Marine bases in Porkkala to the west of Helsinki, and on Nargö rather than Hangö, would have given Stalin greater ability to blockade the Gulf of Finland; however, Finland deemed these areas unsuitable for lease to the Soviet Union, on account of their locations so close to the capitals of both Finland and Estonia.[50] The Petsamo area in the northernmost part of Finland proved of strategic importance as well, because controlling this area, along with access to the Baltic Sea, would give Stalin the power to prevent Great Britain from invading Russia or sending military aid to Finland in case of a showdown between Finland and Russia.[51]

And Germany? Although Russia at the present was on friendly terms with Germany, as noted previously, Stalin was not complacent about the future. "Everything tends to change," he said.[52] "Events have their own logic: we say one thing, but events go another way. With Germany we divided Poland. England and France did not declare war on us, but they might."[53] Finland would clearly prove too small to resist a German invasion, should Hitler decide to set up a base only a few miles from Leningrad.[54] But Stalin's greater concern was that Finland would freely ally with Germany. (Note that Finland allied with Germany first during the so-called Continuation War of 1941–44, for fear of renewed Soviet aggression.) He thus asked that Finland allow the Red Army to enter Finnish soil, arguing that keeping Finland free of German troops would assure the people of both countries greater safety. Restating the wish to remain neutral, Finland refused to abide by the request.[55]

Although Carl Gustaf Mannerheim and a few other government and military officials considered the concessions that Stalin asked for reasonable, the fear that Finland would eventually fall completely under Soviet command, making the War of Independence twenty years earlier futile, made it evident that the use of military force was the only viable option in case of invasion.[56] By October 1939, Finnish men liable for service were called to training designed to coordinate the units and increase the soldiers' familiarity with the terrain near the Soviet border on the Karelian Isthmus.[57] Due to the economic depression, however, Finland had not realized the enormous threat coming from the Soviet Union in time to start building its armed forces, and was thus ill prepared for military action.[58] (Modern research indicates that the Soviet Union had prepared an offensive against Finland as early as 1936.[59])

Although it has been argued that Finland would have benefited from agreeing to Stalin's request for territory, when placed in perspective, and as stated by the Finnish Foreign Ministry in the end of December 1939, succumbing to the demands would have been equivalent in severity to Great Britain's surrender of "the Ilse of Wight, the Channel Isles, Southampton and the Orkneys and Shetlands — all to be fortified by the foreign Power; Cessation of an area extending 50 miles inland from the coast of Norfolk; Destruction of most of Britain's defences."[60] The greatest difficulty lay perhaps in accepting Stalin's request for Hangö. This piece of land was particularly attractive because of its location by the entrance to the Gulf of Finland and thus to Helsinki, the country's capital and center of power. Finland reported to Swedish politicians and military leaders that if the Soviet Union insisted on getting access to the islands in the Gulf, Finland could agree to the demands only if the country was not humiliated and received just compensation. But if the Soviet Union wanted Porkkala, Hangö, or the Åland Islands, the answer was definitely no.[61] Hangö in Russian hands would not only mean the creation of a dangerous gap in Finland's coastal defenses, but also the creation of a bridgehead that could carry a hostile force directly to the country's most vital areas, and would require that Finland split its meager defensive forces between two fronts. Stalin's promise that he would station no more than five thousand troops on Hangö did not decrease Finland's fears, as nearby Estonia which was already under Russian control could easily act as a base for much greater forces. Bomber bases were also located in Leningrad and East Karelia, from where the Russians could reach every city and village in Finland.[62]

Giving Stalin the requested areas posed yet a domestic problem: The permanent move of large numbers of citizens away from the territories bordering the Karelian Isthmus. In the months preceding the war, 130,000 Finns along with their farm animals were temporarily evacuated in the name of safety, while the government waited to see how events would unfold.[63] Some of these families returned home a few weeks later under the impression that the immediate danger was over. Others would never again set foot in the area they had once called home. Additionally, many Finnish families displayed lack of confidence in Finland's ability to defend the people against a Soviet attack, and exchanged their money for Swedish crowns while preparing to leave the country.[64] When the war started, thousands of families were evacuated from the Karelian Isthmus by the Finnish army, their houses burned and their livestock removed to prevent their use by the enemy.[65]

Molotov's Address to the Supreme Soviet of the Soviet Union

On October 5, 1939, Molotov asked that Finland send a delegation to Moscow to discuss important political questions.[66] Four days later, the Finnish leadership expressed concern to Germany about the extent of the Soviet Union's penetration into the Baltic. The secretary of the German Foreign Office reported back to Wipert von Blücher, the German minister in Finland, that the demarcation line with respect to the Baltic states was fixed, and that German interests lay only to the west of this line. Germany therefore had no idea what the Soviet Union might do regarding her interests to the east of the line. At any rate, Germany was not in position to intervene in Russo-Finnish interests.[67] Since Germany's forces were tied up in the west, Hitler would later explain, the country was unable to come to Finland's assistance in the war.[68]

A few days later, Sweden called on Germany, bringing attention to the seriousness of the developing situation in the Baltic and the frightful consequences of a Soviet attack on Finland. It was highly unlikely that Finland would submit to Soviet demands as the Baltic states had done, which meant that war would be unavoidable. Again, Germany answered that the government was unaware of any demands on Finland, and that it was in everybody's interest that a peaceful solution be found to any potential problems.[69] Simultaneously, a commander in the Finnish army noted in his daily log that Soviet military aircraft had flown over the Finnish cities of Joutselkä and Perkjärvi in Karelia.[70]

All German officials were not oblivious to the disaster that was brewing on the horizon, however. On October 10, Blücher sent an urgent telegram to the German Foreign Office:

> All indications are that if Russia will not confine its demands to islands in the Gulf of Finland, Finland will offer armed resistance. The consequences for our war economy would be grave. Not only food and timber exports, but also indispensable copper and molybdenum exports from Finland to Germany would cease. For this reason I suggest you intercede with Russian Government in the sense that it should not go beyond a demand for the islands.[71]

But this statement, too, fell on deaf ears. Germany replied only that it had seen nothing that indicated that demands made by Stalin would result in hostilities that could not be resolved peacefully at the negotiating table. Furthermore, the nonaggression pact precluded Germany from assisting a third party engaged in war with the Soviet Union.[72] The situation proved slightly more optimistic when Scandinavia and the United States expressed moral support for Finland. In Sweden, however, opinions were divided over active interference in a coming war. On October 19, Finland reported a violation of its borders as Russian aircraft penetrated Finnish airspace, and ordered a blackout exercise as a result. A week later, Russian aircraft flew along the entire southeastern coast of Finland, circling above the Finnish fleet based outside of Turku.[73]

The horizon darkened further when Molotov, on October 31, announced in an address to the Supreme Soviet of the Soviet Union (the highest legislative body in the country) that "important changes" that could be felt outside of the immediate borders of Europe had taken place in recent months, three of which required particular attention. The first change, the newly established friendship pact between the Soviet Union and Germany, was important enough that it would likely affect international relations. The second change, the "collapse of the Polish state" as a result of Germany's speedy campaign into the country, was considered a blow to the remnants of the Versailles Treaty. Molotov expressed relief that the treaty could no longer oppress non–Polish nationalities.[74] The third change applied to the war that was developing in Europe. Although it had started as a conflict between Germany and Poland, it had quickly grown to include Great Britain and France against Germany and was expected to continue to grow until it also covered countries outside of Europe's borders. The more complex the war became, the more difficult it would be to define the aggressor. Although Germany's invasion and conquest of Poland had gone rather quickly, Molotov emphasized that Germany was ultimately striving for peace. But Britain's and France's involvement in the war had now made them, and not Germany, the aggressors. There was little chance that there would be a resolution to the conflict any time soon, because Britain and France had declared it their goal to defeat Hitler and everything he stood for. This was not a fight for democracy, Molotov meant. On the contrary, Britain and France who had been great colonial powers were afraid of losing their former might and were striving to establish a new empire. Communists were hunted everywhere and the rights of the working class were ignored.[75]

Molotov talked about the changes that had taken place within the Soviet Union next, with particular emphasis on international relations. To a roar of applause, he stressed how Russia's "peaceful foreign policy," including the newfound camaraderie with Germany and the effort to support the struggle for peace, had enabled the country to strengthen its "international weight." When the Red Army had marched into western Ukraine and western Belorussia, the population had welcomed the Russians as liberators. The pacts signed with Estonia, Latvia, and Lithuania should be viewed as agreements of mutual friendship. The Soviet Union would offer military assistance to these countries in case they came under attack by a foreign power, and in return be granted permission to maintain naval and air bases in the Baltic states.[76] With respect to Finland, Molotov laid down the base for his argument by explaining how Stalin's relations with the Baltic states had allowed the Soviet Union to strengthen its defensive capabilities and promote world peace. The "good will" of the Soviet Union had thus been made clear.

As noted previously, the greatest threat to Soviet territory did not come from Finland but from Germany via the way of Finland, despite the nonaggression pact. If Finland proved unwilling to negotiate, Molotov warned, military action might be necessary. While he acknowledged that negotiations had begun with Finland, he called the accusation that the Soviet Union might attempt to lay claims on Viborg, the northern part of Lake Ladoga, and the Åland Islands an outright lie and fabrication. The Soviet Union, he assured, would ask only for the absolute minimum territorial concessions it would need to successfully defend against outside aggression while continuing to maintain friendly relations with Finland. Establishing military bases on some of the Finnish islands would not only provide for the security of Leningrad, it would simultaneously serve Finland's security needs. A friendly agreement would therefore benefit both countries mutually.[77]

Despite these reassurances, it was not difficult for the Finnish leadership to see how moving the border further from Leningrad would intrude on the Mannerheim Line, a series of field fortifications given their name by foreign war correspondents, and jeopardize Finland's own defenses. If the fortifications were torn down, Stalin's Red Army could move forward unhindered, placing all of Finland under Soviet control. Although Stalin attempted to demonstrate his good intention by offering to compensate Finland with certain territories in East Karelia, the Finnish leadership debated his honesty. If Stalin feared an offensive against Leningrad via the way of Finland, they argued, the border would have to be moved all the way to the Gulf of Bothnia and not just a few miles further west. Simultaneously, they worried about the range of modern weapons and aircraft.[78]

It is also worth noting that the safety of Leningrad depended on the Red Banner Fleet, the part of the Soviet navy that operated in the Baltic. Should a hostile power gain dominion over the Gulf of Finland, the fleet would be confined to its base off Leningrad and be virtually useless. In order to guard against such an occurrence, it was crucial that Finland lease Stalin the Hangö peninsula. Not only was it ice free most of the winter, its harbor was suitable for a wide variety of ships and the town on the peninsula was large enough to accommodate more than twenty-five thousand Soviet troops once the

Finnish residents had left their homes. Stalin had little hope of guarding the stretch of water between Hangö and the Soviet base at Paldiski on the Estonian coast without radar.[79] No educated military man could thus take Stalin seriously when he claimed that his only concern was that the border be moved a few miles further west of Leningrad. If Finland agreed to the concessions, Russia would surely ask for additional territory in the near future. It was also likely that Stalin would interpret any concessions as a sign of Finnish inferiority, which would no doubt empower the Soviet leadership.[80]

How did Sweden react? In a letter to Väinö Alfred Tanner, Finland's Minister of Foreign Affairs, Sweden's Prime Minister Per Albin Hansson commented that Sweden was prepared to resort to diplomatic measures on Finland's behalf without direct military involvement in open conflict. Although diplomacy could likely be used successfully on several points, he recognized that the problem with the Hangö peninsula would be difficult to settle through diplomacy alone. Although expressing little optimism with respect to official military assistance in Finland, Hansson noted that if war broke out, Sweden would most likely reform its cabinet. He refrained from saying whether or not a new cabinet would take a more active stand toward Finland's needs. It might be noted that opinions in the Swedish Parliament were split. The Liberal People's Party and the Agrarian Party were opposed to sending government sanctioned troops to Finland. The right-wing parties, although still opposed, were in slightly greater favor, as was the Social Democratic Party. Everybody, even those in favor, were unsure of the extent of the help they would recommend sending, however, because the details of the demands that the Soviet Union had placed on Finland, and the uncertainty about the length of the war, were still unclear.[81]

Although Finland had kept a watchful eye toward Russia for centuries and acted as a barrier to Russian expansion, the Finnish leadership was taken by surprise at Molotov's speech and the quickness with which events came to unfold. In a speech held on November 23, 1939, Finland's Prime Minister Aimo Kaarlo Cajander stressed that the greatest danger lay not in the Soviet Union's request for territories in Finland, but in the Molotov-Ribbentrop pact or, rather, in its timing. Finland could no longer adhere to the earlier belief that German ideologies were incompatible with those of the Soviet Union. Finland had watched Germany march into Poland. When Poland was on the verge of collapse, it was the Soviet Union's turn to march in and occupy the country. Then Estonia, Latvia, and Lithuania had fallen to Soviet demands. Finland recognized that enormous forces were at play that would likely lead to a long lasting war in Europe, the effects of which would be felt in Finland even if the country managed to remain neutral.[82] In answer to

Cajander's speech, *Pravda* (meaning "truth"), the official newspaper of the Communist Party in the Soviet Union, accused the Finnish cabinet of cowardice and fear of confronting its own parliament, and charged Cajander with wrecking the negotiations by failing to align himself with the will of the people of Finland.[83]

Propaganda leaflets issued to the Red Army in November 1939 further emphasized how Finland ought to be grateful for the independence the Soviet Union had granted the country in 1920. But after having "sank in blood the workers' revolution in Finland," the people had adopted a "hostile policy" toward Russia, had launched an organized expedition for the purpose of plundering Soviet Karelia, and had ambitions to capture all of the northern part of the Soviet Union. Rather than agreeing to a friendly treaty with Russia as the Baltic states had done, now that the European powers were striving for imperial domination, Finland had beefed up its armed forces, practiced blackouts in the cities, and concentrated large numbers of troops on the Karelian Isthmus just thirty-two kilometers from Leningrad. These aggressive acts, which were a direct threat to the Soviet Union, were carried out in spite of the poverty of the common man. The Finnish people had to bear the full burden of the military expenses and suffered enormous hardship under the brutal Finnish government. The local landlords were even worse, the propaganda stated, and evicted families to the streets for the tiniest infraction or late payment of rent.[84] Why did the Soviet Union know so little about Finnish culture and ambition even though Finland had been a Grand Duchy of Russia and the two countries were close neighbors? Russia was after all Finland's traditional enemy and should have known better. Part of the problem rested with the fact that the Communist Party in Finland was illegal and information did not transmit properly. "[I]ts nearest official representative, Arvo Tuominen, lived in exile in Stockholm."[85]

Although it seemed futile to even try to set the record straight, Eljas Erkko, Finland's Minister of Foreign Affairs, expressed disappointment in the European countries, and particularly in England's disinterest and lack of sympathy for the difficulties that Finland and the Baltic states were going through. England's plan, according to Erkko, was to convince the Red Army to advance all the way to the Baltic Sea where it could threaten Germany's northeastern flank from Estonia or Latvia. Then the Russians, rather than the English, could go to war with Germany and bleed for England's cause.[86] England had also expressed the opinion that Finland was inflexible and therefore not likely to reach an agreement in negotiations with the Soviet Union, and that a clash of armed forces was inevitable. It was suggested that Rickard Sandler, the Swedish Minister of Foreign Affairs, act as mediator in the conflict because of his long experience in diplomacy and deep understanding of the special relations that existed between Sweden and Finland.[87] As winter drew near, however, Carl Gustaf Mannerheim believed that the Soviet Union's access to ports in Estonia had contributed to easing the tension a bit, and Erkko agreed that the risk of a Soviet offensive against Finland had declined.[88] Juho Niukkanen, Finland's Minister of Defense, interjected yet anothet viewpoint into the argument. If negotiations fell through, it was possible that Stalin would refrain from attacking Finland for now and that the respective armies would lie in wait by the border all winter.[89] The winter months should therefore be used to strengthen Finland's armed forces so that the country could respond in full against a Soviet offensive come spring.[90]

Sweden's Military Preparedness

Sweden had followed Finland's war preparations with interest while overhauling its own military capabilities. Although Sweden had been a superpower with territories in Bremen and Pomerania, Estonia, all of Finland, and parts of Norway in the seventeenth century, much had changed since the country was forced to cede Finland to Russia in 1809. Sweden's ability to protect Finland against attacks from the great enemy to the east was at best questionable. At the start of World War I, Sweden's armed forces were strong enough to meet hostilities from Russia and Germany and, shortly thereafter, from Great Britain and Norway, if need be. During the war years of 1914–18, Sweden increased the number of officers in the armed forces. The government also created six reserve branches and increased the initial training period for the infantry to 365 days.[91] The wish for sustained peace prompted Sweden to stay neutral, however. At the conclusion of the Great War, political pressure and popular support for disarmament encouraged the left political parties to press for "continued reduction in the military establishment."[92] In 1925, the Parliament decided to eliminate some of the outdated regiments, cutting the six reserve branches and the cavalry entirely. The initial training period for the infantry was also reduced to 140 days.[93] Although Sweden employed universal conscription for men, it soon became evident that the training was too short to fully prepare the recruits for combat.[94] Additionally, conscientious objectors were granted the option of civilian service, and one-fourth of the men deemed suitable for military duty were never called upon to serve.[95]

Although Europe experienced growing tension in the interwar years (some historians consider World War II merely a continuation of World War I, or one and the same war with a twenty-year interlude of peace) and many countries were viewed as "interests" to be divided between the Great Powers, Sweden continued to downsize its armed forces in part because the Great War had ended, and in part because the Swedish people at large had (and have) a negative view of war and lacked enthusiasm for military buildup. The idea that unrest in Europe or Russia would lead to war in Sweden seemed far-fetched. Not all citizens took this stand, however. In the late 1920s, many Swedes kept a watchful eye on the Soviet Union's imperialistic tendencies and were particularly concerned with the future of neighboring Finland. The publication *Antingen–Eller* (either–or) emphasized that *either* the national defense must be organized so that Sweden could successfully execute sanctions against an enemy state for the benefit of Finland, *or* the military preparedness must be such that Sweden could maintain national independence should the country be subjected to direct attack or possible attempts of Soviet expansion.[96] Still, in 1936, the Parliament was determined to make further cuts in defense spending, a decision it would come to regret at the start of World War II when "Russian demands on Finland in the fall of 1939 ... roused Sweden to danger."[97] The total number of personnel in the Swedish armed forces at the time of Hitler's invasion of Poland was estimated at 130,000.[98]

In a speech to the nation on August 27, 1939, Prime Minister Per Albin Hansson assured the people that "our military preparedness is good."[99] There was no reason to panic, he said. Although the tension in Europe was growing, Sweden and many other small nations were not directly threatened. Sweden had no known enemies, and it was not in the interest of other countries to draw Sweden into the conflict. In worst-case scenario, the state had taken necessary precautions to protect the citizens.[100] Hansson further emphasized that Sweden's neutrality would be defended. A country's right to remain neutral was based on international agreements, the most important of which stemmed from the Hague Convention of October 18, 1907, and which stipulated that should a territorial violation take place, the neutral country had an obligation to take appropriate action against the violators (through diplomatic means, by capture of a ship's crew, etc.) to avoid being guilty of internal neutrality breach.[101] It has since come to light that Sweden was much less prepared than Hansson wanted the people to believe. Although the level of danger Sweden faced was uncertain and Sweden was not currently in conflict with any other power, the Soviet Union's demands on Finland, along with the forces that were brewing between Hitler and Stalin regarding the division of the Baltic states, brought the possibility of war dangerously close.

Moreover, in 1939, Sweden relied on a defense plan that was dated to 1927, a time when Germany was still limited by the rules of the Versailles Treaty.[102] The outdated plan focused primarily on the possibility of attack from the Soviet Union or possibly from a Western power other than Germany and stipulated that, should the Soviet Union attack Finland and Russian forces had not yet reached the southwestern part of Finland, the Swedish army would defend the Stockholm area and southern Sweden with strong infantry forces and coast artillery for the purpose of preventing a Russian landing along the eastern and southern coastline. The Åland Islands would also be defended. Should Russian forces reach the Torne River in the north or occupy the Åland Islands, the main part of the Swedish army would defend northern Sweden and focus on cutting Russian communications to Torneå. The defense of Stockholm would remain of utmost importance, particularly if Russian forces succeeded at reaching the Swedish border. The plan against an attack or attempted invasion by a Western power, by contrast, was based on the assumption that the threat would come primarily against the western coastline of southern Sweden. Since Norway was neutral, the border with Norway would be guarded but a large force for its defense would not be dispatched.[103] Thus, the plan did not consider the possibility of a threat by Germany or the Western Allies against northern Sweden.

Although Germany and the Soviet Union acted as checks and balances for one another, and a parliamentary bill from 1924 had characterized Sweden's geopolitical landscape as not immediately threatened as long as Finland and the Baltic states could maintain their independence and act as barriers to foreign aggression, the situation in Europe in 1939 changed drastically when the Molotov-Ribbentrop pact united German and Soviet interests and upset the balance of power in the region.[104] When it became evident that a can of worms was about to be opened and World War II could not be avoided, Sweden started to set aside money for the development of its armed forces. Conscripts, including the whole class of 1923, were called up for recurrent training.[105] According to a government decision of 1894, the king had at his disposal a line of credit to be used in an unavoidable emergency that necessitated buildup of the defense budget in the likelihood of war. If war actually broke out, the king could call together the Parliament and request even greater monetary assets.[106]

Civilians began taking part in air defense practice sessions, and the size of the air force was increased by 50 percent.[107] The relatively modern J8 Gloster Gladiator, although a biplane, proved suitable for the Swedish air force. Two other types of aircraft, both monoplanes, were considered: the Italian Breda and the new Hurricane from Hawker. The Breda was finally dismissed because of difficulties associated with landing in the varied Swedish terrain. Uncertainties with respect to delivery of the Hurricane from the British government led to the Gladiator being ultimately chosen.[108]

It was thus no longer inconceivable that the war might end up on Swedish soil. In September 1939, the political leadership in Sweden, Norway, Denmark, and Finland called a conference in Copenhagen, reconfirming their strong nonpartisan neutrality politics while upholding the right to engage in commerce with one another and the warring nations. The decision was necessary because isolationist policies would likely result in mass starvation.[109] The greater fear was that the Scandinavian countries would end up on opposite sides of the conflict should they be forced to join the war.[110] The common cultural characteristics and emotional bonds, cemented together through hundreds of years of shared history, prompted the need to unite against the rise of German and Soviet power. The possibility of a joint defense of Finland was discussed — an idea that Sweden had considered as early as 1923, although the Social Democratic Party had voiced strong opposition — but further action was not taken.[111] Of utmost concern was the fact that the Soviet Union desired to act as the protector of Finland in case of a global conflict. In the event a hostile force occupied either Norway or Finland, enemy troops could easily spill across the border into Sweden and take control of the country.[112]

But deciding how to proceed in case of violation of Swedish borders proved problematic. Several questions remained to be answered. Would Nazi Germany invade and occupy Sweden from the south, or would the Soviet Union attempt to form a Soviet Republic in the north? Although Sweden must at least entertain the idea of battling it out with either of these military powers, the possibility of war with the Soviet Union was of greater concern than war with Germany. It was speculated that the Russians would likely enter Finland over the Karelian Isthmus and then work their way to the Swedish border in the north. A question of particular importance in military circles was whether it really was in Sweden's best interest to sit back and wait until Stalin's troops reached Finnish Torneå, and then focus on defending the Swedish-Finnish border. Or, might it be better, in the interest of safety, to assist the Finns and actively fight the war on Finnish territory side-by-side with Finnish ground and air units in the hope of stalling a Russian advance before it reached the Swedish border?[113]

Determining strategy vis à vis the Soviets proved equally problematic. Although stationing a large mobile force in Norrland (northern Sweden) seemed like an attractive alternative in the hope that it would act as a deterrent to Soviet aggression against Finland, it could also have the opposite effect and prompt Stalin to act preemptively. Yet an option was for Swedish troops to relieve Finnish troops in northern Finland, who could then be reassigned to the Karelian Isthmus.[114] As the situation grew more intense, guard stations were set up along the border with Finland and plans were made for warding off Soviet air attacks over Swedish territory.[115] A Soviet ground attack against Sweden must also be guarded against which would likely be reinforced with air power, as modern airplanes now had the capacity to reach Sweden from the Soviet air bases in the Baltic states or even from Murmansk. An enemy that would strive to occupy any of the Swedish or Danish islands, or Åland, was of particular concern.[116]

After much debate, Sweden's leadership determined that a coalition of Swedish and Finnish forces would unnecessarily endanger Swedish sovereignty. When Väinö Tanner, in a letter to Per Albin Hansson, asked about the possibility of receiving military assistance from Sweden in case of war, Per Edvin Sköld, the Swedish Minister of Defense, firmly told him that Sweden would not intervene in a conflict between the Soviet Union and Finland.[117] Simultaneously, the Swedish government informed Molotov that Sweden was sympathetic to Finnish interests and asked that the Soviet Union honor Finland's neutrality. The passionate bond that existed between the Swedes and the Finns would prompt Sweden to give full emotional support to Finland during the Finnish-Soviet negotiations.[118] Decisions resulting from Swedish mediation between Finland and Russia could ultimately not violate Finnish neutrality and independence.[119]

Although moral support for Finland increased during the months preceding the war, political opinions were split regarding the extent of active military support Sweden should give Finland. Sweden was clearly concerned about Finland's fate and many Swedes would have liked to see the government support Finland more openly. But Sweden was militarily underprepared and the leadership had to proceed cautiously to avoid direct confrontation with the Soviet Union. If Sweden became a target of Soviet aggression, the whole spectacle could snowball until Sweden was drawn into the war between the Great Powers. King Gustav V Adolf expressed concern about sending any kind of official military help to Finland.[120] He even threatened to abdicate from the monarchy should England be granted permission to help Finland, for example, by sending troops through Swedish territory.[121]

Although Sweden's historical relationship with Russia and Finland might have been responsible for triggering the Swedish people's emotional needs to support their closest neighbor to the east, the situation became extraordinarily complex with newer developments between Germany and the Western Allies. Although many Swedes had sympathized with Germany after the signing of the Versailles Treaty, when Hitler came to power and built a huge and well-trained army, Sweden feared that he would go too far in his desire for *Lebensraum* (living space) in the east.[122] A conflict with Germany would have been impossible to win with the outdated equipment and relatively few trained

Caricature of Stalin extinguishing the flame of the Nordic countries. The candles represent Sweden, Norway, Denmark, and Finland. The four-armed candleholder is commonly seen in Sweden during the month of Advent, the four weeks preceding Christmas (source: Den Svenske Folksocialisten, *December 23, 1939, Krigsarkivet, Finlandskommitten, 1939–1940).*

soldiers that Sweden had at its disposal. Should Germany decide to intervene in the Russo-Finnish conflict on the side of the Soviet Union, Sweden would likely have been able to oppose a German invasion of the Scandinavian peninsula for no more than a week.[123] Simultaneously, Sweden was unprepared to forego its long-standing tradition of neutrality and could not ally with British or French forces.

The Åland Islands Question

Some military leaders in Sweden questioned the rationality behind the king as Commander-in-Chief of the armed forces, and his resistance to sending Finland official military help. What would be the constitutional consequences, for example, if the king refused to send troops to Finland but the people and government expressed a definitive desire to help, or vice versa? The situation was serious enough that many military leaders thought action a better option than neutrality, particularly since the growing Soviet threat against Finland seemed to have triggered a desire in England and France to come to Finland's assistance.[124] A recurring and unresolved question at the start of World War II was the defense of the Åland Islands. Although officially Finnish territory, the group of more than six thousand islands and skerries had a mostly Swedish-speaking population, who for sentimental reasons counted on protection from Sweden in case of war. Located roughly halfway between Sweden and Finland, the islands formed a natural "bridge" between the two countries and constituted an enormously important strategic asset through their ability to guard the "entry to both the Gulf of Finland and the Gulf of Bothnia." If these islands fell into foreign hands, a hostile nation could control the shipping of goods between Sweden and Finland, cut off most of the supply routes, and present a direct military threat to Sweden and the Swedish archipelago.[125] Sweden's worries had roots in the country's geographical location by the Baltic Sea. The access to numerous waters and harbors had been the envy of foreign states for most of the country's history, and had been central to Sweden's status as a military superpower prior to the loss of Finland in 1809.[126]

As noted previously, the Åland Islands had become disputed territory when Finland declared independence from Russia in 1917, and according to agreement were to remain demilitarized. Two years earlier, in 1915, however, Russia had begun to fortify the islands. Although the fortifications were strictly defensive for the purpose of warding off a possible German invasion, their proximity to Sweden and the possibility of conflict in the Baltic Sea had worried the Swedish government who wished to annex the islands. Heated debates between Sweden and Finland prompted Finland to request military assistance from Germany in order to oust the Russians from the islands. During the Russian Civil War, Sweden offered to send a voluntary military force to the islands to prevent Russian garrisons and artillery pieces from gaining a foothold. In charge of this expedition was Vice Admiral Carl August Ehrensvärd, who would later serve as a commander in the Winter War. While the debate between Sweden and Finland continued, a decision by the League of Nations in 1921 declared that the islands should be part of Finnish territory, but be granted autonomy and remain neutral in case of war.[127] In 1939, Sweden and Finland had gained distance from their former disagreements and could reinstate a more harmonious relationship with one another.

The Åland Islands question proved particularly worrisome in the spring of 1939, as the political conditions heated up in Europe and a clash between Germany and the Soviet Union seemed inevitable. If the Soviets managed to take Tallinn harbor in Estonia, they would have a logical base for an attack against Åland and could also threaten Sweden since Soviet aircraft and ships could quickly reach Swedish territory from these harbors.[128] The problem was that the Åland Islands were Finland's responsibility. Yet, both Sweden and Finland recognized that a purely Finnish defense might not suffice and that cooperation between the countries would be necessary. Thus, in January 1939, serious negotiations took place for a preliminary defense plan of the islands. It was suggested that defensive forces should be divided into coast artillery on the southern skerries, obligatory military service of the citizens of Åland, and anti-aircraft artillery located on the main island, in addition to a mobile fleet. At the core of this plan lay the idea that both Sweden and Finland would be able to defend their neutrality better if the controversy over the islands was resolved once and for all. If Sweden and Finland jointly fortified the islands and communicated a clear readiness to defend them, the risk of a hostile power moving through the Baltic and into the Gulf of Bothnia would be decreased significantly. Swedish and Finnish forces could then be relocated to more important fronts. If left undefended, however, the islands would no doubt become a temptation for a hostile takeover that would endanger both Swedish and Finnish coastlines.[129]

Upon the Soviet Union's entry into eastern Poland on September 17, 1939 and the subjugation of the Baltic states, the danger of a possible attack against Åland increased, which hurried Finland's desire to cooperate with Sweden regarding the building of fortifications. Sweden offered to station air and coast artillery on the islands if an earlier decision to keep Åland demilitarized could be reversed. Heavy protests from the Soviet Union, who considered this idea a direct threat, led to Sweden never taking action.[130] As a new member of the League of Nations, the Soviet Union meant that it had equal interest in the defense of the islands' neutrality. (The Soviet Union was expelled from the League of Nations for its aggression toward Finland in late 1939. This decision was a moral victory for Finland, but at the same time it became clear that Finland could not count on military intervention from the Scandinavian countries.) A contrasting view was that the nonaggression pact signed between Germany and the Soviet Union also granted Germany equal interest in the islands, making a joint Swedish and Finnish defense plan less crucial.[131]

Thus, the debate continued. Although certain military leaders argued that Sweden ought to prepare for war by mobilizing parts of the coast artillery and the navy and send Swedish troops to the islands, others favored a more pacifist approach — propagating the view that since Sweden had been able to remain neutral throughout World War I when both Finland and the Åland Islands were part of Russia, why worry about the islands now? Finland also expressed several concerns with respect to a joint defense plan: How would Sweden react if Finland alone defended the islands? Could Sweden contribute with war materiel? If Sweden was willing to get involved, could it coordinate the defense of the islands and actually fulfill the promise?[132] The combined defense plan was based on the assumption that both Sweden and Finland would remain neutral. The fact that Finland was threatened with war made it difficult for Sweden to offer any real military assistance while simultaneously protecting its own neutrality.[133]

In answer to a letter from Väinö Tanner in October 1939, in which Tanner had appealed to Sweden for help defending the Åland Islands, Per Albin Hansson wrote:

> ... the strongly preponderant opinion is to the effect that Sweden should take no steps which might involve the country in any incident. This stand, natural to a small country, is perhaps especially in favor among a people that has enjoyed the blessings of peace as long as Sweden has, and that has become accustomed to regarding its position as pretty well protected from the storms which sweep over the world.[134]

The crown prince of Sweden expressed grave concern for the status of the Åland Islands so close to the Swedish capital, and for Russia's attitude toward Finland and the serious consequences for northern Europe in case of any violence against the integrity of Finland's independence, and went as far as appealing to the President of the United States, as a "trusted promoter of peace and justice," to use his influence to counteract any aggressive attempts by Moscow.[135] President Roosevelt responded favorably to the crown prince's appeal, but in response to criticism of Soviet aggression toward Finland, Molotov scoffed and sarcastically drew attention to Finland's War of Independence twenty years earlier: "[T]the Soviet Union ha[s] given Finland its independence in 1917, but the Philippines ha[ve] yet to receive theirs from the United States!"[136]

In a desperate attempt to resolve the issue, Finland turned to Germany for help, arguing that if the Soviet Union were to take the Åland Islands or any other part of Finland and gain control of the Baltic, Germany's strength in the region would decline. But the timing of the request was poor since Hitler had just signed the friendship pact with Stalin. Germany's Foreign Ministry replied that the country could not intervene in the rising hostilities between the Soviet Union and Finland. Additionally, "Finland lay east of the demarcation line which, it had been agreed in the Treaty with Russia, should divide German and Soviet spheres of interest."[137] Finland's next concern was whether Germany would agree to avoid interfering in the conflict should Sweden decide to come to the assistance of Finland. Germany's leadership replied that their only concern was that the iron ore exports from Sweden were left intact.[138] Hitler claimed to have "no regard for your countries of the North," and did not believe that "Swedish aid would mean much in a really serious conflict."[139] In other words, he did not care what Sweden decided to do about the Russo-Finnish war, as long as no steps were taken "giving the Western Allies access to the Baltic." He refused to give a more definitive answer.[140]

The situation proved even more complex. Control of the Åland Islands was crucial to the defense of northern Finland. As noted previously, Sweden had considered sending troops to northern Finland and taking over the defense of this part of the country. Since the Gulf of Bothnia would be frozen shut in winter, keeping the waters in the Baltic around the Åland Islands open for shipping of war materiel to Finland was absolutely crucial. If shipping went through the southernmost parts of the Baltic instead, Germany might interfere and stop the transports. The ability to protect the transports was therefore directly tied to control of the Åland Islands.[141] To avoid arousing suspicion with respect to Swedish neutrality, the proposed defenses of the islands and northern Finland were discussed in separate documents. In the end, Sweden settled for placing mines in the waters surrounding the islands.[142]

The Shots at Mainila

By the end of November 1939, the Russo-Finnish negotiations had resulted in diplomatic deadlock. Attempts to get Finland to voluntarily cede territory to the Soviet Union had failed, and Stalin was forced to revert to military means. One soldier of the Red Army remembered how he had overheard the top brass talking, "Well, Germans captured Poland in fifteen days, we take Finland in twelve days."[143] Molotov agreed, "[W]e civilians seem unable to get further, so now it will be the military's turn."[144] Nikita Khrushchev later recalled, "When I arrived in Stalin's home in the Kreml, I got the feeling that Stalin, Molotov, and Kuusinen [a former leader of the Finnish Communist Party] were engaged in an ongoing discussion in which they had already decided to present Finland with an ultimatum." It would be a cakewalk. "All we had to do was to raise our voices a little and the Finns would obey. If that didn't work, we only had to fire one shot and the Finns would surely capitulate."[145]

An incident on November 26 cleared the way for Stalin to pursue his objectives. Shots fired near Mainila village on the Karelian Isthmus detonated on Soviet territory, reportedly resulting in the deaths of four Soviet soldiers and nine other casualties. (As reported via radio from Moscow, the deaths involved three soldiers and one noncommissioned officer, in addition to seven soldiers, one noncommissioned officer, and one lieutenant who were wounded.[146]) Prior to this incident, Finnish aerial reconnaissance photos had indicated "massive troop buildups in the Leningrad area and hundreds of tanks, guns, and planes massed openly within easy range of the frontier."[147]

In Molotov's view, the Finnish troops stationed close to the border had acted as a provocation and triggered the conflict. The Soviet government proposed that Finland should withdraw its troops a distance of twenty to twenty-five kilometers from the frontier, so that aggressive acts would not be repeated.[148] Aarno Yrjö-Koskinen, the Finnish minister in Moscow, replied the following day that the Finnish government had ordered an inquiry into the incident and that the shots had not been fired from the Finnish side. In fact, Carl Gustaf Mannerheim, Commander-in-Chief of Finland's armed forces, had ordered all Finnish guns drawn back out of range. Moreover, Finnish troops had observed a grenade explosion coming from the Soviet side. Thus, there were no grounds for withdrawal of the Finnish troops. Finland would be open to conversations leading to mutual withdrawal the recommended distance, however. Koskinen also offered to conduct a joint inquiry into the origin of the shots in order to dispel any misunderstandings.[149]

Molotov replied the following day that the Finnish government had displayed a desire to mislead the public through the refusal to take responsibility for the strikes. The Soviet troops could not withdraw, he said, since they did not present a threat to Finland to begin with. Furthermore, withdrawing twenty-five kilometers inland would place them in the suburbs of Leningrad. Finland's refusal to withdraw, on the other hand, proved that Finland had clear intent to threaten Leningrad. Due to the stubbornness of the Finnish government and the refusal to resolve the issue peacefully, the nonaggression treaty signed between the Soviet Union and Finland in 1932 would be considered void:

> In consequence, the Government of the U.S.S.R. are obliged to state that they consider themselves, as from to-day, released from the obligations ensuing from the Treaty of Non-Aggression concluded between the U.S.S.R. and Finland, obligations which are being systematically violated by the Finnish Government.[150]

In a radio address the next day, Molotov officially renounced the nonaggression pact and severed all diplomatic relations with Finland. By firing the shots and refusing to take responsibility, Finland had clearly indicated that it did not wish to maintain normal relations with the Soviet Union:

> Therefore the Soviet government was yesterday compelled to announce that from now on it considers itself free from the obligations taken on by virtue of the non-aggression pact concluded between the U.S.S.R. and Finland and now irresponsibly broken by the government of Finland.[151]

Although the shots resulted in a terrible uprising among the Soviet troops stationed along the Finnish border, for some reason the seriousness of the event and the soon-to-come Soviet "counterattack" failed to register among the Swedish leadership, who considered it naïve to suggest that Finland, a nation of only three and a half million people, could possibly desire to agitate the enormously bigger and militarily superior Soviet Union by starting a war.[152]

The Finns had clear proof that their artillery was located too far away to reach the Russian border, but Molotov would not hear of it. Finland had failed to act rationally, he claimed. Soviet propaganda broadcasts further suggested that the small states around the Baltic harbored adventurists, who were plotting the destruction of the Soviet Union. As early as 1936, Soviet politician Andrei Zhdanov had promoted the attitude that small countries surrounding the city of Leningrad were scheming within their borders and dreaming up "great adventures." If these nations were not satisfied to mind their own business, Russia might feel "forced to open up our windows a bit wider" and "call upon our Red Army to defend our country."[153] Propaganda leaflets issued by the Russians urged the Finns to rise up against their capitalist oppressors. The coming war would be a combination of propaganda campaigns and military terror as the Red Army poured across the border. The Finns feared that the hostilities would lead to renewed Soviet occupation of Finland.[154] Since the opening of the Soviet archives, however, it has become clear that Finland never fired the shots, and that it was a planned provocation by the Soviet

Union.[155] The report that several Soviet soldiers were killed has also proven false.[156] Russian diaries and personnel records of the event indicate that there was "no shelling or casualties on that date or any engagement with the Finnish Army at any time before the Soviet Union declared war on Finland."[157] Khrushchev explained the event as follows in his memoirs:

> Suddenly there was a telephone call. We had fired our salvo, and the Finns had replied with artillery fire of their own. De facto, the war had begun. There is, of course, another version of the facts: it's said that the Finns started shooting first and that we were compelled to shoot back. It's always like that when people start a war. They say, "You fired the first shot," or "You slapped me first, and I'm only hitting back."[158]

According to Khrushchev, the need to protect against outside threats was justification enough for starting the war. Besides, Stalin was confident that the war would be short-lived and resolved to his liking without too many Soviet casualties.[159] On November 30, Kirill Meretskov, Commander-in-Chief of Leningrad Military District, spoke to the soldiers of the Red Army and the people of the Soviet Union, ordering "the troops of Leningrad military district to march over the frontier, crush the Finnish forces, and once and for all secure the Soviet Union's northwestern borders and Lenin city, the cradle of the revolution of the proletariat."[160] Stalin had built a huge and technologically advanced army and was confident in a quick victory, and without a formal declaration of war he launched an attack against Helsinki. "[F]our Soviet armies with 21 divisions, more than 400,000 soldiers, thousands of tanks, warplanes, and heavy artillery crossed Finland's borders. The invasion [was] almost three times larger than the Allied landing at Normandy on D-day."[161] The Soviet tanks overwhelmed the Finnish army, who had no training in confronting tanks in warfare. The Finnish defense was initially on the verge of collapse.

Early that morning, Mannerheim received the devastating news that the Red Army, after preparing the way with artillery fire, had violated the border on the Karelian Isthmus and was now proceeding in several directions toward the heart of Finland. Hostile aircraft had likewise engaged in attacks against a number of country towns and other areas. In the protection of a thickening cloud cover, the Russian flight squadron that had departed from Stalin's base in Estonia had managed to reach the Finnish capital without drawing undue attention.[162] Was this the "modern way of declaring war," the Finns asked in astonishment when Helsinki was bombed.[163] But Mannerheim considered it simply a continuation of the War of Independence twenty years earlier.[164] He advised the civilian leadership to attempt yet a diplomatic compromise with Stalin, simultaneously emphasizing that under no circumstances should they gamble away the country's independence and ultimately its existence.[165] Simultaneously, he was utterly aware of the dismal shape of the Finnish armed forces and knew that a war with Russia would have devastating consequences. At the time of the invasion, Finland's defensive forces stationed along the frontier amounted to approximately thirteen thousand troops. In relation to the breadth of the area that had to be defended, they were so few and would have to spread themselves so thin that they would be unable to halt a determined Russian advance, even if they simply guarded the terrain without engaging in actual combat. Should the Russians manage a breakthrough anywhere along the line, remaining in the established positions would prove futile and the troops would risk encirclement and/or isolation.[166] When criticized by the United States for bombing Finnish civilians, Molotov denied the action and stated that it must be a misunderstanding, as viewed from America "at a distance of over 8,000 kilometers from Finland," because "Soviet airplanes have not bombarded cities and do not intend to do so but have bombarded airdromes since our Government prizes the interests of the Finnish people no less than any other Government."[167]

When news of the offensive against Finland reached Sweden, the Swedish leadership became fully aware of the seriousness of the situation and immediately heightened the country's war preparations, for example, by denying the infantry regiment in Boden in northern Sweden a previously planned leave. A government meeting with Per Edvin Sköld, the Minister of Defense, proved in order. Government officials further decided to start mobilizing the armed forces in the hope that it would signal to the rest of the world that Sweden was fully prepared to protect its border in the north. They refused to send troops to the Åland Islands, however. According to a letter dated December 3, 1939, and intended only for the inner circle of the Swedish defense department, the Finnish government indicated great disappointment in Sweden's decision not to defend the Åland Islands. Reportedly, Finland's President Kyösti Kallio nearly collapsed when he received the devastating news. But Mannerheim merely shrugged and said that he had expected no other answer from Sweden. Juho Niukkanen, the Finnish Minister of Defense, went as far as suggesting that Finland should offer the Åland Islands to Hitler in return for a German intervention in the conflict.[168]

The Soviet Union's Strategic Plan

Although the Soviet invasion of Finland might have appeared a hasty decision to the casual observer, and likely a product of the division of the Baltic states three months earlier, the war had been long in the making. Stalin had planned an offensive against Finland several months prior to the signing of the Molotov-Ribbentrop pact, even prior to his political speech of March 10, 1939, in which he had talked about the need to aggravate a European conflict in order to weaken the warring powers, clear the way for Soviet intervention with fresh forces, and give the Soviet Union the ability to dictate the peace terms in Europe. In June that year, Stalin approved of General Meretskov's plan to take Helsinki, then called "a counter-offensive blow against Finland," and prepared transports toward Finland two months later.[169] Stalin's generals, impressed with Hitler's *Blitzkrieg* tactics, believed that the Soviet Union's bold violation of Finland's borders from the Arctic Ocean to the Gulf of Finland would lead to a quick victory. Termed a "walkover" expected to take two weeks at the most, the plan called for overrunning Finland with overwhelming force, and through a westward advance attack the Finns from eight different directions.[170] The Soviet divisions, although receiving orders not to violate Finland's frontier with Sweden, were expected to penetrate all the way to the Swedish border.[171]

The 14th army thus attacked from the north in the Petsamo area with the objective of closing Finland's access to the sea, before marching toward Torneå on the Swedish border where it would take control of the vital railway connection to the west. The 9th army struck slightly further south with the objective of cutting Finland in half at the "waist." The 7th army attacked Finland's main defenses, the fortified Mannerheim Line on the Karelian Isthmus, with the objective of pressing through to Viborg and into southern Finland, which housed the main population centers and the capital, Helsinki. The 8th army moved north of Lake Ladoga. Its objective was to cut Finland's internal network of rail and then attack the Mannerheim Line from the rear.[172] The plan ultimately called for dividing the country in half at the narrow "mid-section" by Suomussalmi, however, thereby severing all of Finland's communications with Sweden, which were essential to Finnish resistance.[173] Viborg, the second largest city in Finland, once taken, would provide easy access to Helsinki, after which all of Finland would fall into Soviet hands.[174]

The core of Stalin's plan was based on the Treaty of Nystadt, signed by Tsar Peter I (Peter the Great) and the King of Sweden in 1721, and which had brought the Great Northern War to an end. "The Ladies of St. Petersburg could not sleep peacefully as long as the Finnish frontier ran so close to our capital," Peter the Great had written in explanation of his conquest of Viborg.[175] The treaty had outlined the territories that Russia needed for strategic reasons in order to protect St. Petersburg, including territorial ownership of the Karelian Isthmus, or the land bridge that separated the Gulf of Finland from Lake Ladoga. Control of the Isthmus would force an invader desiring to reach the capital to take the long route to the north of Lake Ladoga, trekking through difficult terrain, particularly if the offensive occurred in winter.[176] As Khrushchev would say later, "Ever since Russia turned back Napoleon's invasion [in 1812], people claimed that winter was our main ally."[177] The day the shots were fired at Mainila, however, little did the Red Army suspect that the many difficulties ahead would be directly attributed to winter operations in rough terrain.

With a population of 170 million and a peacetime army almost two million men strong, the Soviet Union possessed the largest military establishment in the world.[178] A problem at the start of the Winter War was that the country had suffered from leadership and organizational problems for several years. The superior technology and good leadership that did exist often took second place to the emphasis on political propaganda. In the years prior to the war, Stalin had purged approximately thirty-five thousand officers or nearly one half of the total officer corps, including 80 to 90 percent of the colonels and generals, and now had to rely on junior officers with little experience of combat and not enough confidence to lead the Soviet troops toward victory. Still, the Red Army enjoyed a great numerical advantage. The regular army had been increased gradually in size until it was comprised of approximately 1.8 million men organized into 138 divisions of which 108 were infantry. The army was reinforced with approximately eighty reserve divisions, which were comprised of several million more troops.[179] Fifty divisions including approximately three thousand tanks and eight hundred aircraft were sent to fight the war in Finland. For comparison purposes, Finland owned only 45 tanks, most of which were leftovers from World War I, and 146 airplanes.[180] At the start of the war, Finland flew 31 Fokker D-XXI monoplanes produced by the Dutch.[181] Although fairly modern in design, Finland's air force was so small that it was laughable in comparison to Russia's. The ten hours of training in air combat operations per month that the Finnish pilots received was hardly enough for teaching them to defend Finland's airspace. The deficient education resulted in a disproportionally high number of training accidents, which amounted to several losses in lives and aircraft.[182]

On December 2, 1939, Moscow reported "through intercepted radio messages" that a Finnish democratic "people's government" had been formed in Terijoki, the first town that the Russians "liberated," on the Karelian Isthmus. The Soviet Union instituted Otto Vilhelm Kuusinen, a Marxist Finn and former leader of the Finnish Communist Party, as head of the new government.[183] Kuusinen, who had fled to Russia after Finland's War of Independence, had been placed under the protection of the Soviet state just inside the Finnish border.[184] Laurence Steinhardt, United States Ambassador to the

Soviet Union, reported that it appeared as though the Soviet objectives in Finland, through the setup of the Terijoki government, were "to achieve by means of its armed forces the physical seizure of the strategic positions in Finland now desired by the Soviet Government ostensibly for the purpose of defense but actually for the purpose of attaining a dominant position in the Baltic, and to establish in power the Kuusinen government or another regime which will be subservient to the Soviet Government." He further noted that it appeared as though the Soviet Union had no desire to use a third party as a mediator in the conflict, and that the war in Finland was an opportunity for Russia to subjugate Finland in order to "be free to meet possible developments in the Balkans and the Black Sea area or perhaps to strengthen its position vis-à-vis Germany."[185]

The Soviet Union's immediate acknowledgement of the Terijoki government as legitimate allowed Stalin to claim the right to unite the Soviet part of Karelia with Finland.[186] An election of officials was to be held soon after the Finnish "People's Army," supported by the Red Army, had marched into Helsinki. The chief of the military district in Leningrad had expressed in his directives as early as November 23 that the Kuusinen government would eventually be established in Helsinki with the help of Russian troops who did not come as conquerors but as friends of Finland. The Red Army aspired to conquering Viborg within four days, and Helsinki within two weeks.[187] It has since come to light that the Soviet Union had offered Kuusinen's position to another Finnish communist, Arvo Tuominen, living in Stockholm, as early as November 13, 1939.[188] Despite being a zealous communist, Tuominen, who was discouraged by the purges and the new developments between the Soviet Union and Germany, declined the offer, later stating:

> The longer my conscience-struggle continued, the clearer I realized that was not a question of the liberation of the working people of Finland. Instead it was a matter of an unprecedented crime, which I could not go along with.[189]

The day after instituting the new government, Molotov signed a friendship treaty with Kuusinen; a deal in the name of the "Democratic Finland," which stipulated that all questions relating to the border between the Soviet Union and Finland were to be regulated by the Soviet Union.[190] Stalin thus no longer recognized the democratically elected government in Helsinki. These measures were further indication that he intended to turn Finland into a vassal state of Russia.[191] The establishment of the Kuusinen government was also a tactic meant to split the Finns politically and decrease their resistance to the Soviet invasion. Others have argued that no direct evidence exists for Stalin's intent to annex all of Finland, and that his goal was instead to increase Soviet influence in the area and establish bases on Finnish territory in order to protect Russia against the West European forces.[192] It is also possible that Stalin believed that his invasion of Finland would trigger another civil war like the one in 1918, where the communists would stand with Russia against the legitimate Finnish government in Helsinki. In Stalin's view, further negotiations with Finland would then have proven unnecessary, since such a war would have been an internal deal and not an official conflict between Russia and Finland.[193]

Pravda reported on December 4 that it was in the Finnish people's best interest that Kuusinen was chosen President of the new Democratic Republic of Finland. With the support of the Soviet Union, he could defend and protect Finland's independence through the use of armed force against hostile powers.[194] Stalin airdropped a number of propaganda letters over Finnish territory in an attempt to promote positive attitudes toward Kuusinen. One such letter, found by a Swedish volunteer, stated that Finland was a "very dangerous" country that had allowed its army to establish a foothold at the Soviet border. But now that Finland had formed its own democratic republic through the Kuusinen government, the commoners, the heroic Finnish people, could finally rise and defeat the dangerous Finnish army and the capitalists who had treated the peace loving and efficient Finns so brutally. The friendship pact between the Kuusinen government and the Soviet Union would grant the Finns the power to realize their dream of reuniting with the Karelian people. Further Soviet propaganda communicated that the new people's government along with the Finnish populace had met the Red Army with overwhelming enthusiasm while shouting, "Long live the Soviet Union — the true protector of the people."[195] Obviously, no Finn took the propaganda seriously, which also promised "bread for the starving people," yet were followed by bombs dropped over the major cities.[196] These events clearly demonstrated the lack of knowledge the Soviets possessed with respect to the culture and mentality of the Finnish people.

Despite the brutal invasion of their country, the Finns were willing to engage in negotiations with the Soviet Union, as long as any concessions they agreed to would not jeopardize Finland's independence. Although there was hope that a mutual agreement could be reached before too many families had been devastated by the bombings of the cities, the Finnish government did not believe that the Soviet Union would come to the negotiating table in good faith, pointing to that Stalin had already proclaimed the Kuusinen government the only legitimate establishment.[197] More diplomatic difficulties developed on December 6, when the State Secretary of the German Foreign Office sent a telegram to the German minister in the Soviet Union, laying blame on England for halting the negotiations, and further cautioned against expressing sympathy for Finland's position:

> Only a few weeks ago Finland was about to come to an understanding with Russia, which might have been achieved by a prudent Finnish policy. An appeal to the League of Nations by the Finnish Government is the least suitable way of solving the crisis. There is no doubt that British influence on the Finnish Government — partly operating through Scandinavian capitals — induced the Finnish Government to reject Russian proposals and thereby brought on the present conflict. England's guilt in the Russo-Finnish conflict should be especially emphasized. Germany is not involved in these events. In conversations, sympathy is to be expressed for the Russian point of view. Please refrain from expressing any sympathy for the Finnish position.[198]

Events now developed quickly. On December 9, the German Embassy followed up with an urgent and top secret telegram to the Minister of Foreign Affairs in Germany, stating that the Soviet Naval Committee was planning a submarine blockade against Finland in the Gulf of Bothnia, and asking that German steamers in regular traffic to northern Sweden deliver fuel and food in secret to the Soviet submarines. The Commander-in-Chief of the German Navy recommended that Germany stay completely out of the Russo-Finnish conflict and refrain from shipping armaments to Finland, while in the same breath recommending that Germany honor Russia's request for oil for her submarines.[199] These communications demonstrated that Germany was not unbiased and had at least some hand in the war, despite officially insisting that this was not the case.

Despite Germany's favorable attitude toward the Soviet Union, Hitler's inspirational *Blitzkrieg* tactics, and the initial successes of the Soviet offensive against Finland, Stalin had a tough road ahead of him. He had failed to realize that he could not base his tactics on the familiar landscape and network of roads that the German leadership had relied upon in its initial successes in Poland. Moreover, Finland could defend the coastal archipelago relatively easy by placing mines in the waters.[200] Blücher, the German minister in Finland, was able to foresee the gravity of the situation and the difficulties that Stalin was bound to suffer as a result of this war:

> I cannot avoid the impression that with the attack by the Russians on Finland a disaster is also descending upon Germany.... For someone who has had an opportunity here to observe the resolute unanimity of this nation, which, though small, is tenacious, hardened by sports, and militarily proficient, for someone who knows the country with its swamps, lakes, cliffs, forests, and harsh climate, it is difficult to believe that the Russians will have an easy time of it. On the contrary, the war may last a long time, may bring the Russians many a defeat and must cause them severe losses. The war will probably take the following course: The Russians, because of the inaccessibility of the Finnish coast, will forego any landing attempt and will employ their land forces at the

> Karelian Isthmus and north of Lake Ladoga, where they will be forced to fight for every foot of ground. At the same time they will try to destroy cities, factories, railroads, and bridges by air raids on a very large scale, in order to crush the resistance of the Finnish people. Since the cities and large factories have been evacuated, the Russians will cause only property damage by this action.[201]

It was thus clear that the war could not be fought with the same tactics that were common to mass armies. The restricted availability of roads in the area limited the number of troops that could cross at one time, and the only railway ran more than a hundred kilometers from the border. Even if the Red Army managed to use the railway for transport of supplies and troops, the shipments could easily be targeted by Finnish bomber aircraft. If attempting to guard the railway with anti-aircraft artillery, the Russians would have to do so along its entire extent, which would prove an almost impossible task. Additionally, as Blücher had pointed out, the Russians would face several difficulties moving through Finland's interior. Finland's big cities, industrial areas and harbors, and the majority of the population were concentrated in the southern and southwestern parts of the country. The sparse network of roads and numerous waterways would no doubt complicate the movement of the large numbers of motor-driven vehicles the Russians were known to employ. The Finns could also bomb the bridges connecting the land between the many lakes in order to further halt the advance of the Red Army.[202]

Although Stalin desired to fight along a frontier as long as possible in order to take full advantage of his numerical superiority, landing troops by air on Finnish territory did not prove operationally feasible. Whether parachuting in or landing by transport aircraft, troops and equipment would still need to be moved through the wilderness to the industrial areas once on the ground. Large transport aircraft were required if one were to drop any sizable number of troops, but the ability to land such aircraft would be severely hampered due to the difficult Finnish terrain. The Russian pilots could not count on landing safely at established airports since the Finns could easily guard these fields and aim fire at incoming aircraft.[203]

Finland's Defense Plan

Finland's army faced an enemy that had access to two million troops and even greater reserves. Stalin's massive launch of forces across the Finnish border and his bombing of Helsinki were evidence that he had taken Hitler's lead and attempted his own version of *Blitzkrieg*.[204] The march into Estonia and the occupation of military bases along the southern coast of the Gulf of Finland in October 1939, from which the Russian pilots could reach Finland's capital in less than a half an hour flight, had worsened Finland's chances of defending the country against air attacks.[205] Europe expected a quick Soviet victory. Successfully taking and holding territory required a land-based army, however, and in the months prior to the war Finnish headquarters determined that the main attack would likely come across the Karelian Isthmus — the gateway to Helsinki; a city which the Soviet leadership estimated would fall under their dominion within fourteen days — mainly because the terrain in northern Finland would prove too difficult to bridge by a land-based army.[206]

Although it was theoretically possible that an attack could come, for example, against the northern border by Petsamo or from Murmansk, the possibility seemed remote and would not have constituted a direct threat to Finland's capital and main industrial areas. A Soviet offensive over the northern or northwestern border would easily be detected in time for Finland to prepare a counteroffensive because, in order to reach the border, the Red Army must first pass across Swedish or Norwegian territory.[207] From a military perspective, the land route over the Isthmus, "through which run the main railways and roads connecting Finland with Leningrad and the rest of Russia," thus seemed superior to an offensive launched against the northern border or the fortified western coastline.[208] The other option was to move around the northern shore of Lake Ladoga, but this would require a march of approximately 240 kilometers by the invading army, before it would reach a point from which it could endanger the Finnish positions on the Isthmus.[209] A greater threat was possible if the enemy managed to make use of the harbors in Estonia or Latvia, or worse, managed to occupy the Åland Islands.[210] But losing the islands, although they were emotionally important territory, would not necessarily mean that Finland would lose its sovereignty as a nation.[211]

There was thus little doubt that the Karelian Isthmus would become the main theater of operation, not only because it served as a land bridge between Russia and Finland and could be breached rather easily by the powerful Red Army, but also because of its proximity to Leningrad where Russia could base large numbers of troops, who could then march into Finland's interior and main industrial centers. Several questions remained to be answered. For example, what type of strategy should the Finns use when meeting the Red Army on the Isthmus? Would static defense suffice in order to minimize casualties in the already slim army, or would forceful counterattacks prove more valuable? Determining the exact place of the breakthrough was of particular importance since Finland possessed such limited resources and must decide in advance where to stage the greatest number of troops. Part of the answer to this question lay in how much time Finland would have to mobilize its forces before the war became fact. In best-case scenario, the troops would be stationed twenty to sixty kilometers from the border along the Mannerheim Line, which had been strengthened during the summer of 1939 and stretched across the Karelian Isthmus from Lake Ladoga to the Gulf of Finland.[212] The river Vuoksen, which could be crossed via a number of bridges, further protected the line's eastern part. These bridges would become primary targets for Soviet attacks before the ice grew thick enough to support the weight of tanks and other transport vehicles.[213] Should Russia launch a surprise attack, however, the Finnish army would have little time to march to the border, and would then have to station the troops much closer to Viborg.[214]

As the Soviet threat grew stronger in the autumn of 1939, Mannerheim urged Finland to further reinforce the defensive lines across the Isthmus and mobilize the troops in order to ensure them time for refresher training.[215] Gaining familiarity with the terrain now before hostilities started would increase morale and give the troops the mental fortitude they needed to face the trials that lay ahead.[216] Reinforcing the lines required a considerable amount of manual labor. As Finnish students went to work digging trenches and erecting barbed wire obstacles, Soviet laborers likewise started to renovate the deficient rail network and sparse roads on their side of the border.[217] Thus, the drawback in Finland's plan did not lie in a lack of team spirit but in the fact that the country was militarily weak, because the political leadership had failed to allocate enough funds for strengthening the country's defensive forces in the decades preceding the war. Not only did the Finns lack tanks and ammunition, Russian aircraft could fly at more than double the speed of the outdated Finnish aircraft. Finland's limited resources propagated the use of primitive weapons and innovative tactics. For example, the Finns often had to resort to fighting at close combat range armed only with their *puukko* utility knives, which they always carried with them.[218]

Although the use of mobile warfare did not prove feasible without substantial motor-driven equipment, the Finns soon scrapped the idea of a purely static defense plan. Not only would it prove impossible to stand passively against the superior Red Army for any length of time, static defense without active initiative would have a negative effect on morale. A compromise was reached that involved stabilizing the front in order to hinder, or at least delay, the Red Army's march toward the Finnish capital. Another concern was the defense of northern Finland in case of an attempted enemy breakthrough there as well. Since the scarcity of manpower and equipment prevented the Finnish army from guarding the entire frontier from Lake Ladoga to the Arctic Ocean, it became evident that foreign assistance would prove crucial to their success. Finland looked foremost to its closest neighbor, Sweden, in the hope that the Swedish government would agree to supply Finland with material resources and trained military troops and commanders. Simultaneously, Finland realized that an increase in hostilities between Germany and the French-British alliance in the autumn of 1939 could actually be an asset to the Finnish army. It was unlikely that the Soviet Union would manage to stay outside the European conflict for any length of time, and Stalin would eventually be compelled to redirect part of his forces toward Europe. He would then have to fight on two fronts, which meant that he could allocate fewer troops to the war in Finland. Finland's primary goal was therefore to delay the Red Army's advance long enough for international help to arrive, or at least until Stalin was forced to join the European war.[219]

The war against the "Russian Bear" was at its core not about borders, but about national survival and autonomy. The Finns knew that the war threatened their very culture and way of life, and the bombings of civilians only increased their resolve. Stalin's request for territory proved a threat to Finland's existence. Despite the numerically inferior forces, the Finnish soldier was confident "that on a man-to-man basis he was worth several of his opponents. His ancestors, as far back as recorded Finnish history existed, had fought Russians on this same soil and usually won."[220] Finland was a nation forged from conflict. If Finland lost this war, the people would no longer be Finns. The Soviets had "overwhelming military superiority"; the Finns "little more than the will to resist."[221] But if the enemy succeeded with a breakthrough on the Karelian Isthmus and reached the inner parts of the country, how long could Finland's population retain their fighting spirit? Blücher, who continued to follow the developments with interest, acknowledged the Finnish resolve but expressed more concern for his own country than for either Russia or Finland:

> Within a matter of a few months this flourishing country, which in the twenty years of its independence has doubled its agricultural production and tripled its industrial production, will be transformed into a heap of rubble. This will not mean the defeat of the people, for all elements are willing to return to the most primitive conditions and continue their fight for freedom. But for us this means that Finland is eliminated as a supplier of very important raw materials for the war copper, molybdenum, and possibly later nickel and iron and also animal foods, especially fish from the Arctic Ocean.[222]

When the Finnish troops had recovered from the initial shock of the Soviet invasion, they managed to hold the border on the Karelian Isthmus until the turn of the year. They knew the terrain well, used horses over motor-driven vehicles, and could endure temperatures occasionally dipping as low as -40 degrees C. But they could not hold out against the "Russian Bear" forever and defend every part of the country's thousand kilometer long border with the Soviet Union. Although there was hope that the rest of the world would sympathize with Finland and offer military assistance, Mannerheim, who understood the detrimental conditions the soldiers would suffer as a result of their numerical inferiority, recommended that peace be sought.[223] He had displayed pessimism over Finland's ability to defend against an invasion as early as September 30, 1939, and held the view that Finland should give Russia the islands in the Gulf of Finland that Stalin asked for in order to preserve the peace.[224] When the Finnish government refused, he suggested that Finland ask for soldiers and weapons from Sweden.[225] Although Finland's defensive plan was extensive, it came with no guarantees of success beyond the first day of fighting.

Sweden Reacts to the War

Finland's remarkable resistance to the Soviet invasion astounded the world. Countries throughout Europe followed the war with interest and cheered the Finns for their attempts to secure democratic values and retain independence. Yet, when the war started, Swedish foreign policy with respect to Finland was not clearly defined.[226] Sweden's leadership was not as surprised at the Soviet invasion of Finland as they were at the time Stalin had chosen for launching the offensive. Winter had already come to the northern latitudes; in some places the snow cover was two to five decimeters thick. The severity of the weather seemed to benefit the defenders and should have made Stalin less eager to launch an assault this time of year, particularly since most of the Soviet troops were untrained in winter operations.[227] Thus, in the days following the shots at Mainila, Sweden waited, cautiously hoping that Stalin had merely attempted to frighten Finland into compliance and that nothing more would come of it. But when the Kuusinen government was formed, it became clear that Stalin had a definite plan with far-reaching consequences.[228]

Both foreign political relations and domestic politics affected how Sweden reacted to the conflict. Since Sweden took pride in democratic values, the opinions of the people mattered and could not be ignored. Of utmost importance was also that the government remain united and no party stray too far from the general wishes of the people. The failure of Rickard Sandler, the Swedish Minister of Foreign Affairs, to gain approval for his suggestion that Sweden should take concrete military action in Finland with particular focus on the defense of the Åland Islands, led to his resignation and subsequently resulted in Sweden, on December 13, 1939, forming a coalition government

Caricature of the Communist and Social Democratic parties in Sweden, and the shunning of communists that occurred after the Soviet Union invaded Finland. "Why don't you say hi?" asks the communist. "I am sorry, but I don't think I know you," the socialist answers (source: Den Svenske Folksocialisten, *January 20, 1940, Krigsarkivet, Finlandskommitten, 1939–1940).*

under the leadership of Per Albin Hansson. This new government consisted of representatives from the four most prominent parties, and had at its goal to garner as much lateral support as possible for keeping Sweden outside the war.[229] The communists, who sided with the Soviet Union, were banned from representation.[230] (Finland had likewise established a coalition government on December 1, 1939, the second day of the war, under the leadership of statesman Risto Ryti.[231])

In order to avoid conflict within the government, Hansson found it necessary to establish a common view of how to proceed politically. Domestic issues were placed on the backburner, and neutrality became the base for foreign policy. There were four major concerns: Sweden must start immediate mediation between the Soviet Union and Finland; the Soviet forces must be kept in check in the meantime; a quick peace agreement was of utmost importance, particularly since England and France had indicated a desire to assist Finland militarily; and English and French troops should not be given permission to transit through Sweden on their way to Finland. The danger was that it could lead to a foreign occupation of northern Sweden and the iron ore mines, which would likely trigger a German invasion of Sweden. Sweden was thus in principle threatened by four countries from different directions: England, France, Germany, and the Soviet Union.[232] Despite the desire to set aside ideological and political barriers, the coalition government became a hampered entity that found it easier to agree NOT to do anything at all than to take action in any particular direction.[233]

Christian Günther, the new Minister of Foreign Affairs, when asked about the possibility of sending government sanctioned troops to Finland, emphasized caution. In order to prevent a run of emotions and loss of reason, the consequences of such an action must be considered before any decisions were made, or political balance and preservation of Swedish neutrality could not be achieved. Several questions must be asked: If Sweden officially assisted Finland, how great was the risk that the country would get pulled into the war in Europe? If it did not assist Finland, would Stalin's troops advance to the Swedish border and become a threat also to Sweden's independence? The greater parts of the Finnish troops were concentrated in southeastern Finland; thus, the points of weakness were northern Finland and the Åland Islands, with the likely attack lines located across the Petsamo-Rovaniemi area or toward the Torne River. However, as long as Finland's defense in the southeastern part of the country held, a Soviet offensive against Sweden seemed improbable. Air attacks were improbable as well, despite earlier fears. The Russians had few bases in Balticum, East Karelia, and Murmansk, which limited their use of airpower. An attack coming by sea from the Russian bases in the Baltic states was not really considered a threat at this time, because of Russia's mediocre resources in the area. If Stalin's troops managed to occupy Finland, however, the situation would change drastically.[234]

Although Günther did not perceive an immediate threat to Sweden by the Soviet Union, he was more leery of England and France. He considered it particularly crucial to be vigilant of Germany's intents and thought a German invasion of Sweden via Denmark possible. Hitler must not be given a reason to invade Sweden, as might happen should Sweden grant British or French troops transit rights through Swedish territory. Blücher had already warned the world about the dangerous effects the war might have on the Swedish exports of iron to Germany:

> And finally it can in no wise be predicted how far the conflagration in the North will extend now that Russia has hurled the torch of war into Finnish territory. Questions such as the ore supply from Sweden arise inevitably.[235]

Furthermore, a report issued by the Commander-in-Chief of the German Navy and sent to Hitler on December 12 indicated concern over the negative public opinion in Norway with respect to the Winter War, and the consequences it might have for Germany's ability to secure iron ore from Sweden. If England managed to exercise influence over Norway and get Norway to agree to English occupation, Norwegian coastal bases would disrupt German naval warfare in the Atlantic and the North Sea, which would interrupt or completely halt the transports of iron ore from Narvik. If England could dominate both Norway and Sweden, the war would be carried into the Baltic Sea, which could lead to a decisive Allied victory fought on Swedish soil.[236]

Despite the neutrality concerns, when the Soviet Union attacked Finland unprovoked, public support in Sweden flared up and surged like an ocean wave through all parts of the country. Hans Ruin, a renowned author and professor of philosophy at Turku Academy in Finland and at Lund's University in Sweden and a great proponent of the defense of Finland, kept the people informed by reporting about the war to Swedish newspapers.[237] Class and political differences disappeared and people from all walks of life came together in support of their Finnish neighbors. Simultaneously, the dislike of communists grew stronger, and the positive view that many Swedes held of Germany declined because of Hitler's recent friendship pact with Stalin.[238] Although Sweden had not seen war since 1814, the Swedish people had a long record of voluntarily fighting for the underdog. Thus, in December 1939, Swedish volunteers once again stood at the threshold of war, this time for the purpose of assisting Finland against the Soviet invasion of the Karelian Isthmus.

2

Volunteer Recruitment and Training

Popular Sentiments and Opinions

In order to better understand the severity of the situation that prompted Sweden to send materiel and voluntary manpower to Finland, an overview of the military events that preceded the arrival of the Swedish troops at the front is in place. When Stalin broke the diplomatic ties with Finland on November 29, 1939, Soviet soldiers violated the border at the Fisherman's Peninsula on the Arctic coast and took prisoner some Finnish border guards. The next day the war started without an official declaration. Soviet troops invaded the Karelian Isthmus at several places, opened fire against the villages north of Lake Ladoga, and bombed Helsinki. The Finnish troops stationed on the Isthmus were initially forced to retreat, but soon thereafter managed to hold their ground against the Soviet break-through involving more than a thousand tanks. It soon became evident that the war would be long-lasting and amount to more than a "walkover," as expressed earlier by the Soviet leadership. The Soviet Union's invasion of Finland brought strong criticism from Europe and the United States. Finland, this tiny country, could not possible do any conceivable harm to the Soviet Union, it was reasoned. The Finns clearly wished only "to live at peace as a democracy."[1]

The next few weeks proved turbulent but initially seemed to favor the Finns. On December 11, the Russians reached Tolvajärvi to the north of Lake Ladoga, but were defeated by a skilled counterattack and forced to retreat. The Battle of Tolvajärvi proved particularly dangerous, because it directly threatened Viborg. Meanwhile, the attacks on the Isthmus were acting as a distraction, giving the Red Army an opportunity to develop their forces in the north. Russian soldiers poured over the Finnish border wherever the network of roads permitted, and launched a strong offensive in the direction of Suomussalmi at Finland's midsection and Salla in the north. On December 14, the Finns scored an impressive victory in Suomussalmi, defeating two Russian divisions. The Russians landed additional troops at Petsamo but were again forced to retreat. Although the Finns had managed to halt the Soviet advance on the Karelian Isthmus, the Mannerheim Line was in danger and the threat to northern Finland proved extremely serious. By the beginning of January 1940, however, the Finns had taken around 3,000 prisoners and acquired from the Russians 102 cannons, 54 tanks, and 10 armored vehicles.[2] As reported in an article in *Life* magazine:

> The first phase of the Russo-Finnish war is now at an end, with the repulse of all the Russian attacks over the whole stretch of frontier between the Arctic Ocean and Lake Ladoga. Finland is thus temporarily freed from any further anxiety in the North, and the Russians appear likely for the present to confine their attention to attempts to break through in the South by sheer weight of numbers.[3]

According to one war correspondent, Finland's impressive counteroffensive was "worthy to rank with Napoleon's famous 1796 campaign in Italy, or Jackson's operations in the Valley of Virginia," and had "for the moment saved Finland."[4]

But Russia garnered strength and started a new offensive that involved powerful artillery and air attacks against Finnish ground troops. North of Lake Ladoga, the Red Army advanced toward Salmi and Suijärvi, driving the Finnish guards away, although Finnish battery pieces located on an island in Lake Ladoga opened fire against the Russian flanks. Russian bombers, many based in Estonia, engaged in almost daily terror attacks against Finnish cities and fired at civilians with automatic rifles. In the week of January 7 to 13, as reported by Finland's Minister of Defense, the Russians dropped more than 2,000 bombs over 42 different localities. In the week of January 14 to 20, the weather benefited aerial attacks and the Russian air force flew an estimated 450 aircraft over Finnish territory, dropping 6,667 bombs (not counting bombs dropped at the front) on nearly 200 cities and other localities. The attacks resulted in 18 dead and 109 wounded Finns (not including those killed or wounded at the front). Turku, on January 20, experienced 33 aerial attacks. The relatively few civilian losses were likely a result of the Finnish population's ability to seek cover in a hurry. The great majority of bombs also fell in forests and lakes. By the end of January, the Finns reported having acquired, destroyed, or downed 204 enemy aircraft (confirmed hits, with an additional 30 suspected hits), 434 tanks, and 189 cannons.[5]

Meanwhile, Sweden reacted with anti–Soviet propaganda, harshly criticizing the Swedish Communist Party who defended Stalin's political views and agreed with the newly established Kuusinen government in Terijoki. The Swedish leadership worried that the Soviet Union would recruit the communists living in Sweden in an attempt to overthrow the government,[6] or that hostilities reaching the border in Norrland might trigger a civil war between communists and non-communists, much like the war that had raged in Finland twenty years earlier. According to the political election in 1938, one-fourth of the populace in the north was communist.[7] In contrast to the industrialized cities in southern Sweden where communists were generally shunned, poor education and a large unemployment rate in the north likely contributed to the communist-friendly attitudes. Northern Sweden also housed the iron ore mines which employed large numbers of blue-collar workers, and was headquarter of the communist publication *Norrskensflamman* (the Flame of the Northern Lights), founded by the workers of the iron ore fields several decades earlier. Swedish commander Magnus Dyrssen noted in his diary in the end of January 1940 that communist activities in Norway, as reported by a Norwegian newspaper, were on the rise and the leader for the Norwegian Communist Party had been arrested. Many Finnish communists had likewise fled from the Petsamo region to Norway. Should Russia prove successful in the war with Finland, however, Sweden might be unable to prevent Stalin from forming a north–Scandinavian Soviet Republic.[8]

At the start of the war it was thus the Soviet Union rather than Nazi Germany that presented the greatest threat to Sweden's democratic principles. But when the political right suggested that the Communist Party be forbidden to hold seats in the Swedish Parliament, the Socialist Party insisted that this idea could be enforced only if the Nazi parties, too, were forbidden to hold any kind of power. The friendship and compassion that the Swedes felt for the Finns nevertheless resulted in that several actions were taken against the Communist Party, some of which might be viewed as ethically questionable at best for a democratic country. For example, the political opinions of Party members were recorded and their mail and telecommunications monitored. Many communists were harassed at their work places. On February 10, 1940, the police searched more than a thousand homes of Party members.[9] But harassment and verbal expressions of distaste seemed insufficient to some activists, who considered the time ripe for driving the communists from all positions of importance, thereby completely halting their influence among the working class in northern Sweden.[10]

On March 3, 1940, the newspaper offices of *Norrskensflamman* were set on fire. The incident claimed the lives of five people, two of them children.[11] The suspects were caught but ordered to serve only a lenient five-year sentence.[12] The husband of one of the women and father of the children who died in the event, and who was not at home at the time, never recovered from the shock of losing his family and later committed suicide.[13] The military leadership in Luleå in conjunction with *Finlandskommittén* (the Committee for Finland) also attempted to stop all supply of paper to the printing offices of *Norrskensflamman*, and threatened to permanently close down the publication. It was from this coalition that the terror group formed that organized the arson attack against the paper.[14]

Several other problems related to foreign policy. As military hostilities in Finland intensified at the turn of the year, some people speculated that the Soviet Union and Sweden were really engaged in a form of "mini-war" with each other. Despite its neutrality status, Sweden experienced Soviet aggression on an almost weekly basis. In early January 1940, a Russian submarine attacked a Swedish steamer in Swedish waters, forcing the crew to save themselves in lifeboats while leaving the steamer to sink. Not much later, the Soviet Union dropped bombs over the airport at Kallax at the top of the Gulf of Bothnia, although with little effect. In February 1940, seven Soviet aircraft dropped approximately fifty bombs over Pajala by the Swedish/Finnish border, again without causing any casualties, although several buildings were destroyed. The Soviet Union defended the action, claiming that the pilots had lost track of their whereabouts and unintentionally violated Swedish airspace.[15] Critics, however, believed that these incidents were "diplomatic" attempts by the Russians to communicate that Sweden was neither neutral nor a noncombatant with respect to the war in Finland. It was around this time that Sweden "answered" by rounding up communists and burning the offices of *Norrskensflamman*.[16]

Swedish General Archibald Douglas, Commander of the Northern Army Corps, believed that the safety of Sweden could be served best if the country assisted Finland militarily, and introduced the idea of using the offices of *Norrskensflamman* for printing documents in support of his views. A staunch supporter of Finland, he further propagated the idea that Sweden should completely empty the northern part of the country of communists, by recruiting them for "military duty" in a form of concentration camps set up specifically for citizens with radical political views.[17] The Swedish Communist Party was thus severely decimated. By the end of the war three months later, it had lost one-third of its members. In May 1940, a temporary law granted the Parliament power to forbid certain parties or organizations from existing, if deemed dangerous to Swedish democracy.[18] An article in *Svenska Dagbladet*, a Swedish daily newspaper, noted that the government was united in its desire to defend Swedish neutrality, and would forbid both communist and Nazi actions in the country and press.[19]

General Douglas, who had spent the last three years in Boden responsible for defending northern Sweden, further noted that the Red Army was tactically inferior to the Finnish troops but strategically more dangerous than anticipated.

If Stalin could not be stopped, he believed, Soviet troops would break the Finnish defense in the north around March 1940 and establish themselves by the Swedish border before the ice broke in spring. Despite their tactical inferiority, the Russians would surely learn from their mistakes during their battles with the Finns and gain strength once they had overcome the first hurdles. When reaching the Swedish border, they could use the summer months to replenish their forces and improve the railway and road connections through northern Finland. The Swedes, meanwhile, would be unable to establish any defensive measures that even remotely resembled the Mannerheim Line, and would thus be forced to engage the Russians in mobile warfare. Douglas predicted that the Red Army would likely gain a foothold around the iron ore fields in northern Sweden, and proceed to establish a Finnish-speaking Soviet Republic. He further believed that the material help and volunteers that Sweden had sent to Finland were insufficient. The volunteers would need considerable time in training if they were to gain any kind of unity and military efficiency, he argued, and continued to press the political leadership (to no avail) to send official military forces to Finland.[20]

Yet a problem was the fact that, although the Swedish defense in Upper Norrland focused on guarding the iron ore mines, the troops lacked experience in winter warfare. Most of the troops would be adequately trained first after the end of the Winter War. In a letter to Karl Gustav Westman, Minister of Justice, Douglas argued that if the leadership were to utter only a word or two in favor of sending official assistance to Finland, it would likely trigger a burning enthusiasm among the civilian population at large, and not just among adventurists or idealists. In an attempt to persuade the politicians of his views, he hinted at any case he could find in history which indicated that the Swedish government had chosen the wrong fork in the road because of cowardice, weak leadership, or lack of insight and forethought.[21]

Opinions among the citizens of Sweden were split, however. The Swedish people at large stood on the side of Finland, but some of those who waved an accusatory finger at the Soviet Union would not have done the same had it been Germany or England who had invaded Finland. Others thought it okay for Stalin to conquer Finland, as long as Sweden, Norway, and Denmark sided with Hitler. Still others believed that even if Stalin's campaign in Finland proved successful, Sweden would ultimately not be endangered by a continued Russian campaign across the border, because Hitler, who was in desperate need of the iron ore shipments, would check Stalin's advance. There were also groups who dreamed of the time when Sweden was a superpower and would have liked to see Sweden enter the war for the purpose of reclaiming its former empire, which had included all of Finland and parts of Norway and Germany.[22]

Although a significant distance separated Sweden from the European hostilities and dampened the fear of Nazis, when Stalin invaded Finland, the war was suddenly brought to the Swedish people's backyard.[23] Finland's initial successes at stopping the Russian advance indicated that the big enemy to the east could be conquered, but it required help from other nations, as would become painfully apparent during the second phase of fighting.[24] When the Red Army made a comeback in the end of January and beginning of February 1940, they "dispelled the halo of the Finns' invincibility and thrashed them several times," as expressed by the Soviet military leadership during analysis of the war after it had ended.[25]

Carl Gustaf Mannerheim, Field Marshal and Commander of the Finnish forces, asked for reinforcements from Sweden in early December 1939.[26] Mannerheim had been instrumental in guiding Finland toward a Scandinavian orientation, and now President Kyösti Kallio had given him the supreme command of the country's armed forces.[27] Born of a Swedish-Finnish aristocracy and having served in the military of Imperial Russia, Mannerheim understood the Russian psyche and was therefore particularly suited to lead the Finns against the Red Army.[28] His thirty-year career in tsarist Russia had given him insights and perspectives that would have been impossible to gain had he foregone this option and instead remained in Finland all his life.[29] Finland's best chance of surviving a crisis, he believed, would come by strengthening the armed forces and steering the country toward Western ideals in the hope that Sweden would ally with Finland in the event of war. Initially, Mannerheim's main problem was not lack of manpower, however, but materiel. Sweden's geographical location would prove crucial to Finland's success or failure, because military equipment from other countries had to be transported through Swedish territory in order to reach Finland. Swedish mass media were divided on the issue. Part wished to ensure continued Swedish neutrality, and part wished to support Finland militarily. Questions remained: Was it wise to risk sabotaging Sweden's good relations with Germany? Did Sweden have the economic ability to support Finland with equipment and troops, particularly if the war became long-lasting? Sweden's wish to remain neutral, and the fear of retaliation from Germany should Sweden get involved in the conflict, made Mannerheim's hopes for a strong and active ally in Sweden less probable.[30]

Material Assistance for Finland

During the negotiations preceding the war, King Gustav V Adolf had informed Finland not to count on a military intervention from Sweden and emphasized that the Swedish government, led by Prime Minister Per Albin Hansson, would retain the country's noncombatant status.[31] At the start of the war, Swedish politicians dealing with foreign policy debated three issues of primary concern: First, if Sweden decided to assist Finland materially, how much materiel should be sent and how should the shipping of such be organized? Second, in what ways could the Swedish government make itself useful for mediating in the peace process between Finland and the Soviet Union? Third, how could the government ensure that the "little war" between Finland and Russia was kept separate from the "big war" between Germany and the Western Allies? Since these problems seemed related, Sweden believed that it was obligated to assist Finland in some way in order to facilitate an end to the war and a satisfying closure to the conflict. Moreover, if Sweden acted as a mediator for peace, it might be able to prevent the two wars from becoming one big war by decreasing the risk of intervention from Britain and France.[32] The government thus agreed to help Finland to the extent possible, as long as it would not put Swedish neutrality at risk. Some actions had to be concealed in the name of safety. For example, the Ministry of Foreign Affairs decided that Finnish submarines could be repaired in Sweden, on the conditions that the crew avoided wearing uniforms and agreed to be called shipbuilders rather than sailors.[33]

The scarcity of equipment and manpower in the Finnish army proved a serious problem. Although the Finns had spent some time preparing for war and had undertaken training maneuvers on the Karelian Isthmus since August 1939, they possessed only a few dozen antiquated tanks and no efficient defensive procedures against enemy tanks whatsoever. The materiel shortage was so severe that, in order to avoid spreading itself so thin that it would lose its military effectiveness altogether, Finland had to focus all efforts on the Karelian Isthmus where the major Russian offensive was expected to take place. The greater Finnish frontier with Russia that stretched north for hundreds of kilometers would be protected only with a few pockets of troops scattered across the wilderness.[34] The Finnish people's devotion to their cause was superb, however, and the populace trusted that the government had taken precautions with respect to the country's military preparedness and established necessary diplomatic connections with friendly states.[35]

But the Finnish leadership failed to anticipate many of the coming difficulties. Although several countries openly displayed friendship toward the Finns, their ability to assist Finland with artillery pieces was restricted because of their own lack of excess equipment as Europe progressed deeper into war. Additionally, ammunition from other countries was difficult to come by on account of the unique calibers in Finnish and foreign artillery pieces, which complicated the cross utilization of ammunition. Before the war's end in March 1940, however, Finland was able to acquire and use several artillery pieces from England, France, and Sweden.[36] Of some help was a prior decision from 1928, when Finland had considered the possibility of war with the Soviet Union and examined the likelihood of getting assistance from Sweden. The Finnish government had then decided that the caliber used on Finnish artillery pieces should coincide with that used in Sweden, in order that Swedish ammunition would be easily transferable to the Finnish weapons.[37]

The equipment sent to Finland was sorely needed, not the least psychologically. Mannerheim had predicted at the start of the war that the Finnish supply of ammunition would last two weeks at the most.[38] He had given the troops strict orders to fire only when directly threatened by Soviet forces.[39] One officer of the Finnish army estimated that Finland would need a minimum of fifteen thousand cartridges of ammunition per day in order to have any chance at all to stave off the Russian advance along the Mannerheim Line. If this could not be provided, the officers might as well prepare the troops for an immediate retreat to Viborg. Moreover, the estimation was based on the amount of ammunition the army would need in a purely defensive war. As it turned out, the resourcefulness of the Finns allowed them to fight offensively all the way from the Gulf of Finland to Petsamo on less than ten thousand rounds per day, even during the heaviest fighting which took place in the months of February and March 1940.[40]

In an effort to offer relief to the Finnish troops, Sweden agreed to send one-third of the country's total air force fighter squadrons to Finland, ready to defend the northernmost parts of the country by early January 1940, in addition to a wide variety of firearms and ammunition.[41] Transports went via rail to Torneå where the equipment had to be unloaded and reloaded onto Finnish train cars due to the fact that Sweden and Finland used different gauge railway tracks.[42] Although Sweden donated several hundred cannons (in addition to approximately 80 cannons that Finland purchased from Sweden), 90,000 rifles, and 42 million cartridges to Finland,[43] the first shipment of antitank guns from Bofors, Sweden's developer of defense systems, was uncrated just weeks before the war broke out and proved barely enough to supply each regiment with one or two guns.[44] The antitank guns were crucial to Finnish success, as they had the ability to penetrate the armor of "most light-to-medium Russian tanks."[45] The equipment was financed through loans from the Swedish government.[46]

The Swedish leadership worried that supplying Finland with weapons and ammunition would create a shortage at home, should the war between Germany and the Western Allies spread to the Scandinavian peninsula.[47]

Volunteers inspecting a damaged Russian tank (source: Krigsarkivet, Förbundet Svenska Finlandsfrivilliga, Volume 29 of photograph collection).

England had also ordered weapons from Bofors, and these orders had to be fulfilled.[48] Although both Britain and France delivered large amounts of weapons and ammunition to Finland, according to Väinö Tanner, "Sweden was especially important to us as a source of munitions, since as our closest neighbor it was capable and desirous of assisting us quickly. Without this aid the war could by no means have been fought."[49] Although Germany supported Finland with rifles and ammunition for a short time in secret (as reported by Mussolini's Minister of Foreign Affairs),[50] it had to stop when a Swedish journalist leaked the news and Hitler's nonaggression pact with Stalin came into question.[51] The Russians would likely have discovered the German deliveries of weapons eventually, anyway, even without the help of Swedish journalists.[52]

In addition to material help, Sweden engaged in humanitarian missions, accepted thousands of refugees, and participated in a massive operation to evacuate approximately ten thousand Finnish children to Swedish foster care.[53] A number of organizations were enlisted for this purpose. Among these were *Centrala Finlandshjälpen* and *Filadelfiaorganisationen*, which focused on placing thousands of women and children, many of whom originated in Karelia and who had fled Finland, in Swedish homes. The so-called *Nordiska Hjälpen* assisted with the transport of Finnish citizens to Sweden. *Röda Korset* (the Red Cross), *Rädda Barnen* (Save the Children), *Fredrika Bremerförbundet*, *Frälsningsarmen* (the Salvation Army), and *Lottakåren* (from the Lotta Svärd organization; a women's auxiliary) were also involved.[54] The extremely cold temperatures and the shortage of motorized equipment prompted Finland to use approximately sixty thousand horses in the Winter War. The Swedish *Röda Stjärnan* (Red Star; later, Blue Star) veterinary services sent veterinarians to Finland to care for the great numbers of horses that were wounded in the war. Approximately 670 horses, of which 60 had to be put down because of the severity of their injuries, underwent treatment for war wounds.[55]

The Committee for Finland took charge of the collection of monetary donations.[56] On December 29, it was reported that the donations in Sweden had reached the sum of 800,000 crowns.[57] Some industries encouraged the employees to work on the Swedish holiday of January 6, 1940, and donate their salaries for Finland's cause. Ninety thousand Swedes showed up to sacrifice and raised nearly one million Swedish crowns for the war effort. (According to today's currency conversion rates, one million Swedish crowns equal approximately 130,000 U.S. dollars. In the 1940s, this was a significant amount of money.) During a bandy match between Finland and Sweden on February 11, the spectators arranged a money drive for the benefit of Finland.[58] (Bandy is a sport similar to ice hockey and is played on a sheet of ice.) People also donated jewelry, primarily gold rings. By March 1, 1940, the collection of donated gold rings would reach 1,500.[59] Additionally, private individuals and industry, particularly the bigger companies and banks, contributed with 97 million Swedish crowns for the war effort, an amount that constituted more than half of Sweden's yearly defense budget. It was estimated that the cost of forming, equipping, and sending a volunteer force for a period of six months would cost an additional 55 million Swedish crowns.[60] If converted to today's currency value, the total sum donated, including clothes and food and credits or loans given by Swedish banks, would amount to approximately 13 billion Swedish crowns, or 1.6 billion U.S. dollars; a large sum for a country as small as Sweden.[61] State-supported credits that Sweden offered Finland during the war were calculated to exceed the amount that Sweden offered its own defense forces in the same period.[62]

As the fighting grew more intense, many Swedes viewed the Soviet bombings of civilians as war crimes. The women in particular focused on collecting money to buy Finland additional aircraft as defense against the Soviet bombers; a form of humanitarian help, it was argued, since the cities housed thousands of defenseless men, women, and children whose homes were left in ruins. The elderly and young alike were forced to seek cover in the forests for hours at a time in temperatures dipping well below freezing.[63] It is estimated that every third Swedish woman knitted, crocheted, or sewed clothing for the Finnish troops. Sweden also donated to Finland hundreds of thousands of meters of fabric for overcoats, which became crucial to the Finnish soldiers' ability to survive in the sub-zero temperatures.[64] (The Finnish women, too, knitted gloves for the troops, employing a unique design by leaving a hole for the trigger finger for the rifle.[65]) It is also worth noting that many countries other than Sweden offered emotional and material support for Finland. For example, on January 13, the coffee growers in Rio de Janeiro donated sixty thousand bags of coffee to Finland. Several other countries including Norway, Hungary, Switzerland, Italy, and Belgium donated large amounts of artillery pieces and clothing to Finland, which demonstrates that the support for Finland was widespread.[66] As expressed in a poem by Swedish Prince Vilhelm, the "battle" moved through every home, and every stitch sewn was a greeting to the men at the front.[67] Women continued to sew and crochet mittens and hats for the volunteers who came to serve at the front, and who struggled with a limited supply of winter clothes because the government had underestimated the number of men who would ultimately apply for duty in Finland to only four thousand when more than twice that many showed up.[68]

As a result of the generous donations, just about every Finnish soldier on the Karelian Isthmus was in possession of a warm winter coat by Christmas 1939. By the time the severity of winter set in after the New Year's celebrations, access to felt boots was so good that only a minimal number of soldiers came to suffer frost-injured toes.[69] To further demonstrate the enormity of the emotional support that Sweden offered Finland in the early stages of the war, on December 6, 1939, which was Finland's Day of Independence, Swedish scholars, authors, and others of renowned character held speeches in Stockholm, to which two thousand people showed up and filled every seat in the auditorium. Six thousand others stood outside in the winter weather, listening to speakers hung in the trees. These types of gatherings, always well attended, continued throughout the war, until nearly one thousand such meetings had been held in different parts of the country.[70]

But arms and clothing were not all that was needed to fight a war. There must also be soldiers, particularly since Finland had to face an enemy several times superior in numbers. Although Sweden had entertained the idea of sending twenty-five thousand men to the Karelian Isthmus to build fortifications for the Mannerheim Line,[71] when the question of voluntary manpower arose, a whole new set of problems developed: How many men could Sweden realistically afford to send without cutting itself so short that it would jeopardize its own safety should the threat from the Soviet Union (or perhaps worse, Germany) spread to Sweden? Sweden was utterly unprepared in the event it had to use military force to defend against an invasion, particularly along its northern border with Finland, and had halted all scheduled leaves of military personnel. Full government support was absolutely essential before a volunteer corps could be formed. Men with duty to perform military service within Sweden must secure permission before leaving the country, and officers needed a guarantee to return to their former military posts after the war was over. Equipping the volunteers likewise required the cooperation of the government.[72] There were also problems with foreign policy. If large numbers of men in their prime went to Finland, it could appear as though Sweden had taken an official stand in the war. The country could then no longer retain its noncombatant status. The government thus set a "ceiling" for volunteer help and decided that no more than 8,000 men would be granted leave. On February 8, 1940, the government would raise the limit to 12,000 volunteers and 540 permanent military personnel.[73]

Recruitment Propaganda and Motivations for Volunteering

On November 30, 1939, the Committee for Finland started a campaign for the purpose of motivating Swedish men to apply for voluntary combat duty in northern Finland.[74] Christian Günther, Sweden's Minister of Foreign Affairs, coined the phrase, "Finlands Sak Är Vår" (Finland's Cause Is Ours). Posters were printed in an attempt to hurry the recruitment effort.[75] As remembered by Orvar Nilsson, a highly decorated officer in the Swedish army and who served in the Finnish Winter War, the Continuation War, and in nearly two dozen other foreign missions, "The strangest thing was that the volunteer corps seemed to grow out of nothing. It started as a paper organization. They owned not even as much as a shoelace."[76]

Much of the work associated with recruitment had to be done in secret to avoid arousing suspicions about Sweden's noncombatant status. Since the volunteer corps was prohibited from advertising in public, it began running a small newspaper ad that simply read "FINLAND," with an address and phone number, in the hope that people would get the message.[77] An article in the publication, *Sverige Fritt* (Sweden Independent), later criticized the

Information brochure about the volunteer corps (source: Krigsarkivet, Finlandskommitten, 1939–1940).

government restriction on advertising. Had the volunteer corps been allowed to advertise freely, the article argued, between 20,000 and 30,000 volunteers would no doubt have enlisted to serve in Finland by the year's end, and not just the 1,700 to 1,900 who had registered under the current conditions.[78]

Although agreements that stemmed from the Hague Convention of 1907 stated that "[c]orps of combatants [could not] be formed nor recruiting agencies opened on the territory of a neutral Power to assist the belligerents," the restriction did not apply to "persons crossing the frontier separately to offer their services to one of the belligerents."[79] Sweden capitalized on this statement by opening a recruitment office in central Stockholm the first day of the war. Soon thereafter, 125 such offices had opened across the country. Those interested in serving Finland were encouraged to present in person. Anyone younger than twenty-one years of age needed written permission from a parent or legal guardian before signing a contract.[80] The recruitment center in Stockholm also housed an office for a marine division, which would come to organize an anti-aircraft artillery battery at Turku manned by 35 Swedish sailors from the fleet, 4 Finnish telephone operators, and 6 women from the *Lotta* organization, although, 305 volunteers had expressed interest in serving at this battery.[81] The fact that many marine-educated and skilled artillery shooters applied to go to Finland led to the establishment of several independent combat groups that were complemented with Finnish personnel.[82] (Note that a marine soldier in Sweden is not the same as a marine soldier in the United States, but is part of the Swedish navy or fleet.)

How did the process of volunteering work? A man walking into a recruitment center to volunteer would first get a medical exam, vaccinations, and general information about the assignment including how he would be compensated. Upon passing the medical, he could expect to wait a few days before receiving notification about acceptance and orders to appear at the training center in Torneå. Background checks were conducted to the extent possible in order to avoid recruiting criminals or others with questionable backgrounds, such as Nazi or communist sympathizers. Mannerheim requested as many volunteers as Sweden could manage to send. The total number was less important, however, than that the process was hurried and the troops were sent as soon as possible. A quick response, even if just a few volunteers showed up, would likely communicate to other countries that it was prudent for them, too, to offer help.[83]

By December 3, the plan began to take shape. It was determined that the volunteer corps would consist of three combat battalions reinforced with artillery in addition to an air force and a number of special forces units, and would require the service of approximately seven thousand men stationed primarily in northern Finland. A Finnish commander reported

FÖRBUNDET SVENSKA FRIVILLIGKÅREN

ARSENALSGATAN 4 · WAHRENDORFFSGATAN 8, 4 TR · TELEFON 10 02 15
STOCKHOLM den 4/9 1940.

Letterhead for the Swedish Volunteer Corps. Note the four hands representing the Nordic countries of Sweden, Norway, Denmark, and Finland (source: Krigsarkivet, Finlandskommitten, 1939–1940).

that Finnish headquarters were less concerned with the present activities on the Karelian Isthmus than with the front in northern Finland, particularly in the Petsamo area where Russian troops had advanced far into Finnish territory, and expressed hope that a well-equipped Swedish volunteer force could help ease the situation.[84]

Although Sweden had a history of permitting volunteer service in foreign states, the numbers of volunteers had traditionally been limited to a few hundred. This time would be different. One of the major hurdles was how to dress the troops. They could not wear the regimental uniform because it would indicate an official stand by the Swedish government. It was thus decided that the volunteers should wear the new model uniform that had not yet been incorporated into the Swedish armed forces.[85] Three hundred women worked on replacing the buttons depicting the Swedish "three crowns" symbol with buttons of Finnish design depicting the lion.[86] The combat battalions, named Group I, Group II, and Group III, each received its own emblem sewn onto the uniforms: a cross bow for Group I, a moose head for Group II, and two crossed swords for Group III.[87] Additionally, the emblem of the volunteer corps, the four hands representing the Nordic countries of Sweden, Norway, Denmark, and Finland, was fastened on the collar along with the slogan, "Nordens Frihet—Ära, Skyldighet, Vilja" (Nordic Independence—Honor, Duty, Purpose).[88] General Ernst Linder, a veteran of Finland's War of Independence, was placed in charge of the volunteers. On February 25, 1940, General Linder would come to accept total responsibility for the defense of northern Finland, and would also help oversee the activities of three Finnish battalions.[89]

Propaganda poster depicting a Finnish and Swedish soldier on skis, for the recruitment of volunteers for Finland: "Finland's cause is ours! For a greater fight, join the Volunteer Corps" (photograph: Martina Sprague, displayed at the Army Museum in Stockholm, Sweden).

The support from the people and the excitement of forming the volunteer corps proved intense. But the recruitment efforts were dampened somewhat by the uncertainty of the government's stand on the issue and the nearness of the Christmas Holiday.[90] Germany's reaction was also watched carefully. The Swedish efforts in Finland could not lead to open confrontation with the

Soviet Union, as this could force Hitler into action due to his nonaggression treaty with Stalin.[91] So far, Germany had remained silent. In a discussion between Swedish Count Eric von Rosen and Hermann Göring, a leading member of the Nazi Party, Göring assured Rosen that if Sweden became officially involved in the war on the side of Finland, Germany would not assist Russia, but would remain a friend of Sweden.[92] But the Swedish leadership proved skeptical with respect to German promises.

Once the restrictions on advertisement for the volunteer corps were lifted just before Christmas 1939, as many as six hundred new volunteers expressed interest to serve each day. New advertisements were printed sporting the text, "Nu vet världen vad det är att vara finne. Visa Du vad det är att vara svensk" (Now the world knows what it means to be a Finn. Show the world what it means to be a Swede.)[93] The propaganda posters were reinforced with the statement, "Finland's fight is the fight of the Nordic countries, which is the fight of the Western world,"[94] and the slogan, "För Nordens Frihet — Sveriges Ära" (For Nordic Independence — Sweden's Honor).[95] A letter with the heading, "Finland's Cause Is Ours," called Swedish men to go forth with weapon in hand in Finland's struggle for survival, securing the future of the Nordic countries. According to one propaganda letter, if Finland fell under the Russian onslaught, the cause was not lack of money but lack of soldiers: "Defend Western Culture, Democracy, and Freedom — Volunteer for Finland."[96]

The famous Swedish author and historian Vilhelm Moberg, perhaps remembered best for his four-part novel, *The Emigrants*, published a letter to Sweden's farmers expressing concern for the threat in the East:

> The Red Army is on the march toward Scandinavia. Swedish freedom and Swedish territory lie in the shadow of this threat. Sweden is the oldest state in the region with a continuous history of independence. The failure to give everything we own, even our lives, in defense of Sweden, will mean the betrayal of our ancestors through generations, as well as the betrayal of our children. The Finnish farmers are offering their blood in defense of their nation, but how long will their struggle last if we fail to step forward and offer our assistance? What we do for Finland will ultimately benefit our own security. This is the time for Swedish farmers to show the world the value they place on the culture they have nurtured for a thousand years.[97]

Support for Finland was most notable, perhaps, in the composition of the group that went eastward. Far from homogenous, the volunteer corps included students, industrial and construction workers, farmers, and independent businessmen.[98] In addition to those enlisting for combat were men who could work as drivers, firefighters, or veterinarians, and others in possession of valuable technical skills.[99] Approximately two-thirds of the volunteers were between the ages of twenty and thirty, and one-fifth had no prior

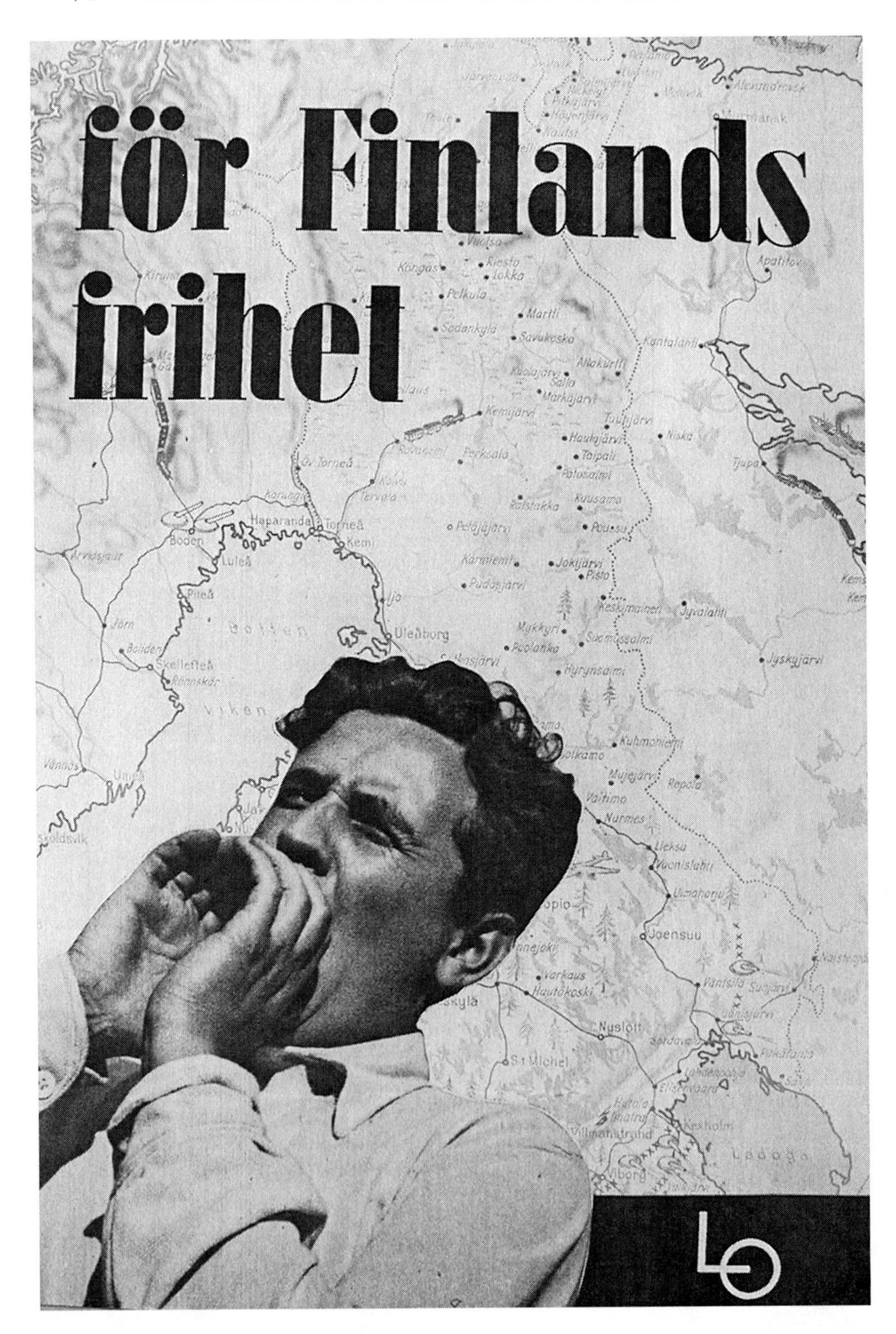
för Finlands
frihet
Haparanda
Torneå
Kemi
Boden
Luleå
Uleåborg
Joensuu
Nuslott
LO

experience in handling firearms or other weapons.[100] Despite the social class differences, the volunteers were united in purpose. Naturally, some rotten apples ended up in the group, for example, those with unhappy family relations or large tax debts, or criminals looking to escape the law. Many of the volunteers, however, came from financially stable backgrounds or were business owners.[101] A letter from the Committee for Finland to the superintendents for the recruitment centers, dated January 21, 1940, emphasized that the volunteer corps in Finland must be as strong as possible if it were to make a true combat contribution. As the only bread winner of the family, many men who were considering applying as volunteers were forced to decline. These sorts of difficulties had to be resolved as quickly as possible whether in the form of an extra one-time payment to families in need, or in the form of monetary donations from private citizens.[102]

What drove them? Some men volunteered for no other reason than because they believed that the Finns might be in need of someone "who could care for the horses."[103] Others had an adventurous spirit. Two young men mutually promised each other to fight also in the Continuation War. Naturally, they did not know at the time that there would be a Continuation War, but promised each other to fight for as long as Finland needed them, a promise which they also fulfilled. They later admitted that nobody in his right mind would make such a promise absent a longing for adventure.[104] One volunteer from the Swedish island of Gotland noted in hindsight that it was the madness of youth that drove him to volunteer, and he would not do it again.[105] Another man admitted that it was the boy in him, the childhood memories of World War I, and the dream of taking his place in the columns of marching soldiers that led him to the recruitment office. To actually get to wear the uniform in battle was an ambition out of reach for a boy in neutral Sweden. Now, he had a chance to make his dream come true.[106] Still another man declared that his desire to volunteer for Finland was based in his view that the Finns should have a right to live according to their beliefs without becoming subjects of an oppressive regime. The courage the Finns displayed fighting an enemy as numerically superior as the Soviet Union became this man's primary motivation to enlist. The spirit of the Finns lit the hope that the volunteers, with weapon in hand, might be able to "rehabilitate" Sweden's pacifist image on the international scene.[107]

Opposite: *Propaganda poster, "For Finland's Independence," issued by LO—Landsorganisationen (Swedish Trade Union Confederation), organizer mainly of blue collar workers and founded in 1898 by members of the Social Democratic Party (source: Krigsarkivet, Finlandskommitten, 1939–1940).*

On a more negative note, a small number of the applicants were also looking for "an honorable way to end a hopeless life."[108]

When news of the bombings of Helsinki came over the radio, Mannerheim requested that aerial assistance be made available as soon as possible. Several Swedish pilots reportedly got up from their morning coffee and walked directly to the squadron chief to volunteer.[109] The desire to fight for Finland proved so strong that three of the pilots departed on November 30, 1939, the same day that the Soviets violated the Finnish border and two weeks prior to receiving official permission from the Swedish government to fly in Finland.[110] On December 14, more progress was made when the government cleared the way for the organization of a volunteer air force, whose duty it would be to protect the cities in northern Finland against Soviet air attacks. Secondary motives were to eliminate Soviet hegemony of the airspace, defend the railway between Sweden and Finland, and detect the movement of Soviet troops toward the Swedish border.[111] Carl August Ehrensvärd, a veteran of Finland's War of Independence, had by December 7, in a confidential letter to the chief of the air force, requested names and information about permanent as well as reserve personnel wishing to join the fighter/bomber wing in northern Finland. Sweden commissioned twelve attack and twelve bomber aircraft to Finland, although only four of the twelve bombers were actually used. The squadron would be ready to fly combat missions around January 10, 1940.[112] The recruitment process of pilots posed few problems. The volunteers asked to be released from the Swedish air force with promise of being rehired upon their return, and formally applied for duty within the Republic of Finland. The fact that the pilots fought under Finnish flag meant that the Swedish government could deny official involvement in the war. For political purposes, the pilots were now Finns, not Swedes, but still reported to a Swedish commander.

In January 1940, the Soviet government voiced opposition to the volunteer corps. Stalin's envoy in Stockholm, Madame Alexandra Kollontay, protested on behalf of her government against the recruitment of volunteers and a number of animosity articles that Swedish media had written about the Soviet Union.[113] Sweden answered the accusations ten days later, defending its freedom of the press and also denying any involvement in the recruiting process. Despite the fact that a number of Swedish officers had asked to terminate their employment with the Swedish military and sign up under Finnish flag, Sweden notified the Soviet Union that it had no responsibility for the actions of private citizens going to Finland on an entirely voluntary basis.[114] The Soviet News Agency *Tass* would later falsely suggest that Sweden had freed all domestic prisoners and sent them to Finland as volunteers.[115]

Although admitting that their superiors who briefed and questioned them encouraged participation in the war, the volunteer pilots unanimously denied that any coercion took place. Recruitment was done on a strictly voluntary basis.[116] Toward the end of February 1940, new rules regarding the recruitment of volunteers would grant officers and noncommissioned officers the right to solicit men directly from their units. For example, an officer might tell his unit that he would volunteer and invite others to join him. This new recruitment strategy allowed a unit to deploy together. The idea was that soldiers and officers who had trained together could reach combat efficiency quicker. The officers were still prohibited from using any form of coercion or accusations of cowardice when attempting to motivate personnel.[117]

Only hours after the government had cleared the air force for action, eleven men had expressed interest to serve in Finland. They were skilled aviators; inexperienced at flying combat missions, but in possession of extraordinary attitudes and desire for adventure. Their love of aviation and the drive to assist Finland had been planted in childhood years through songs and stories of Finnish war heroes.[118] Upon arrival in Finland, the pilots covered the swastikas on the Finnish aircraft with the skull and crossbones to further communicate their anger over the Russian invasion.[119]

Why did they do it? "We were rookie officers," explained one pilot. "We had just finished our training and we were in possession of relatively modern aircraft. We believed that we were the cream of the crop; we were ready to make a go and find out what we were made of." Many Swedes, caught up in the massive atmosphere that had gripped the country, felt contempt for the Soviets and did not think twice about participating in the war. Although the pilots expressed a heartfelt desire to assist Finland, volunteering also became a way of proving their worth. They wanted positive confirmation that they could do what they had been trained to do. Personal ties to Finland and a sense of common ground also served as factors of motivation. Some of the pilots were half–Finns or had close relatives living in Finland. Others were bored with the status quo, had a desire to further their careers and gain some practical experience in warfare, or were simply striving to fulfill a personal need for glory and adventure.[120] They also held the belief that their service in northern Finland would ultimately protect the Swedish border, should the Red Army and communism manage to spread that far.[121]

The Swedish pilots would accumulate more than six hundred hours of flight time during the war. They would shoot down or destroy six bombers and six fighter aircraft, attack Soviet ground troops and Soviet bases, and interfere in several Soviet bomb attacks. Their contribution would result in stabilizing the front in northern Finland.[122] In the first combat mission, Sweden would lose three bombers and suffer one pilot casualty. Two more would die in combat related activities before the war was over. The Soviets would take two Swedish pilots prisoners but release them after the war. When placed in perspective, however, the losses proved minimal. For comparison purposes, seventeen Swedish pilots had lost their lives during training missions that took place in peacetime in 1939.[123]

Arrival and Training in Torneå

As noted previously, the Swedish leadership worried that the military would spread itself too thin and have too few troops available to defend the country should the war reach Sweden. A plus was that the combat units that departed for Finland would be well-trained upon completing their service against the Red Army.[124] The first four hundred ground troops left from the Central Station in Stockholm by train to Haparanda in northern Sweden on December 21, 1939. When crossing the border into Finland and the war, it was with the knowledge that they would be making history helping their neighbor. Most men were painfully aware that they might meet their destiny on Finnish soil.[125] When recruitment could take place openly with the government's approval, several train cars at once could be seen reserved for the volunteers' journey north.[126] In addition to troops, several hundred medical personnel along with transport cars were sent to Finland, primarily to care for wounded Swedish soldiers in Märkäjärvi.[127] Väinö Tanner, Finland's Minister of Foreign Affairs, officially welcomed the volunteers to Finland through an interview with Swedish media on New Year's Eve 1939.[128]

The volunteers were transported first to Torneå, where they were equipped and trained, and then to Kemi. Although there were good reasons to use the volunteers on the Karelian Isthmus where the heaviest fighting would likely take place, there were also valid reasons for placing them in northern Finland where they not only could protect Swedish interests but the railway between Sweden and Finland. Northern Finland seemed the better choice also because of lack of combat experience among the Swedish troops. If they were sent to the Isthmus, they would likely take heavy casualties early in the game, or might even be a hindrance to the more experienced Finnish troops. Too many casualties right off the bat would likely damage popular support for the war back home.[129]

Upon arrival in Finland, the volunteers had to sign a contract with the Finnish government in order to legitimize their service. Should they be taken prisoners by the Russians, they would be regarded as citizens of Finland, not

Sweden.[130] The identity cards they were issued were to be carried on their person throughout their service in Finland. They were also taught to shout in Finnish, "don't shoot," and, "I am a volunteer," in order to prevent taking fire from Finnish troops, should they end up behind enemy lines.[131] Learning the phrase proved particularly important to the men serving in the air force, who risked getting shot down by the Soviets. The volunteers were compensated between fifteen and ninety Swedish crowns per ten days of service depending on their military rank, which amounted to a pretty sorry sum. Although they had not volunteered for the purpose of making money, many had families and financial obligations to fill at home.[132]

Few of the troops proved to be skilled skiers and an even smaller number had military experience; 628 men had not yet turned 20 and 238 were older than 45 years of age.[133] The Swedish commanders, not entirely satisfied with the group that had arrived, wondered if they had the caliber to be good soldiers. Many were adventurists; others lacked basic military training and were unfamiliar with operating in subarctic climates. A few communists were caught and sent back to Sweden.[134] Magnus Dyrssen, chief for Combat Group I, was confident that the "bad apples" would make themselves known at the New Year's Eve party once they got some alcohol in their bodies. They could then be sorted out and returned back home.[135] He also complained that a number of officers were "running around ... getting in the way of each other," and expressed concern about how teamwork would proceed between General Linder and Mannerheim, and whose orders should be given priority if they differed.[136] However, the most important question was whether the volunteers would be tough enough to pass the training requirements. Would they be able to endure the cold temperatures, living in tents for several weeks, or even months?

There were also concerns about foreign nationalities masquerading as Swedes. According to an entry made on New Year's Eve 1939 in the diary of Magnus Dyrssen, several foreigners had arrived, including some Danes who were practically useless, and a prince Lichtenstein (likely Prince Ferdinand Andreas of Lichtenstein who had expressed interest in volunteering in Finland).[137] Sweden also agreed to place 727 Norwegian volunteers under Swedish command, because Norway could not afford to send any of its own officers to Finland.[138] If the total number of volunteers for Finland could have been utilized at the front, it was argued, they would have become a valuable force in view of Finland's vanishing reserves. Still, the Swedish-Norwegian troops gave Finland a meaningful reinforcement, and their presence in the struggle helped lift the spirit of the Finnish people.[139] Danish volunteers, however, were trained separately from the Swedes, since the Swedish commanders considered the Danes unsuitable for winter warfare in northern Finland on account of Denmark's geographical location by Sweden's southern tip.[140] Because of the difficulties inherent to accepting volunteers of different nationalities and languages and get them to function as a unit alongside of the Finnish troops, after considering generous offers from numerous countries, Finland replied that volunteers must be "trained men and come in organized groups under their own officers and with their own supplies and arms." Due to conflict of interests, Russians or Germans would not be registered as volunteers. By the middle of January, Finland realized that it was almost impossible to bring together a substantial volunteer force based on the earlier requirements, and thus agreed to also take untrained men.[141]

One evening after their arrival, the volunteers listened to a motivational speech with focus on duty, cohesion, and the will to defend Finland. The following day, a reconnaissance patrol reported that the situation in Petsamo had not yet reached a significant degree of danger. It was worse in Salla. Although the Russians had suffered heavy losses, the Finnish troops were exhausted, which further emphasized the need for Swedish reinforcements both on the ground and in the air. Dyrssen reported that Stockholm would send an additional 300 volunteers for the ground troops in addition to 150 men for the air force. There were also reports from Germany confirming that Hitler would accept the fact that Sweden had sent volunteer help to Finland, but would object to any official intervention by the Swedish military and would take action if Sweden failed to respect his wishes. It was evident that Germany worried about a possible intervention by the Western Allies via the way of Sweden. Dyrssen considered it "best to allow the whole Swedish army to be employed officially under Finnish flag."[142]

He continued to worry about the composition of the volunteer force. On January 5, he reported that quite a few of the men did not even know how to ski: "I wonder how some men look inside, who apply without even being apt at the basics?" Although the men were willing to fight, it was clear that many had no idea of what they had committed themselves to. Dyrssen further reported that the equipment that Sweden had sent was generally good, although the shoes were too small and had to be exchanged. Gloves and fur hats were also missing, although both the overcoat and the pants proved practical for the conditions.[143] The ski boots issued to the volunteers, of the same model as those issued to regular Swedish army personnel, proved ill-suited for the harsh conditions in the far north. Felt boots were undoubtedly the better option for keeping the soldiers warm. Flexibility in the sole allowed for better movement of the foot and therefore better blood circulation. Regular boots could be used, however, if they were sufficiently large to allow for a felt

Car at a road crossing covered in snow 31 kilometers from Salla. Note the skis and poles on top of the roof (source: Krigsarkivet, Förbundet Svenska Finlandsfrivilliga, Vol. 29).

insert. The Finnish leather boots filled with hay proved much warmer than the Swedish issued boots, but tended not to last long during heavy usage.[144] Additionally, cars had difficulty starting in the cold temperatures. Getting enough equipment for the volunteers was really the only significant problem during the preparations in Torneå, and was due mostly to the fact that the government had initially counted only on a force of four thousand.[145]

A new entry in the daily log on January 15 indicated that at least 100 men were deemed unsuitable for combat and had to be sent home. Another 150 were mildly sick, mainly with the common cold, which delayed their training.[146] In temperatures of -30 degrees C, it was not strange, according to Dyrssen, if some men, particularly those from southern Sweden, would come to regret their decision to go to Finland.[147] One volunteer noted that the odd collection of "soldiers" reminded him of a hastily combined group of tourists.[148] For example, hardened veterans from Finland's War of Independence were made to serve together with young men still wet behind the ears. Political, age, and class differences vanished, however, in light of the greater goal: A fight for Nordic independence and Sweden's honor.[149]

Creating useful combatants required a short but intense training program. The goal was to construct a homogenous group of soldiers with the capacity to oppose a numerically superior enemy; not an easy task in the short time allotted. The physical preparations involved an evaluation of the group's general conditioning, then five to ten minutes warm-up gymnastics in the morning and heavier exercise later in the day, sauna, sufficient rest, nutritious food, and no consumption of alcoholic beverages. Those deemed unsuitable, either too weak or afraid of physical exertion, were identified, weeded out, and returned to Sweden.[150] The combat training focused mainly on teamwork and coordination of movements between units. Skiing was practiced first in easy terrain, gradually becoming more intense to include various exercises both on and off skies. The uneven and hilly terrain at Salla would require confident skiers, particularly after dark.[151]

The volunteers learned how to maintain and handle their weapons in cold and snow, disassembling and reassembling their rifles until they could do so blindfolded. They were taught to set up bivouacs and tents, make fire and cook outside, stand watch and protect their peers, handle anti-aircraft artillery, and attack tanks with improvised explosive devices such as Molotov cocktails.[152] When practice-throwing "cocktails" against advancing tanks, one man would simulate the tank while another would throw snowballs to simulate the "cocktails."[153] These methods demonstrate the simplicity of training due to the scarcity of materiel. The volunteers also took advantage of the knowledge the Finns possessed of the enemy, by watching films from the Salla front and by inviting Finnish officers to tell their stories.[154] Magnus Dyrssen would comment after the training march to Rovaniemi in February that he continued worrying that soldiers as well as horses were undertrained, however. Although they displayed plenty of courage, they lacked good discipline.[155] But, as it turned out, fighting in Finland required not physical strength or a broad-shouldered build. The greatest asset was the will to fight for a good cause. Although the Finnish soldiers were vastly superior on skis, one volunteer reminded the critics that the Swedes had not come to fight the Finns. In comparison to the Russians, the worst Swedish skier was still better than the best Russian skier.[156]

The volunteer pilots' transport to Finland took place in civilian clothing. Upon arrival, they received the new Swedish uniforms with the Finnish lion buttons. The contract they signed required that they agree to serve Finland on a voluntary basis under Swedish commanders. The volunteer would bind himself to the rules, orders, and disciplinary actions of the Finnish armed forces that were currently in effect. He could terminate the contract one month after official request to do so, the earliest of which would be May 31, 1940. Should the volunteer be deemed unsuitable for service, the contract would no longer be enforced. Should mobilization occur within Sweden for Sweden's own defense, the volunteer would be given the opportunity to return home. From the day he signed, the volunteer would be considered equal with a Finnish pilot of equal rank with respect to pay and other benefits. Should he be wounded during his service in Finland, the same rules and compensation in effect for Finnish pilots would apply. Should he die from injury or disease, his widow and children would get the same compensation as a Finnish pilot in a similar circumstance.[157] Although the pilots would operate under Swedish command, the Finnish air force was responsible for giving directives and promoting teamwork between the squadrons.[158] The men who signed up for air force service in Finland included 25 pilots and 230 ground personnel. Two women, one working for the Red Cross and one as a secretary, followed the flight squadron north.[159]

F19's ground personnel receive information by chief Björn Bjuggren regarding their coming duties upon their arrival in northern Finland (source: Krigsarkivet, Svenska Frivilligkåren, Kriget 1939–1940).

Although nobody honestly believed that the Swedes would decide the war, the volunteer efforts would supplement the Finnish army and air force, contribute to stalling the Red Army's advance, and give the Finns a fighting chance. But the situation still proved dire. In the days before Christmas, one Finnish commander reported that although the Finnish troops had already achieved considerable routine fighting in the difficult terrain and climate, many soldiers were so tired that they displayed signs of apathy. A surgeon reported that five lightly wounded soldiers had died on the operating table from sheer exhaustion. In an attempt to inspire the failing troops, an officer reminded them that if they died from exhaustion and not from enemy fire, they would leave the roads to the inner parts of Finland open and give the enemy a painless advance into the cities and industrial centers.[160] The relief the Swedish volunteers offered at the front came not a moment too soon.

Continued Political Difficulties

Swedish war propaganda sent over the radio and printed in the newspapers discussed the bitter cold temperatures the Finns had to endure, and their heroism. Swedish military leaders explained that the Finnish and Swedish forces would soon unite and stop the advance of the "incompetent and helpless" Soviet troops.[161] On February 1, 1940, the Finnish statesman Risto Ryti noted that Finland had suffered great losses that amounted to approximately twenty thousand dead, wounded, or taken prisoners, and that the troops were exhausted and in desperate need of rest. But when he asked if Sweden could deliver reinforcements comprised of two divisions and approximately twenty thousand men, Per Albin Hansson explained that it was not possible to reach these numbers by relying on volunteers alone. The volunteer corps had to decide on its own how large it should grow. If the issue were pushed, aside from the fact that Hansson would be engaging in questionable neutrality politics, it could backfire on the government, and men whose turn it was to get conscripted for military service within the country might refuse by arguing that Sweden was not at war with anyone. If the country could afford to send large numbers of soldiers to Finland, it would obviously not need them at home.[162]

Toward the middle of February, Väinö Tanner complained to Christian Günther that recruitment of volunteers had been ongoing for a month and a half, but no troops had yet appeared at the front. The training seemed to drag. A new request was made for official troops from Sweden. When the Western Allies offered to supply Finland with twenty thousand soldiers, Tanner further criticized the Swedish government, who on account of the country's neutrality declaration denied Finland direct help by denying the Allies transit through Swedish territory.[163] But Günther was afraid to jeopardize the Soviet Union's relations with the Western Powers, particularly if Britain and France decided to join in the war. Hitler would then be forced into action as well, in order to prevent them from establishing military bases in Scandinavia.[164]

In defense of his decision, Günther pointed to the agreements formed during the Hague Convention of October 18, 1907 with respect to the rights and duties of neutral powers, which stated that with the exception of transportation of the sick and wounded of belligerent armies, no military personnel or war materiel belonging to a belligerent state could be transported through neutral territory.[165] Thus, if Sweden agreed to send government-sanctioned troops to Finland or grant the Western Allies transit rights through Swedish territory, hostilities would escalate on the world scene and Sweden would get dragged into the war. Tanner would not budge but reminded Günther that Finland was fighting this war also for the safety of Sweden, as would be perfectly clear if one just took the time to examine the totality of the situation.[166] It was a Catch-22 for Sweden: Either break the country's neutrality, send trained troops to Finland, and become officially involved in the war. Or do not send troops to Finland and risk becoming part of a drawn-out war anyway, when the Western Powers and Germany turned the Scandinavian peninsula into a battleground and laid claim to the Swedish iron ore fields.

Further debate indicated that official Swedish involvement might have a negative effect on Russian prestige. While Tanner believed that the Soviet Union would be eager to hurry a peace agreement if Sweden took an official stand by Finland's side, Günther believed that sending large numbers of trained troops to Finland might create a backlash. Soviet prestige, he argued, would require that Russia continue fighting in order to demonstrate that the Red Army was capable of winning a decisive military victory. The situation proved even more complex. Finland had offered to negotiate with Russia, but Russian demands were too heavy and Stalin was unwilling to back down even a little. Finland had therefore no choice but continue the war.[167]

As late as February 23, 1940, Sweden's Ministry of Foreign Affairs notified Finland that no changes were forthcoming regarding Swedish-Finnish political relations. Sweden would not send official troops to Finland, but would continue to provide support in the form of war materiel and volunteers. The Swedish newspapers criticized Prime Minister Hansson for his decision to withhold military support, and the Swedish envoy Wilhelm Winther expressed concern that unless some great miracle happened that would force Stalin to fight on more than one front, it was only a matter of time before the superior Soviet forces would annihilate the Finns.[168] Meanwhile, the Swedish volunteers,

Generals Arthur Nordensvan and Carl August Ehrensvärd (source: Krigsarkivet, Förbundet Svenska Finlandsfrivilliga, Vol. 29).

unaware of the political difficulties, started their march to Märkäjärvi at Salla in northern Finland, which would become the battleground for some of the war's toughest fights.

The March to the Front

General Ernst Linder, who had participated in Finland's War of Independence under Carl Gustaf Mannerheim, had been elected chief of the volunteer corps. The 71-year-old general of Finnish descent had served in the Swedish army since 1887. In the War of Independence, he was the first Swedish officer to appear in the Finnish army and participated in several combat missions. More recently, during Finland's preparatory training on the Karelian Isthmus in the late summer of 1939, Linder had promised Mannerheim, his comrade-in-arms from earlier times, that he would come to Finland's assistance if need be.[169] Linder's outstanding military record, it was reasoned, his prior service in Finland, and his personal friendship with Mannerheim clearly outweighed the drawbacks of his advanced years.[170] Magnus Dyrssen, chief for Combat Group I, noted in his diary on January 7, 1940 that Linder appeared physically weak, and that it would come as no surprise if he collapsed and died suddenly. He admitted, however, that Linder meant well and did not suffer from lack of intellectual acuity.[171]

Directly under Linder served the 47-year-old Carl August Ehrensvärd, Magnus Dyrssen, Viking Tamm, and Martin Ekström, also veterans of Finland's War of Independence. Their prior experiences fighting for Finland on the side of the "whites"—Martin Ekström had also fought in Persia and the Baltic countries—and the enthusiasm these military men displayed for the job made them particularly suited for leading the volunteers in combat.[172] Not all army generals at home shared their enthusiasm, however, but would rather have kept the experienced military leadership in Sweden, prepared to defend the country against a possible Russian or German invasion.[173]

General Linder proceeded to organize three battalions, each consisting of three rifle platoons (considered the core of the volunteer corps), a heavy artillery platoon, a *jäger* platoon (special forces), a signal platoon, and a snowplow platoon, in addition to an air force and a number of support units consisting of independent *jäger* platoons and medical platoons. The Swedish army supplied the volunteers with weapons and equipment, primarily of Swedish design.[174]

Training lasted through the month of January. In early February, Mannerheim asked the Swedish commander "to take his men from training depots and use them to replace Finnish battalions tied down on the quiescent Salla front."[175] The primary duties of the volunteers after relieving the Finnish troops in northern Finland included preventing or delaying a Soviet advance across the border, and protecting the railway communications between Sweden and Finland.[176] The railway was essential for the transport of troops and materiel. Thought to be the primary target of air attacks in the north, it would prove difficult to defend. Toward the end of the month, the volunteers would be responsible for the defense of all of northern Finland.[177] As noted previously, although the main battlefield was the Karelian Isthmus and the area to the northeast of Lake Ladoga, the Soviet goal was to conquer Petsamo in the north by cutting Finland in half at the "waist," preventing Finnish troops from mounting an effective defense. The Red Army would then attempt

Jäger *platoon with dogs (source: Krigsarkivet, Förbundet Svenska Finlandsfrivilliga, Vol. 29).*

to gain control of Viborg and Helsinki and advance toward the Torne River, the biggest river in northeastern Sweden bordering Lapland and Finland. Cutting Finland's communications with Sweden and the rest of the Western world would then be relatively easy.[178]

On February 3, Group I, a battalion of approximately 1,500 men reinforced with artillery operating under the leadership of Lieutenant-Colonel Magnus Dyrssen stood ready to ski to Rovaniemi for continued train transport to Kemijärvi.[179] The 130-kilometer stretch was estimated to take a week to complete and would be followed by an additional long ski-march of 60 kilometers (three days) to Märkäjärvi, the purpose of which it was to prepare the volunteers for the rigors of winter warfare, test their equipment, and form unit cohesion.[180] Meanwhile, two more battalions were organized, and a few days later Group II, under the leadership of Lieutenant-Colonel Viking Tamm, departed by train from Kemi to Kemijärvi on the way to Märkäjärvi

Lieutenant-Colonel Viking Tamm and soldiers from Combat Group II (source: Krigsarkivet, Förbundet Svenska Finlandsfrivilliga, Vol. 29).

at the front.[181] The two groups would reunite for a three-kilometer stretch on skis to the battlefield just north of the road Kemijärvi-Märkäjärvi, where they would disburse into smaller groups with a Finnish soldier as guide.[182] On the day of the march, the troops received reports that Swedish pilots had downed two Russian bombers over Rovaniemi; however, the news from the Isthmus were less gratifying, where the Red Army had made significant advances.[183]

Several deficiencies in equipment, training, and planning became apparent during the march to the front. Dyrssen reported in his daily log that many of the volunteers were not used to the exercise. He had approached the situation with some forethought and brought forty light sleds of Finnish design which were better suited for the terrain than the Swedish sleds. The Swedish tents were outstanding, however, warm and tight against the wind.[184] Still, medical platoons removed more than a hundred men due to illness. The cold temperatures froze the soldiers' sandwiches and coffee to ice, and nights, some of which the troops had to endure in the open, saw temperatures dropping to -40 degrees C.[185] Getting enough food to the soldiers proved problematic, because of the long distances between the combat groups and the food transports.[186] The volunteers maintained morale by transferring their sufferings onto the enemy. "If we were hungry," explained one soldier, "we would say, the Russians must surely be starving now. If we were cold, we would say, the Russians are freezing to death now."[187] The horses' pace, how fast they could walk, and how often they needed to stop and rest determined the speed of the march.[188]

To make matters worse, Group II misinterpreted the map, and the expected twenty-eight kilometers of planned marching distance turned into forty kilometers and thirteen hours of legwork, much of which took place in -45 degrees C and at night in order to avoid detection by Soviet aircraft. Icicles formed in the men's half-grown beards, in their nostrils, and in the corners of their eyes. When stopping to give the horses a rest, the men were encouraged to continue moving in order to maintain blood circulation in the extremities. In the early dawn, they checked their closest comrades for frost injuries which would appear as white blotches on the face. One man is said to have rubbed his nose right off his face when attempting to warm it. He later suffered several amputations of fingers and toes. Of the 1,500 men who partook in this nightly march, approximately 80 suffered severe frost injuries including amputations, and had to be sent home to Sweden.[189]

When Group II arrived in Märkäjärvi, it became evident how primitive the surroundings were. The Finnish soldier acting as guide the last bit of the way showed a trench he had dug only a few decimeters deep in the hard ground. That was the best he could do. Thus, not much protection existed against enemy fire. When seeing the hesitation in the eyes of the Swedish troops, the guide offered the following consolation in the typical Finnish drawl: "Over there where the forest starts are the Russians. They shoot a little sometimes, but it is not so dangerous. Believe me, boys, war is not that bad."[190]

Combat Group II would guard against Soviet attacks north of the main road while preparing a counterattack to the southeast. They would also maintain communication with Combat Group I, stationed by the main road, and send food to the soldiers via dog sleds.[191] Each company had brought ten to twelve dogs for this purpose.[192] The working rule stated that no soldier could leave his post until receiving orders to do so or was forced to leave because of threat of encirclement. Although few volunteers deserted, in order to maintain as many

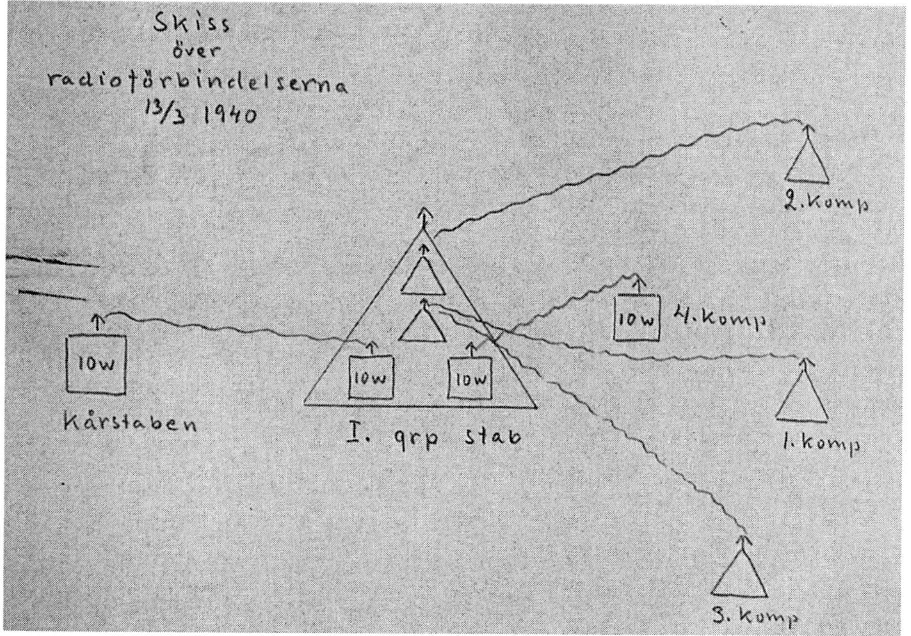

Top: *Dogs with caretaker. Dogs were used to pull sleds with food (source: Krigsarkivet, Förbundet Svenska Finlandsfrivilliga, Vol. 29).* Bottom: *Drawing of radio communications (source: Krigsarkivet, Svenska Frivilligkåren, Kriget 1939–1940).*

men as possible, Swedish authorities declared that anyone disobeying orders or leaving the front would not face disciplinary action upon his return.[193]

The conversations between officers and soldiers focused mainly on battlefield tactics and how to place the defensive positions. The Swedes operated mostly independently, saw few Finnish units, and acted according to Swedish doctrine. While the greater Finnish experience in warfare benefited the Finns, the Swedes believed that specific tactics must be adapted to the mindset of the Swedish soldier. According to one volunteer, the main difference between the Swedes and the Finns was the Finns' slightly more cautious attitude and ability to patiently wait for an opportune moment to counter a Soviet attack. For example, the Finns preferred to launch surprise attacks against enemy field kitchens instead of engaging in conventional warfare, understandably so, because their risk of loss was great.[194]

3

Combat Operations

The Finnish Army's Perspective on the War

The Finnish victories in the early stages of the war demonstrated the importance of mastering Arctic warfare and exercising patience. The clothing — boots lined with reindeer hide and layers of heavy woolen underwear and socks under a lightweight white snow cape serving as camouflage — allowed the Finns to hunker down for hours, as close as ten feet from the passing Soviet patrols without being detected.[1] The Arctic winter became the Finns' greatest ally, and allowed them to follow the Russians deep into the forests and shoot them or simply let them freeze to death.[2] Despite their initial successes at halting the Soviet advance, the Finnish losses proved devastating. By mid–December 1939, the casualties amounted to one-fourth of the total fighting force.[3] The troops faced attrition as their main problem. The government had to call upon new recruits without prior military experience — some were so young that they were technically not obligated to report for military duty until the following year — and reservists, some as old as forty years of age.[4] Many officers lacked experience in warfare and the different divisions were unable to cooperate effectively.[5] More than a hundred thousand women served in support roles in the *Lotta* organization and relieved the men for combat duty at the front.[6] Countless Swedish volunteers have praised the Finnish *Lottas*, some of whom were only in their mid-teens, for their hard work, their competence and compassion. One volunteer called them "a true national treasure."[7]

As noted previously, Finland's armed forces were numerically inferior to the Russian war machine. The troops lacked ammunition and weapons, in particular large artillery pieces, and could therefore not count on decisive support from the artillery. The extreme shortage of materiel made it impossible to defend the extensive frontier with the Soviet Union; a 1,300 kilometer stretch of forests, lakes, and rivers. When the war began, the inventory indicated that ammunition would last two months at the most, and no more than a few weeks for some artillery pieces. Aviation fuel was in even shorter supply and was estimated to last no more than a month.[8] The army was forced to contract with civilians for the use of horses and motor-driven vehicles.[9] Additionally, Finland's geographical location placed nearly one-third of the country above the Arctic Circle. Although the influence of the Gulf Stream tended to make the climate bearable, the winter of 1939–40 proved the second coldest in more than a hundred years (since 1828).[10]

The Finns had in their possession only a few antitank guns purchased from Sweden and were forced to retreat. Unconventional warfare was clearly the only option if they were to have a chance against the massive Red Army. Although the situation seemed hopeless, they would soon learn to draw strength from their nationalistic spirit. Their familiarity with the terrain

Finnish anti-aircraft artillery Lottas *on duty. The Finnish* Lottas *from the Lotta Svärd organization were described by one Swedish volunteer as "a true national treasure" (source: Krigsarkivet, Förbundet Svenska Finlandsfrivilliga, Vol. 29).*

around the Karelian Isthmus, which contained few well-maintained roads, and their skill on skis would earn them the envy of the world. The Finns possessed extraordinary willpower, as they had demonstrated during the War of Independence twenty years earlier.[11] *Sisu,* as explained by Aulikki Olsen, a veteran of the *Lotta* organization, was the personal "ability or spirit that every Finn [was] supposed to have, that when things [went] wrong, you [didn't] give up."[12] But much had changed since the War of Independence. The Finns were no longer politically split. This time the mission included more than freeing the country from the grip of foreign oppression. What lay ahead was a journey of historical importance with focus on protecting Western culture and values.[13]

A basic understanding of nature meant the difference between life and death, and the Finns began to thrive in the extreme weather. They knew plenty of tricks that enabled them to survive the freezing temperatures. Quick communication from one man to another ensured decreased risk of enemy detection. Certain types of brush proved better suited than others for making fires that minimized the smoke. Likewise, fires built in the morning tended to produce less smoke than fires built in the afternoon because of the fair amount of natural mist in the air after the long night.[14] Creative ideas, some as simple as knitted knee warmers for kneeling in the snow when shooting, kept the troops warm and improved morale.[15] Removing and drying one boot at a time ensured readiness to engage the enemy at the spur of the moment, or depart quickly if need be. A cover of evergreen twigs when sleeping in the open helped one cope with the low temperatures at night, as did foods high in protein and fats. Sufficient fluid intake likewise proved important. Hot tea, however, would literally cause one's teeth to crack.[16] The psychological value of a nutritious diet could not be ignored. As noted by one Finnish soldier, good food did wonders for morale, physical strength, and fighting spirit.[17] As the temperatures fell with the arrival of Christmas, the Finns started talking affectionately about "Russian weather," suitable for engaging Stalin's troops who would likely suffer severe setbacks the colder it got.[18]

At the start of the war the Finnish defense retreated to a series of field fortifications made of wood, concrete, barbed wire, and natural terrain such as trenches, tree stumps, and boulders. This fortified line extending from Lake Ladoga to the Gulf of Finland, a distance of approximately 130 kilometers, had been erected in the 1920s as a result of the War of Independence, and came to be known as the Mannerheim Line.[19] The more than a hundred small concrete buildings served primarily as nests from which to launch artillery fire against an approaching army, and could also house and provide protection

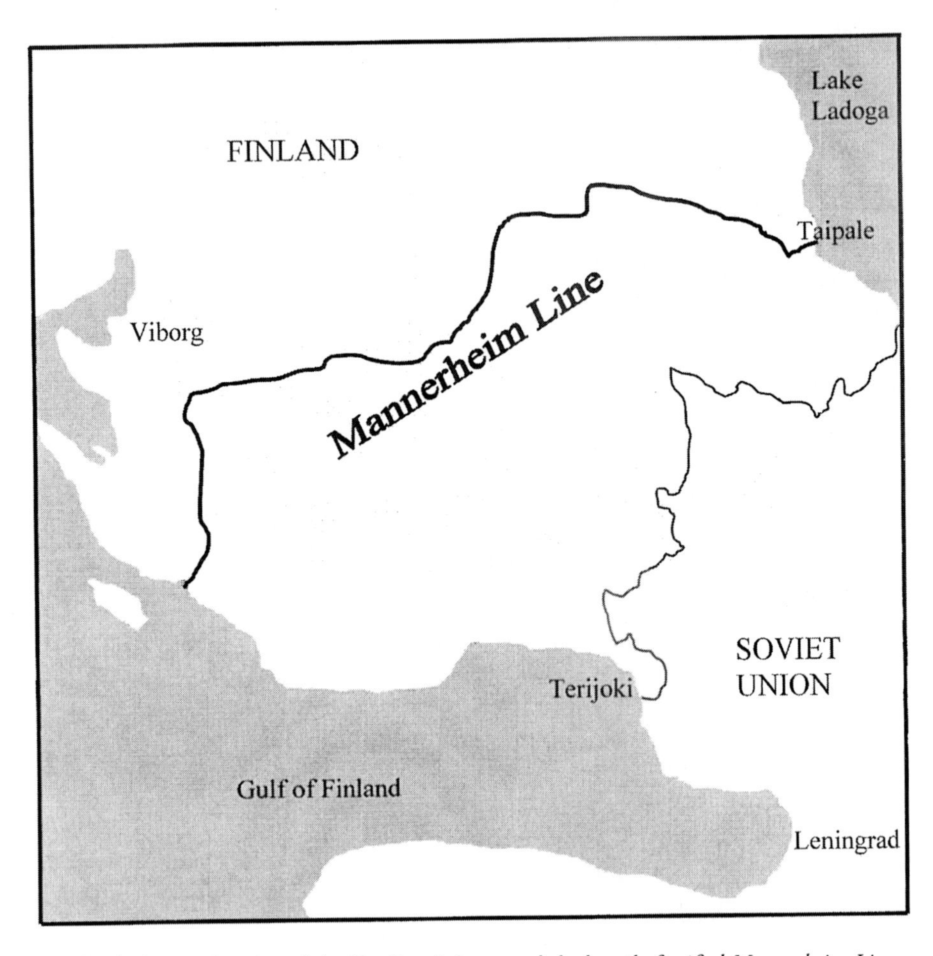

Sketch showing location of the Karelian Isthmus and the heavily fortified Mannerheim Line stretching from Lake Ladoga to the Gulf of Finland, along which many of the Winter War's toughest battles took place (source: Martina Sprague).

to several troops.[20] The first of three defensive lines, the Mannerheim Line was officially presented as nearly impossible to breach. A second line existed further north, and a third line consisting of eighteen bunkers was located near the city of Viborg.[21] The rear line was strong by nature, since Viborg, with its moats and fortifications, served as a psychological barrier to an invading army. The Finnish troops had no prior experience fighting in urban areas, yet Mannerheim's main worry was for how long an exhausted army would be able to hold the third defensive line after a massive retreat.[22] He had earlier considered expanding the second and third lines until they resembled the Mannerheim Line, but this idea never materialized.[23]

Some of the Winter War's toughest fighting took place not by the city of Viborg, however, but along the Mannerheim Line where the Finns managed to stave off the Russian advance for nearly two months.[24] Tanks approaching the line would first face a variety of traps such as mines and ditches.[25] By calculating distance and firing angle, the Finns could generally stop enemy tanks breaching the first obstacles.[26] If not, after confronting fire from the Finnish artillery, the Russians would face more ditches and rocks and a barrage of hand grenades, followed by antitank cannons along with regular infantry and reserve troops deploying even more antitank weapons.[27] Despite its strength, the line was not without problems and did not serve the Finnish defense as well as it could have. The direction of the line proved faulty and, according to one Finnish commander, lacked elasticity and depth and ran too far to the northwest. A breach, if not halted immediately, would jeopardize the strength of the whole line. Much of the line was also located along marshy lowlands that were easily observable by the enemy, and the concrete fortifications were aged and modeled after the defensive lines in France in World War I.[28] Some of the barbed wire and other barricades proved of little value because time constraints had not permitted the Finns to extend the depth of the line. The coast artillery, however, did a reasonably good job protecting the line's flanks at the Gulf of Finland and Lake Ladoga.[29] Although the fortifications along the Mannerheim Line served a psychological purpose, the respect afforded the line was likely a result of learned habits. Toward the end of the war the Russians discovered that they could defeat Finnish counterfire by placing their tanks in front of the firing openings in the bunkers, preventing the Finns from aiming at the Russian troops.[30]

Although providing shelter and an opportunity to preserve strength, the defensive fortifications restricted the Finns to a passive type of warfare. Defeating an enemy required active resistance and offensive maneuvering, and the Finns knew that they could not force the enemy to retreat or "lock a country's borders" indefinitely through defense alone.[31] They were thus forced to resort to guerrilla-type warfare. Intelligence indicated that the Red Army only maintained consistent strength along the front during daytime hours. At night they withdrew most of their troops one or two kilometers to fortified bivouacs in the rear lines, which were further guarded by stationary or slowly moving tanks.[32] This winter was exceptionally cold, however, with temperatures consistently measuring below -20 degrees C, and the ice on the Gulf of Finland by the city of Viborg, the gateway to Helsinki, would soon reach a thickness that would neutralize the natural defensive barrier of the Gulf and permit the transport of motorized equipment including tanks across the ice. Should the Red Army manage to break through the Mannerheim Line, neither the second

Russian horse bivouac (source: Krigsarkivet, Förbundet Svenska Finlandsfrivilliga, Vol. 29).

nor the third defensive line would likely halt their advance.[33] Luckily, the dense and forested terrain around the main battlefield on the Karelian Isthmus lent itself to innovative tactics. The mission of the Finnish army was not to take and hold ground, but to harass the Soviet troops, break them up and inflict casualties, and then disappear quickly. Finnish snipers, nicknamed "the white death" by the enemy, would wait for the right moment to pick off the Soviet troops one by one.[34] Other creative ideas involved filling coveralls with hay and placing them in the terrain in the hope that the Russians would attack thinking they were Finnish troops, and sign their own death sentence by paving the way for a strong Finnish counterattack.[35]

Close combat operations against enemy tanks with nothing more than handmade explosives came to characterize much of Finnish tactics, and required exceptional courage and skill.[36] Although most Finns had never undergone training scenarios involving tanks — Finland could not justify buying and maintaining the expensive equipment on account of the country's strict defensive policies — the "Molotov cocktail" saved the day more than once. This improvised explosive devise consisted of a bottle filled with a mixture of alcohol, tar, resin, and kerosene with a rag stuck into the opening and then lobbed onto the tank engine decks.[37] "The flaming gasoline would get sucked into the engine, the tank's fuel would blow up, and for the price of half a gallon of gas you could destroy an enemy tank."[38] Some of the more powerful "cocktails" consisted of a "blend of gasoline, kerosene, tar, and chloride potassium, ignited not by a dishrag but by an ampoule of sulfuric acid taped to the bottle's neck." Even more potent versions "included a tiny vial of nitroglycerine."[39]

The liquor industry assumed the role of supplying the soldiers with approximately seventy thousand empty bottles.[40] In the same vein, the chief for the alcohol company in Viborg offered to send nearly ten thousand liters of brandy to the front for consummation by the Finnish troops. Fully aware of the Finns' affinity for drinking, however, and in reference to the heavy responsibility the troops had of defending the homeland, the military leadership unanimously declined the offer and asked instead that as much coffee and tobacco as possible be sent to the front.[41]

In a nutshell, Finnish strategy called for splitting the enemy into smaller groups called *motti*,[42] which could be encircled and defeated even with primitive weapons. The Finns would delay the enemy's advance, attack his flanks, cut his supply lines so that he could neither advance nor retreat, and let the cold temperatures do the rest.[43] Successful *motti* tactics required fighting at extremely close range. The Finns learned that, as long as they covered their faces, they could run through the fire of flame-throwing machines and suffer only a scorched snowsuit.[44] (Hospital records from this period indicate a high percentage of facial wounds, however.[45]) The *motti* tactics allowed the Finns to enjoy the spoils of war, including cannons, trucks, horses, and tanks, which complemented their own general lack of equipment.[46] Finnish guerrilla tactics also involved plenty of "dirty" fighting; for example, placing mines in the terrain and under the ice of newly frozen lakes to prevent the enemy from crossing. An article in *Pravda* noted that the Finns were "masters of foul play." Not only did they fill their village wells with earth to prevent the Russians from fetching drinking water,[47] they shoved logs and crowbars into the wheels of the enemy tanks, which "often stripped a tread and immobilized them."[48] When the enemy came out to make repairs, the Finns would attack with machinegun fire. They commonly struck after dark and in poor visibility, in fog and snow.[49] They also planted mines to both sides and in the center of the paths that led through the forests. This activity naturally required expert memory in order to avoid stepping on a mine by accident.[50]

The situation at the front turned night into day, as little work could be done before midnight when the Russian artillery fired nonstop and forced the soldiers to stay in their dugouts. After midnight when the enemy firing had quieted down, the Finns came out and went to work. Instead of digging trenches by hand, they detonated mines to blow up the earth. One dugout at the front, as described by a Finnish soldier, could accommodate fifteen men. The stove in the corner made it so hot on the second level of bunk beds that "[s]weat covers the forehead even if one takes almost all the clothes off."[51] They would also take cover in the holes made in the ground by the Russian shells, then open automatic fire to prevent further enemy movement.[52]

The Finns realized several victories in the first week of the war. On December 6, the Russians attacked in frontal assault against the heavily defended Finnish lines, enabling the Finns to wipe out entire Russian battalions and capture several caches of weapons to be redeployed against their former owners.[53] They damaged 108 Soviet tanks (80 in just the first five days of fighting) through the use of the Molotov cocktail in combination with cannon fire, mines, artillery, and grenades.[54] Mannerheim complimented the troops and compared the Soviet mass assault that took place in December to "a badly conducted orchestra, in which the instruments were played out of time. Division after division was thrown against our positions, but the cooperation between the different arms remained bad."[55]

By seizing the initiative and actively engaging the enemy instead of passively waiting behind their fortifications, the Finns learned that the Soviet forces could be decimated and their spirit broken.[56] Even though the enemy's advance along the front looked threatening, aggressive action proved the best alternative. The Red Army's method of advancing in columns separated by miles of desolate terrain prevented them from using their numerical superiority, accessing their modern equipment, and uniting for a full-force attack. By attacking the enemy columns in the rear or flanks one at a time, the Finns could gain a strategic advantage without jeopardizing their own communications. When a long column had been cut in several places, each part would be defeated individually in fights that could last well over a week. The Russians fought with utmost determination but employed ill-organized tactics. Although division after division attacked the Finnish positions, as Mannerheim had noted, the coordination between the different combat arms proved poor. The artillery wasted ammunition and tanks opened fire but retreated before the infantry had arrived.[57] The number of tanks that the Finns destroyed through their innovative tactics may well have turned the war to their advantage had they been fighting any enemy other than the Soviet Union, who seemed to have an unlimited supply of weapons and manpower.[58]

Defeating the advancing enemy before they had passed the border area proved crucial. They could not be allowed to reach the more populous regions where the network of roads and the railway would ease their advance. Despite the initial successes, several factors came to complicate the Finnish combat operations. Since they received few instructions from their leaders, the Finns had to resolve problems as they occurred and as they saw fit in the best manner possible. Success naturally required great flexibility.[59] When conditions necessitated, cars were driven with lights turned off in order to avoid arousing enemy suspicions. But the drivers often found themselves stranded in a ditch or involved in an accident due to their inability to see the snow covered roads in the dark. The necessity to transport workers, construction materiel for shelters, food, weapons, and ammunition became an exceptionally frustrating undertaking on the narrow snow-covered roads.[60] Their radio equipment proved poor and unable to withstand the harsh exposure to the weather, and many of the Finnish operators had not been trained in the use of codes. Control of telephone lines proved crucial if they were to secure communications and make their "intentions unknown to Soviet intelligence."[61] The frontline signalmen, forced to improvise, started to converse in "a slang-riddled mixture of Swedish and regional Finnish dialect." By imitating Russian signals, they managed to convince the enemy to drop much needed supplies into Finnish positions.[62]

Despite the surprise bombing of Helsinki and the negative experiences on the Karelian Isthmus, the destruction that the Finnish troops had caused their enemy strengthened their morale and allowed them to renew their efforts in the main theater of operations where approximately two-thirds of the forces were stationed. They proved adamant at defending this piece of land, whose actual value could be contested but which, nevertheless, constituted an important part of Finland's future as a sovereign nation.[63] In the long run, however, the Karelian Isthmus proved less suitable than expected for guerrilla tactics against an enemy as numerically superior as the Soviet Union. Although the forests, lakes, and marshes contributed to the strength of the Mannerheim Line, the 168 concrete bunkers, machinegun nests, and barbed wire proved insufficient against heavy Soviet tank artillery.[64] From a defensive-fortification perspective, some Finns considered the line "a myth invented by foreign media correspondents." Mannerheim himself asserted that in reality it was comprised only of the strength of the individual soldiers standing in the snow.[65] The architects of the Maginot Line, erected along

France's border with Germany after World War I, would have found it laughable.[66] The line held as long as it did, he explained, only because of the tenacity and courage of the Finnish troops.[67]

Mannerheim thus had to make one of the most painful decisions of his career. All indications pointed to that the main forces stationed on the Karelian Isthmus would soon become subject of a great enemy offensive. The troops must therefore be reinforced with all available reserves in the hope that the line would maintain its cohesion a little longer. But since the enemy was making quick advances also in the north, Mannerheim was forced to send the main parts of his sparse reserves to Tolvajärvi and Suomussalmi.[68] By December 14, all of Tolvajärvi was in Finnish hands. As new struggles ensued along the front on the Karelian Isthmus as well as further north, the Finns continued to prove to the world that they would not give in to Russian demands. On December 21, *Dagens Nyheter*, a Swedish daily newspaper, reported that a Russian massed attack on the Karelian Isthmus, supported by several hundred tanks, had resulted in two days of intense fighting. Yet, the Red Army had failed to break through the Finnish positions. The Finns managed to take twenty tanks from the enemy. The previous day, more than two hundred Russian bombers had attacked several parts of the Finnish mainland as well as parts of the Finnish archipelago, and the Finns had shot down twenty Russian bombers, fourteen of which were downed by Finnish fighter pilots.[69]

In the following week, the Russians advanced a hundred kilometers through the desolate terrain along the Salla front without encountering any resistance. But when attempting to cross the Kemi River, an ambush toward their flank resulted in battle that claimed the lives of eight hundred Russian troops. The Finns acquired five tanks, thirty cars, several automatic rifles and cannons, and two hundred horses. As reported from the front that day, Russian cavalry, infantry, and artillery had been completely annihilated and the battlefield was "littered with the dead" who "the intense cold had turned into grotesque figures."[70] By December 24, two thousand Russian soldiers had fallen in battle at Tolvajärvi-Ägläjärvi north of Lake Ladoga. Simultaneously, aerial attacks against the Finnish coastal cities had caused little damage. The Russian pilots appeared to be dropping bombs arbitrarily, likely a result of inferior maps which made it difficult to locate exact targets.[71]

More than four thousand fallen Soviet troops could ultimately be counted along the main road, and approximately six hundred prisoners and considerable war booty had been taken. Yet, the Finnish victories in these battles proved expensive and the losses amounted to 30 percent of the officers and 25 percent of the soldiers. In relative terms, these losses were greater than in any other battle of the Winter War. Still, the victory at Tolvajärvi had a strategic and psychological effect on the Finns, and motivated troops along other parts of the front to rise even more strongly against the enemy. Finnish civilians likewise regained confidence in the efficiency of their armed forces. They supported their government and understood that the war must go on, despite the fact that, by the year's end, nobody could escape noting how dark the future looked. The prestige of the Soviet Union was at stake. The Finns understood that the Red Army *must* win, no matter how large their losses.[72]

On January 9, 1940, the weather at the front indicated light snowfall and a temperature of -17 degrees C. Sudden enemy fire forced the Finns to seek cover in the numerous trenches along the road. As reported by a Finnish commander, one regiment comprised of Swedish soldiers from the Finnish province of Österbotten east of the Gulf of Bothnia proved exceptionally skilled at returning the fire at the Russians who were stationed only a hundred meters away, and the Finns could soon rise from behind their covers. On January 17, the thermometer indicated -48 degrees C, the coldest yet measured. When momentarily stepping outside, one soldier remembered how it felt as if his face "were suddenly cut with a knife."[73] Then, in early February, the situation worsened when the Red Army launched a big offensive on the Isthmus. The Finns found five Russian parachutes and started a hunt for the Russian troops. Muffled rumbles from artillery fire could be heard in the direction of Summa, an indication that the war was in full swing. By evening, an incoming report informed the Finnish leadership that seven Russian parachutists had been shot and killed, and one had been taken prisoner. An additional six parachutes had been found, and more than 120 enemy bombers had been sighted. Enemy tanks broke through the first lines of defense, closely followed by infantry. The Russian air force fired against Finnish ground troops each time they attempted to interfere with the Russian advance.[74]

But the Finns stood their ground. On the third day of the offensive, the Swedish newspaper, *Den Svenske Folksocialisten* (The Swedish People Socialist), reported that the front on the Karelian Isthmus had not yet broken.[75] The Finns reported having destroyed seven tanks and killed at least a thousand enemy troops. As observed by one Russian captive, the Red Army's losses were catastrophic. The road to the south of Summa was littered with demolished cars and tanks, and the terrain was covered with the dead. The countless wounded and frost injured Russian troops in the trenches received little assistance from their army, and their screams could be heard throughout the night.[76]

Although the exact hour and day of the offensive had been kept a secret, the Finns had made detailed observations and analysis of enemy activities on a daily basis from the end of January. Russian tactics indicated that the prime objective was not to win territory through an overwhelming surprise attack,

Karelska fronten håller!

De röda kastas tillbaka — Vad de ryska fångarna ha att berätta — Ett besök i ett övergivet karelskt hem

I januari 1940.

En tidig gråkall morgon "någonstans". Det heter så på militärt språk. Det var nämligen i Karelen, närmare bestämt på Näset låg en bataljon finska soldater på ett relativt smalt näs och inväntade fienden. Sedan dagar hade man klart för sig, att någonting därborta höll på att ske. Det var ett ryskt anfall som begynte. På vanligt sätt satte det ryska fältartilleriet igång med en våldsam kanonad, som gudskelov mest var skräckinjaganda genom smällarna och ej genom resultatet. På utsatt tid kom det genom diset en tung gråkall massa, som vällde fram mot de finska linjerna. Vad bestod den av? Utbildade specialtrupper särskilt lämpade för förtruppsstrider? Tanks eller vad? Nej, boskap — levande boskap, **människor**, en gråtung massa av polska fångar, kvinnor, politiska förbrytare mot den nuvarande regimen i Ryssland. De drevos fram med bajo-

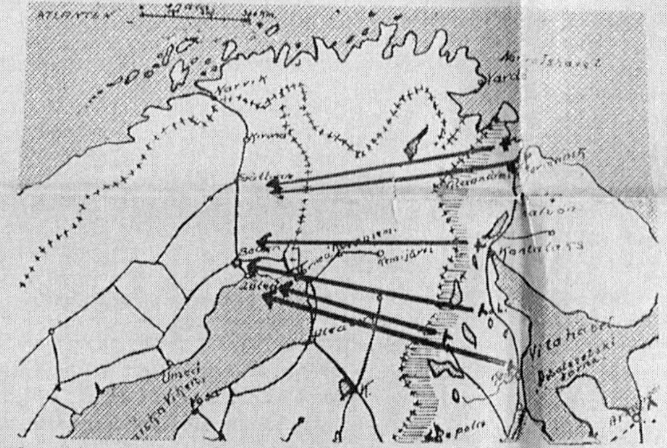

Ovanstående karta över norra Skandinavien visar de ryska flygbasernas läge i förhållande till de svenska försvarslinjerna. Bombfällningen vid Luleå understryker vårt utsatta läge. Trots detta är norra Sverige så gott som blottat på luftstridskrafter.

"The front on the Karelian Isthmus intact," reads the heading. The map indicates the locations of the Russian air bases in relation to the Swedish defensive lines in northern Finland (source: Den Svenske Folksocialisten, *February 3, 1940, Krigsarkivet, Finlandskommitten, 1939–1940).*

but to use a form of attrition warfare where action in escalated intensity would eventually wear the Finnish troops thin. Their plan had worked. Following the big offensive, ammunition among the Finns became so scarce that they were restricted to firing sparingly and with precision. It was estimated that the Red Army could be kept at bay one more week at the most. In fact, the 105-millimeter battery imported from Sweden, capable of firing a distance of eighteen kilometers, had only thirty rounds of ammunition left. On February 10, Viborg came under heavy bombardment. Finnish anti-aircraft artillery answered the threat, but was unable to sight the Russian bombers through the cloud cover and had to fire only against the sound of the machines.[77] Although the Finnish forces fought courageously and without letup against their mighty enemy, there were few encouraging signs. According to Gunnar Laatio, a veteran of the war, when the Russians resumed their offensive and bombarded the Mannerheim Line with more than two thousand artillery pieces each day for the next ten days, "[i]t felt like hell. Of course, I have not actually been there, but I can't imagine it could be any worse."[78] February 11, according to one Finnish officer, was "a horrible day, the most difficult so far."[79]

As the Russian artillery intensified, it not only threatened the frontline Finnish defenses, but also the rear lines. Some of the aerial attacks initially seemed insignificant, likely because the airfields had not been plowed since the heavy snowfalls and prevented takeoff and landing. But on February 28, to the dismay of the Finnish troops, the barometer rose indicating "Molotov weather," clear days with good visibility which heightened the risk of bombing attacks.[80] Moreover, the winter no longer favored the Finns and Soviet tanks moved unhindered over the hard frozen lakes.[81] Defending the western shore at the Viborg bay area, a stretch of more than twenty kilometers, would prove impossible since the ice was now so thick that it could carry trains, and the Finnish army lacked the resources in manpower to place mines along the entire stretch. It was only a matter of time before a land-based attack would come against Viborg. In the Lapland area, Stalin's troops attempted to halt Finland's communications with Sweden, but fortunately Sweden's volunteer air force prevented the Soviets from shutting down the railway. North of Lake Ladoga along the Finnish border with Russia, the Red Army experienced greater success and managed to advance deep into Finnish territory. On March 8, an intercepted Russian radio transmission informed the Finns that Viborg, due to "the celebration of some important gentleman's fiftieth birthday, ought to be conquered today." The Red Army was promised an unlimited supply of brandy as a reward.[82]

The Soviet Army's Perspective on the War

Finland's suspicion that the nonaggression treaty it had signed with Russia in 1932 would be an ineffective barrier to hostilities was confirmed when more than 600,000 Soviet troops "poured across the frontier [all the way to Petsamo in the north] behind a massive artillery bombardment, vastly outnumbering Finland's total combat army of only 250,000."[83] The greatest advantage that Stalin enjoyed may have been the magnitude of his forces, which totaled many times the strength of the Finnish and Swedish troops combined. One Finnish commander admitted after the war that the Finnish leadership had possessed little intelligence with respect to the quantity of the Russian troops.[84] The Russian air force alone amounted to approximately 3,800 airplanes of which 1,500 were fighters, 1,700 bombers, and 600 reconnaissance aircraft. Although not all would be sent to fight the war in Finland, the Soviet Union virtually owned the airspace. On the first day of the war they bombed sixteen Finnish towns while encountering only meager resistance.[85] One Russian soldier claimed that he did not see "a single Finnish airplane throughout the whole war." Even if they had been flying, the Finns would have presented little danger to Russian ground troops who "were always camouflaged from the air with white sheets of linen," and would likely have escaped detection.[86]

The Soviet pilots' lack of proficiency in night operations — only twelve of twenty-two pilots from one flight squadron had received training at night — proved of little concern since they risked virtually no counterattack by Finnish aircraft.[87] A favorite Soviet tactic involved dropping "Molotov breadbaskets," a form of cluster bombs that opened at five hundred meters and spread several smaller incendiary bombs over the target.[88] (According to propaganda, the Soviet Union was not dropping bombs but merely delivering "food" to the starving Finnish masses; thus the term "breadbaskets."[89]) On December 19, 1939, the Russians bombed the big cities of Turku, Hangö, Helsinki, and Viborg.[90] The bombings forced the Finnish civilians to run from their homes and seek cover in the nearby forests. Not until the last week of the war would Finland's fighter pilots realize some success attacking Soviet troops marching across the ice on Viborgska Viken, a deep bay near the city of Viborg in the northeastern part of the Gulf of Finland.[91]

Stalin could not take the country by air power alone, however, but launched a massive attack in the north between Lake Ladoga and the Arctic Ocean on December 8, 1939.[92] When ordering the Red Army to attack Finland's "midsection," it was with the goal of dividing the country in half, then attacking Suomussalmi and driving through all the way to the Gulf of Bothnia.[93] The main Finnish resistance was concentrated in the fortifications along the Mannerheim Line, which the Finns used not for passive defense but as a "springboard" for action, as expressed in a debriefing session between Stalin and his generals after the war.[94] The open areas of the Karelian Isthmus seemed perfect for tank battle and the Soviets entrusted their lives to their tanks. The Red Army's heavy reliance on motorized equipment and the troops' general inability on skis forced them to stay along the roads.[95]

Although Stalin had discounted the possibility that the Finns might refuse to fight a conventional war, at least two of the Soviet commanders had taken prior notice of the difficulties that awaited them. General Kirill Meretskov submitted a report to the high command just before the start of hostilities: "The terrain of coming operations is split by lakes, rivers, swamps, and is almost entirely covered by forests."[96] Lakes and swamps had not yet frozen strong enough to support the weight of the motorized equipment, and would prove as destructive to a tank as dry ground to a ship. Moreover, the Finns could easily anticipate a Russian advance along open terrain and litter the roads and fields with mines and other obstacles.[97] A disastrous incident later in the war nearly caused a whole Russian battalion to drown in the Gulf of Finland, when a shell or mine broke the ice upon which they were walking. They saved themselves only by clinging to a tank in front of them on the ice.[98] The Molotov cocktails the Finns threw proved one of the greater obstacles to motorized warfare and would keep the tanks burning for up to two days. When asking about the fires he saw in the distance, one Russian soldier learned that it was the burning tanks of his comrades.[99]

Thus, as the Finns had predicted, the winter caused severe setbacks for the Red Army. Although given modern firearms and plenty of ammunition, the cold temperatures and difficult terrain prevented the troops from using the equipment as intended. Their rifles, jammed by chunks of frozen oil, frequently refused to fire,[100] forcing the Red Army to assault the Finnish bunkers only with bayonets.[101] When coming under heavy fire from the Finnish artillery, the telephone connections frequently broke and lines could not be repaired under fire. The Red Army thus had to go without connection for several hours. The Finns were relentless in their pursuit in spotting and jamming Russian radio stations.[102] Additionally, the Finns preferred to attack at night, which resulted in a great deal of hand-to-hand fighting with bayonets in the trenches.[103] As reported by a Russian soldier of the 100th Rifle Division at the battle of Summa in January 1940, during an encirclement attempt, hand grenades thrown into the trenches were quickly grabbed and thrown back before they detonated. The Russian heavy machine guns finally managed to force the Finns to retreat through the forest.[104]

The Russians were not only undertrained in winter operations. Thinking that the war would end with an easy victory before his birthday on December 21, 1939, Stalin had outfitted the troops in old fashioned summer and autumn uniforms.[105] They possessed no overcoats for the first weeks of the war, but had to acquire whatever clothing they could from the dead Finnish soldiers. They even cut fur coats into smaller pieces in order to make socks.[106] When the winter uniforms finally arrived, the greatcoat, although warm, interfered with movement and complicated the use of weaponry.[107] As described by one Russian soldier, the greatcoat on top of a sweater and padded jacket was "hard to turn around in ... not to mention fighting the war."[108] Additionally, the armored shields the Soviet forces were issued proved highly unsuitable for the conditions. Although sufficient for passive defense, the shields were too heavy to carry and quickly exhausted a soldier running through the forest or crawling in the snow. The shields also provided a false sense of security, prompting tired soldiers to drop down for cover when sighting the enemy but refusing to rise when the danger had passed. The Finns, by contrast, took advantage of the slow advance of the Red Army and found opportune moments to fire at the Russian infantrymen. Even distances of 100–200 meters would take a long time to cover in the deep snow.[109]

Downtime between battles proved not much better. The lack of tents in which to seek shelter from the wind forced the troops to use dugouts in the snow. Campfires would make them easy targets of aerial attacks once the Swedes arrived to defend northern Finland.[110] "We slept in all kind of ways," one Russian soldier recalled. "We tried to use burnt down ruins, cellars and so on. Sometimes we slept on pine tree branches. Sometimes, when it was windy, we would dig holes in snow to hide from the wind. We did not set up tents, although we had them in our bag packs. We were not allowed to lit fires during the night."[111] Another soldier noted that they had no place to boil or cook food after their field kitchen had been destroyed by a mine, and had to resort to eating biscuits and drinking melted snow.[112]

Staying warm proved difficult no matter how one dressed or ate, however. "Our battalion was very well equipped," explained one Russian soldier. "[We had] sheepskin coats, felt boots, padded jackets and pants, woolen gimnastyorkas [army shirts], warm underwear, warm foot wrappings, a woolen helmet liner that would only leave the eyes and nose exposed to the elements. Catering was excellent — we had 100 grams of vodka every day, lard and other things."[113] Conversations with the Russians in the days following the cease fire revealed that they had received rations consisting of one and a half hectograms (150 grams) of bread a day, one can condensed milk, 100 grams butter, 100 grams sugar, and 200 grams vodka. Those serving in the foremost lines received extra rations.[114] Confessions from Russian prisoners, however, indicated that the soldiers were suffering from lack of food, shelter, and fighting spirit.[115]

The Winter War was "very complicated," noted one lieutenant of the Red Army. The maps were poor and bore little resemblance to the actual terrain. Approaching the Mannerheim Line without a map and not knowing what lay ahead proved particularly treacherous. The Finns had set up barbed wire, then a rock fence and a minefield. If the Red Army made a passage through the fence, the Finns would repair it at night. These measures naturally led to frustration and slowed progress.[116] Movement for the Red Army was particularly cumbersome due to the fact that much of the area was covered by forest, and also by rivers and lakes which were normally traversed through bridges. But the Finns destroyed the bridges and left the wreckage at the riverbeds. Not until cranes had been brought in to clear the wreckage could the Red Army continue their march. Additionally, the roads in the Petsamo region were only four to six meters wide, with forests on both sides. The Russians were finally forced to build a road from Murmansk to Petsamo, along which the whole army moved.[117]

When battle erupted, the troops took cover behind the bodies of their dead comrades, which quickly froze to solid ice in the low temperatures and became "shields" good enough to stop a bullet. Yet, by December 17, 1939, three Russian divisions employing massed attacks had failed to breach the Finnish defenses at Taipale between the western shore of Lake Ladoga and Lake Suvanto, and were mowed down to the last man despite the Finns' scarcity of automatic firearms.[118] A journalist for the *New York Times* reported on December 25, 1939, that the "ice-covered forests" and the cold brain-numbing Arctic air on the Russo-Finnish frontier had turned living men into statues, still in their "fighting attitudes ... frozen in half-standing positions," some with "their bayonets within each other's bodies."[119] One Russian soldier recalled how one of his dead comrades had frozen solid in his pose, "his hand froze in the lifted position — he was either throwing a grenade or tried to protect his face." As further described, everywhere one looked there were "dead men lying ... like heaps of grass during harvest."[120] With the next snowfall, the frozen bodies of the Red Army would become indistinguishable from the rocks, tree stumps, and branches in the forest.[121] The war also tested the confidence and spirit of the Finnish machine gunners, who had to commit this slaughter of enemy troops running into the fire.[122]

But it was not only the merciless cold that made the Winter War so complicated. Efficient movement through the terrain on the Karelian Isthmus required athletic ability and skill on skis. Every Finn knew how to ski. Children went to school on skis. The Finns were not only adept skiers and could ski without poles, as observed by one Russian soldier, they had fastened reindeer hide to the bottom of their skies which made them glide easily through the snow.[123] Recognizing the need to keep up with the vigorous Finnish troops, Stalin started recruiting trained athletes of superior physical strength and endurance. The experiment turned into disaster. Nikita Khrushchev recalled how the Russian sportsmen were "ripped to shreds," and not many came back alive.[124] Other unrealistic expectations have left the impression that nobody, not even the Soviet leadership, knew in any depth what types of terrain and enemy the troops would encounter. A revealing example is how a Soviet division from Ukraine was handed a pamphlet suggesting how to fight at close range with bayonets, while still wearing skis.[125] It was the treacherous tactics that the Finns employed that caused the greatest worries, however. Despite Finnish denial, the Russians swore that snipers (called cuckoos) were sitting in the trees.[126] "We couldn't see them anywhere," explained a Soviet colonel who was taken prisoner by the Finns, "yet they were all over the place.... This invisible death was lurking from every direction.... Hundreds, even thousands of men were slaughtered."[127]

At least one Russian soldier doubted that there were Finnish snipers in the trees. The moment the war ended and the guns fell silent, he observed his company commander walking toward a Finnish officer and shaking his hand, after which all Russian and Finnish soldiers got out of their trenches. The Finnish soldiers were so well camouflaged in white that they were nearly invisible, and the Finnish officer explained that there was no need to sit in the trees in order to avoid being seen. In addition, it would have been exceedingly difficult to fight from such a position. Not only would one need to take food and water up in the trees, one would surely freeze to death if sitting there for any length of time. A ladder would also be needed in order to get up there, which would have given away one's position, and shelter would be poor due to splinters from enemy artillery, which were constantly flying through the air.[128]

The lack of training in the Red Army forced a learn-as-you-go approach to battle, which was "torture" and resulted in high numbers of casualties.[129] One soldier claimed to have received 120 hours of training in "fire, hide and camouflage" before being sent to the front.[130] Yet, at the start of the war, a stunning 47 percent did not know how to handle the weapons they were issued. The officers were not in tune with the soldiers and could not identify with their needs and offer moral support.[131] Poor reconnaissance and inability to communicate orders clearly posed major problems that resulted in severe losses among the commanders.[132] "[F]rom 1937 to 1939 was a period of persecution of the officer corps," recalled one lieutenant of the engineering platoon. "The whole academy [where we attended military training] did not have a single officer. We, men with very little experience, almost ignorant, were appointed commanders."[133] Still, personal opinions as to the effectiveness of the military leadership varied:

> Teachers in the academy were mostly honest and highly trained, former officers of the Royal Russian Army. They tried to teach us not only artillery science, but also traditions of the Russian Officers' Corps — honesty, unanimous obedience to the superiors, accuracy in following orders, preciseness in work, politeness, fitness, cleanliness and tidiness in uniforms, quick analysis of the environment and good decision-making. We the graduates of the academy could very well read the map, could quickly build our own maps, carry out forward observation and fire adjustment, write battle reports and draw maps of battle areas.[134]

Despite the impression that the Red Army was utterly unprepared for the war, many Finnish soldiers considered the Russians no easy take. One Finn who later served in northern Karelia in the Continuation War described the Soviet border guards as elite soldiers, highly skilled at their profession, and in exceptional physical condition.[135] At least some of the Soviet leadership took quick notice of their failures and adjusted their tactics. For example, when discovering that the Finns fought in small groups along the wide front, one Russian commander decided to arrange his division "in three columns and advance with a powerful concentrated force in three directions." This tactic yielded good results and enabled the Russians to break the enemy resistance. At the comeback during the big offensive in February, "[t]he highroad and the railway were chosen as the direction of the main thrust, as motor vehicles could operate nowhere else."[136]

The maps showing the borders revealed that "[t]here were fortified areas everywhere. Every metre was fortified," recalled one soldier, "and we took every metre by force." A fortified area could not be penetrated off the march, however. "First, reconnaissance by fire should be laid on to disclose the enemy's fire-system."[137] The Red Army achieved favorable results during the attack on February 11, laying down two and a half hours of preparatory fire before getting the attack under way without further delay. As noted by one Russian soldier:

> When the guns stopped firing, we transferred the fire some hundreds of metres forward. The Finns cracked our method. They knew that artillery preparation came first, followed by an infantry attack. Therefore, they left their trenches and met our infantry with fire. We began using different methods of artillery preparation. We deceived the enemy by repeated false transfers of fire and finally completely destroyed the troops fighting against our infantry. The ruse made it possible for the 123rd Division to pierce the enemy's fortified area boldly.[138]

The breakthrough clearly demonstrated that artillery was the primary arm for breaching "a modern fortified area." Since concrete works could not be easily destroyed, one had to damage the defenses and shake up the enemy before ordering the troops to advance. Or, as Stalin would later say, "Artillery does have its music. Yes, it does."[139] When the benefits of artillery had been fully realized, the explosions became so frequent that the "earth stood up like one huge black wall," as described by a senior sergeant of the 3rd Battalion, 85th Rifle Regiment. The Finns finally retreated from their trenches. Yet, when the Russians ran up to their bunkers, "they were gone." One Red Army troop reported having seen no dead or wounded. "I only saw a large thermos there, with steaming macaroni in it. I must say I had not seen a single killed Finnish soldier in the war."[140] The Red Army also used opportune moments to attempt to negotiate surrender with the Finns, but to no avail. Stricter measures were taken. The commanders ordered the men to surround the bunkers with explosives, and shouted for the Finns to come out with their hands up if they desired to live to see their families again. But when the blast went off, most of the bunkers held, and the Finns were still safe. Had the Red Army had such bunkers, noted one commander, they could have stayed there for three years waiting out the war, because no enemy could get in.[141]

The Red Army's hope for an easy victory began to fade with growing Finnish resistance. Letters and diaries found on fallen troops have revealed propaganda stating that the war would end on Stalin's birthday. This idea had been so heavily circulated that it was not possible, for the sake of the country's honor, to reconsider the wisdom of continuing in the current direction.[142] Morale fell among the troops. The Finns had sleds on which to transport the wounded to safety. The Soviets, by contrast, were forced to carry their comrades, sometimes for distances up to thirty kilometers, which proved an almost impossible task. The bodies of many Russian soldiers could be recovered and transported back home first after the war. Every soldier in the Red Army understood the necessity of moving the border in order to protect Leningrad. Yet, it was difficult to sympathize with this war of invasion. How could they be motivated to fight when every Finn supposedly owned a hundred times more land than a Russian?[143] When the Soviet district artillery chief, Nikolai Nikolaevich Voronov, received orders that they had less than two weeks to secure the victory, he remarked that he would be happy if the war could be sorted out in three months.[144]

Stalin was thus forced to change his plans. Rather than cutting Finland in half, he focused all efforts on breaking the Mannerheim Line. The strategy turned to accepted attrition rather than quick victory, which also meant large numbers of casualties in the Red Army. Although costly, it would eventually compel the Finns to return to the negotiating table.[145] In the middle of February 1940, the Russians broke through the line, forcing a Finnish retreat to Viborg.[146]

The Swedish Army's Perspective on the War

The Swedish volunteers assumed responsibility for the front at Märkäjärvi near Salla in northern Finland toward the end of February 1940, "releasing five experienced [Finnish] battalions and a handful of artillery pieces for redeployment on the gulf coast."[147] The troops, hunkered down only 80–300 meters from the Russian lines, had to be on constant guard against enemy movement, firearms, and grenades.[148] The volunteer engineering team improved the prior Finnish posts, installed barbed wire along the most sensitive parts of the defensive line, and placed other barriers such as mines in the environment after dark in order to avoid detection. One-third of the force

Ski patrol at Tohmo near Kemijärvi in northern Finland (source: Krigsarkivet, Förbundet Svenska Finlandsfrivilliga, Vol. 29).

stood guard for two hours at a time, while others patrolled on skis also at night, which required keen eyes and ears. The situation was naturally tense. Many of the volunteers lacked prior experience in warfare. Moving shadows cast by the northern lights and sounds in the forest due to the low temperatures took a heavy toll on the nerves. A jumpy trigger finger could easily cause inadvertent firing against friendly Finnish troops in the area.[149]

The first battle-ready unit to enter the war — an anti-aircraft battery supported by artillery and antitank guns — set up to defend a bridge on the Finnish side of a river bordering the Soviet Union. Magnus Dyrssen, chief for Combat Group I, noted that a good defense system could be arranged with the available weapons even if the defensive line was stretched a bit, which would also create a stronger reserve force for backup. By moving the line partly to the east, positions could be established for attacking the enemy flanks with automatic firearms.[150] He also noted that troops could march upright along the front line, because the Russians were passively "sitting in their bunkers" a hundred meters away.[151]

Three tactical alternatives existed: a head-on attack against the enemy, an encirclement attempt with attacks toward the right or left flank, or a strictly defensive position. The volunteers quickly discarded the last alternative because of the negative psychological effect the possibility of a protracted war would have on them. They had come to Finland to fight and not sit in passive defense. They deemed the head-on attack too risky since the Soviet forces

Entrance to a Russian bunker below ground (source: Krigsarkivet, Förbundet Svenska Finlandsfrivilliga, Vol. 29).

were numerically superior and hiding behind armored posts. This left them with the choice of encirclement and attacking the flanks using the Finnish *motti* tactic, if possible, to split the enemy forces into smaller units that could be combated separately. This option presented good chances of success, particularly since the Russians were dependent on roads for transport.[152]

Lieutenant Anders Grafström together with the Group II *Jäger* Company set out to determine the efficiency of the Soviet defense and the suitability of the terrain for travel northeast of Märkäjärvi.[153] The operation that followed was one of the more daring maneuvers of the Winter War, and would claim the lives of six Swedes and approximately two hundred Russian soldiers in heavy fighting.[154] It started March 1, when several volunteers reported that they had seen the enemy but refrained from opening fire. Soon thereafter, a Swedish patrol ran into an ambush and suffered three dead soldiers and four taken prisoners. The next day, a firefight broke out between the Swedes and the Soviets.[155] Combat Group II then received an operational order to attack the Red Army toward the village in Märkäjärvi. The first alternative — encirclement of the enemy from the north — prompted the Swedes to send out *jägers* for reconnaissance. Heavy artillery had to be used, so the probability of a successful attack from the north had to be determined beforehand. The terrain consisted of open fields in all directions except to the south, where a grove of trees complicated the issue. The volunteers expected the enemy to march from the south directly toward this grove. Group II placed sentries in all directions and prepared for attack, and around noon received information that approximately sixty of the enemy troops were moving forward on skis.[156]

The original plan was foiled, however, when a Swedish soldier extinguished a campfire with snow, releasing a huge cloud of smoke that ascended toward the treetops. The Russians decided to await the arrival of reinforcements, then approached the grove from the east and surrounded the Swedes from the south, east, and west. Despite this mishap, several factors would work to the volunteers' advantage. When the firing started, the enemy's aim proved too high to cause significant damage. The Soviets also advanced across the field with large gaps between individual soldiers. When they came within five hundred meters of the Swedish forces, the Swedes opened fire. Suffering considerable losses, the Soviets retreated and awaited reinforcements of 150 troops, who arrived toward evening. They reorganized their forces and prepared to encircle the volunteers. But a heavy Swedish counterattack again halted their advance. The battle came to close quarter hand-to-hand fighting, in which the volunteers lost four men to injuries. An additional six men died during the breakaway and seven were reported missing.[157]

Fol XIII:

Översikt av underrättelser rörande Identifiering

Underrättelse n:r	Underrättelsens innehåll	Iakttagelsen gjord den	av
	Myrtala; Korvala; 273 + ett spakomp /88 div.; Sex skidlkomp +2. gräns bev reg; Salla; 88 div; Kelloselkä; 426?; Kairala; 3. reg?; 122 div; 596; 78; 420; Märkäjärvi; 715; Märkävaara; Pyhäjärvi; N; 1:300000		
3	Fältbefästa ställningar: 2500 m VNV byn Märkäjärvi – genom en sänka 2500 m VSV byn – södra delen av Märkävaara Smal front ömse sidor om landsvägen i höjd med Pyhäjärvis sydspets. Även NO Märkäjärvi (Jfr XIII:2)	26/1	W:s besök Torne

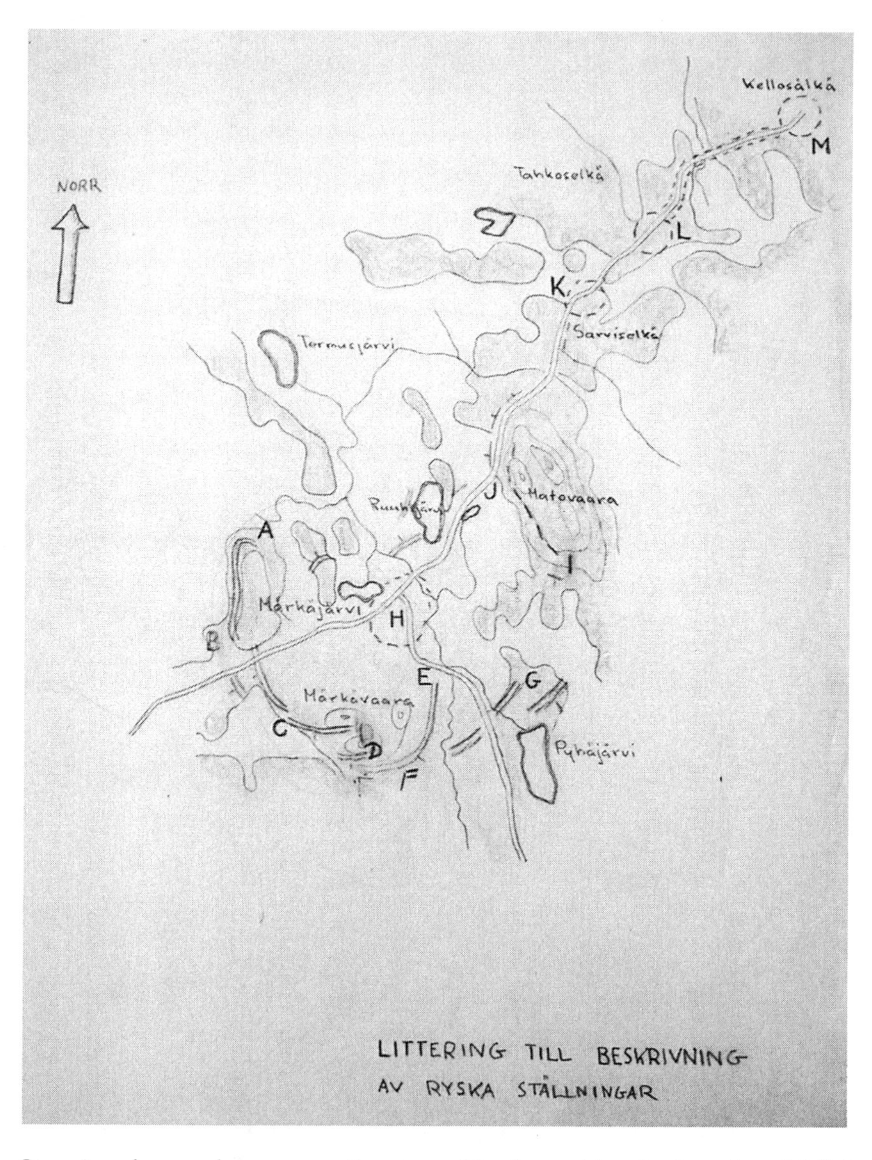

Opposite, above and next page: *Drawings of Russian positions in the region of Salla/ Märkäjärvi (source: Krigsarkivet, Svenska Frivilligkåren, Kriget 1939–1940).*

The Grafström Raid, as this incident came to be called after its inventor Lieutenant Anders Grafström of the Group II *Jäger* Company, was one of the more significant battles the volunteers endured during their two-week stint at the front and taught them a great deal about the skill and equipment of the Red Army. A report detailing the raid concluded that the Russian troops

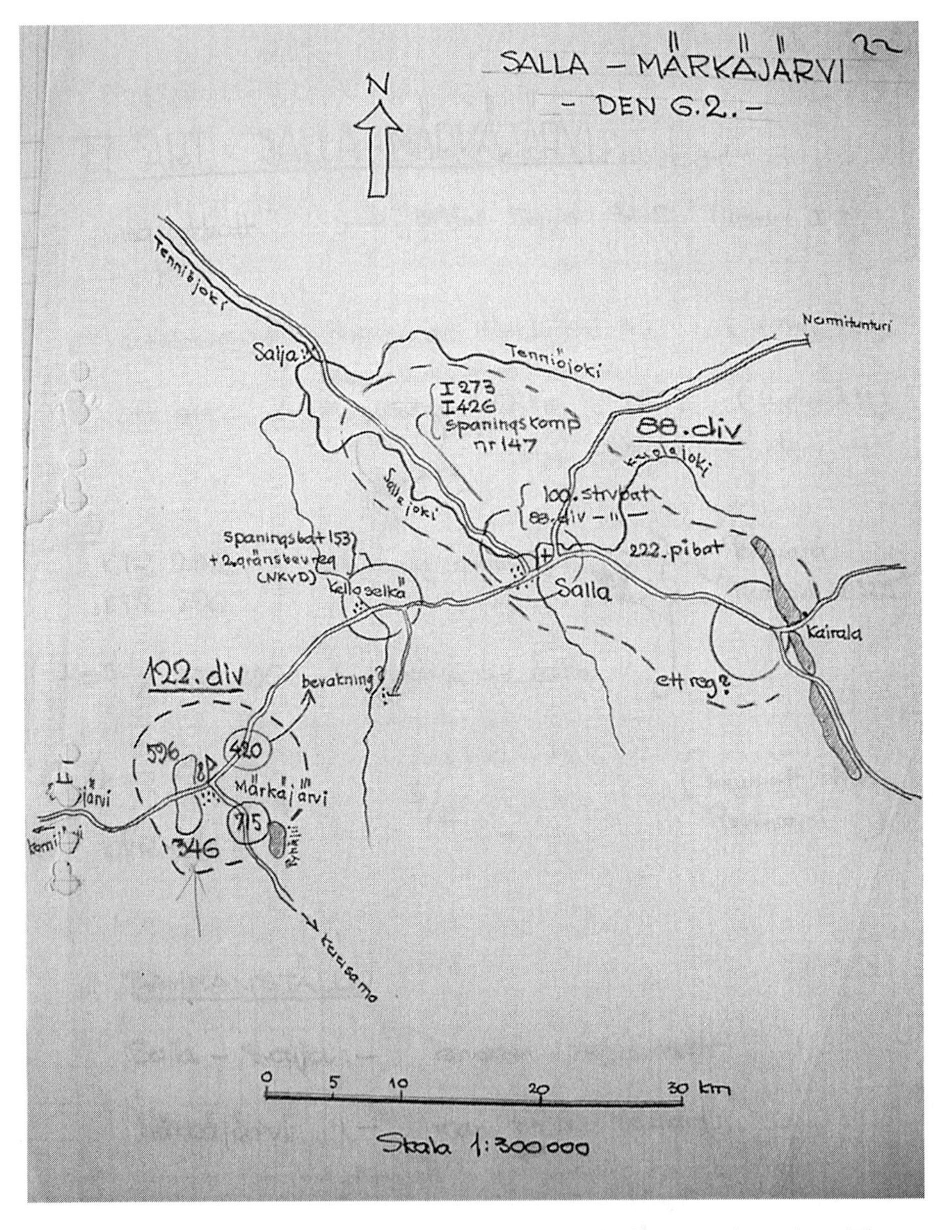

appeared well educated and were skilled in both skiing and combat. They used the terrain to their advantage during advance, although both officers and soldiers appeared intoxicated with vodka and often fired high. Soviet prisoners of war later confirmed this claim.[158] Moreover, one officer of the Finnish army reported that an attack on the anniversary of the formation of the Red Army (February 23) was being celebrated in the Russian lines by intoxicated and loudly singing troops, who "hopefully will drink so much vodka tonight that their attack tomorrow will come to suffer."[159] An exception was the isolated snipers, who were notably skilled and had plenty of automatic weapons available for use. Russian elite troops proved superior both to Finnish and Swedish soldiers in their ability to hold onto and take advantage of conquered terrain.[160] They were also tough-minded, known to have waded through the chest-high freezing waters of a creek in order to advance their position.[161]

Although several Russian troops feigned death in an attempt to set up ambush, mislead the Swedes, and hopefully save their own lives, the volunteers did not fall for the trick but used their bayonets to "take the temperature," as they said, of the Russian soldiers. Many wounded Russians tried in vain to crawl back to their own lines. Some of the survivors were taken prisoners and others, too wounded to march, were reportedly shot dead. Note that no true light has been shed on the claim that the volunteers killed prisoners. It has been speculated that since the Soviet Union did not observe the Hague Convention of 1907, Finland was not responsible for treating prisoners according to the laws and customs of war. The Swedish volunteers formally operated under the Republic of Finland. Although given instructions to treat prisoners in their care humanely, they could be vague with respect to established procedures. Prisoners wounded so badly that they were unable to move by themselves would have constituted a continued danger to the volunteers had they simply been left on the battlefield, and might possibly have been shot dead.[162]

The success of the Grafström Raid was overshadowed by the devastating loss of Magnus Dyrssen, who fell as the first in his group from grenade shrapnel to the head on March 1, when the Russians opened heavy artillery fire against the terrain occupied by Group I. When the initial shock had settled, his death resulted in a great deal of self-reflection. Swedish and Finnish blood had mixed for a common cause: for Nordic independence. Dyrssen's death thus became a motivating force for unity, for continued resistance against the Soviet superpower. The volunteers knew beyond a shadow of a doubt that they had a duty to fulfill and must stand ready to die for Finland's cause.[163]

On March 5, low-flying Soviet aircraft, busy attacking the region through the intermittent snowfall, targeted a car column transporting troops to the battlefield. Seeking shelter underneath the vehicles or in the snow to the side of the road, the volunteers took no casualties, although one of the cars was badly damaged in the firefight.[164] On March 6, two more volunteers died. A Swedish reconnaissance patrol had moved behind enemy lines when hostile fire severely injured one of the Swedes in the leg. The patrol, in need of a sled, was unable to evacuate the gravely wounded soldier who was not expected to live. Upon later examination, it was determined that the volunteers had failed to bring a sled despite orders to do so, and attempted instead (unsuccessfully) to carry the wounded man to safety on a pair of skis.[165] When no progress was made, the lieutenant in charge decided to stay with the wounded soldier while ordering the rest of the men to retreat. One volunteer explained that soon thereafter he heard two shots fired. When he returned to the place of battle, he found both the lieutenant and the soldier dead, shot in the head. Presumably, the lieutenant, when recognizing the futility of the situation, had shot the soldier and then shot himself.[166] Contradictory arguments exist as to what actually transpired. Another volunteer claimed that both the lieutenant and the soldier were killed by enemy fire.[167]

On March 10, the volunteers experienced yet a military triumph when they defeated a Soviet patrol and caused approximately fifty enemy casualties. It started with Viking Tamm, commander of Combat Group II, sending out an order preparing for an attack against "Kalotten" on Ristelivaara (a hill), where the Russians kept approximately ten soldiers and other forces of unknown numbers in the immediate surroundings to the south. The attack was planned for March 11 around 4:30 A.M. Group I *Jäger* Company set out to secure the trail leading to the top of the hill to

Fallen Russian soldiers after the firefight of March 10, 1940. The Russians were unable to retrieve many of their wounded who were left to die of blood loss and exposure during the night (source: Krigsarkivet, Förbundet Svenska Finlandsfrivilliga, Vol. 29).

prevent the enemy from fleeing toward the north. A Russian telephone line, found a few days earlier and intercepted for an hour at the start of the mission, had allowed the volunteers to relay information about the enemy's whereabouts. The plan called for an attempt to convince the Russians to surrender. If they refused, fifteen minutes of artillery fire and grenade throwing would follow, while Group II *Jäger* Company would pursue the hill from the north. If successful, one platoon would be left at the top until replacements arrived. This plan, too, was foiled, however. Telephone reports a quarter past two in the afternoon of March 10 noted that approximately twenty Russian troops stood ready to attack. A firefight ensued shortly thereafter. One volunteer remembered crawling through the barrage of grenades, then digging himself down in the snow. The Russian attacks grew in intensity. It is estimated that approximately a hundred grenades detonated in the immediate vicinity of the volunteers. The firefight continued throughout the afternoon, but the volunteers skillfully warded off the assaults with automatic firearms and grenades. Their successful defense has been attributed to good reconnaissance and quick action when first discovering that they were under attack. The Russians did not retreat until midnight.[168]

At nightfall, the bodies of the Red Army casualties that were left on the battlefield froze to ice in the cold temperatures. Wounded men screamed for

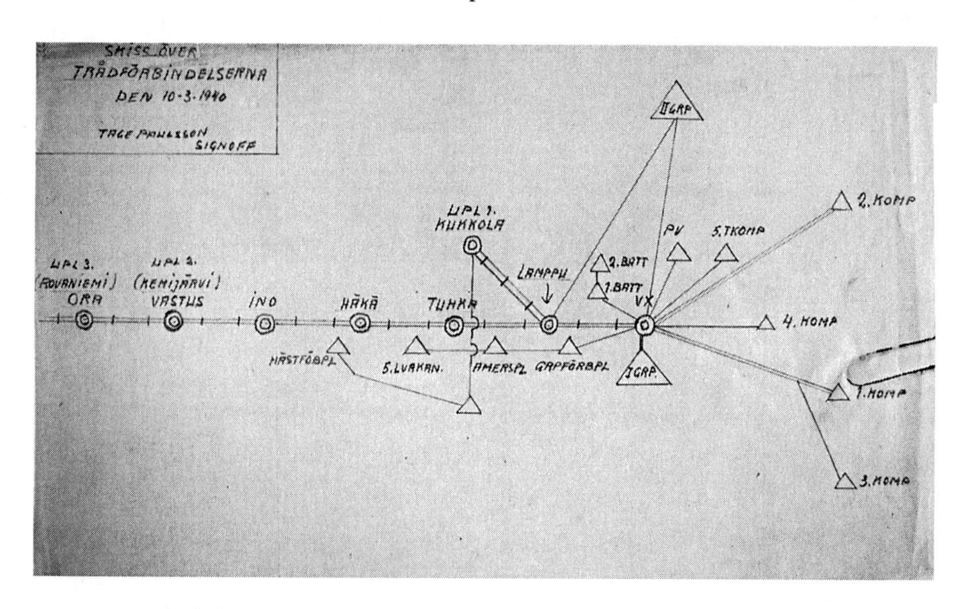

Drawing of telephone communications (source: Krigsarkivet, Svenska Frivilligkåren, Kriget 1939–1940).

Sergeant Svante Engström, chief of the rifle platoon that scored several victories in the firefight of March 10, 1940 (source: Krigsarkivet, Förbundet Svenska Finlandsfrivilliga, Vol. 29).

help, until their cries faded one by one as they froze to death in the -40 degree C temperatures. The volunteers, unable to tend to the injured enemy troops because of the dark and fear of ambush, left them there to die. Never trust a Russian, the saying went. By midnight, all was quiet. The body count the next morning indicated forty-six dead enemy soldiers, their bodies frozen into abnormal positions.[169] Trails discovered in the snow, however, suggested that quite a few of the wounded had been saved by their own and brought back behind Russian lines. Upon examination, it was concluded that the Russian soldiers were well dressed, wearing thick pants and undergarments, felt boots, and gloves lined with fur. Unlike the volunteers who had no opportunity for a shower or change of underwear, the Russians were clean, and several carried a toothbrush and razor for shaving in their pocket.[170]

The firefight on March 10 also led to the acquisition of considerable war booty. The volunteers captured five semi-automatic rifles, two fully automatic rifles, several other rifles, ten grenades, and much ammunition. They confiscated large numbers of skis, which were later used as fuel for the tent stoves since the tar applied to grease them made the wood burn well. Several of the dead enemy also carried postcards and Polish coins, an indication that at least some of them had participated in the attack against Poland in the autumn of 1939. At least one of them carried a wallet containing a photo of what was likely his family. The volunteers acquired mainly rank insignia, however, and important papers from the dead in order to provide evidence of their combat platoon.[171]

Toward evening on March 11, Group II reported seeing what appeared to be a strong body of enemy troops moving in a southwesterly direction across a field. Group I *Jäger* Company prepared to move but failed despite the moonlight to spot the Russians. The following evening a reconnaissance patrol from Group I encountered a Soviet patrol, reinforced with approximately four hundred infantry troops on skis traveling toward the Swedish troops. At 6:45 A.M. heavy artillery fire started, which lasted until 10:50 A.M. The firing resulted in only marginal losses for the Swedes (one wounded soldier).[172]

Although able to hold their own against the Russians in these major combat operations, the volunteers' clothing, living conditions, and material resources proved ill suited for Arctic warfare. The fur hat, for example, designed to be pulled down over the ears also inadvertently covered the eyes. The ski cap, too, proved unsuitable since it failed to provide sufficient cover for the neck, ears, forehead, and temples. The amount of underwear sent to the front, two pairs per person, was totally insufficient. Between February 11 and April 1, the volunteers had opportunity for no change at all.[173] The extreme cold at Märkäjärvi made it crucial to wear double layers, particularly for troops on guard duty. But this was not possible, since each troop was only issued two pairs of underwear and needed access to one clean change. A request was put forth for four pairs per troop, with an opportunity to wash at least every fourteen days.[174] Personal hygiene in the wilderness thus proved terrible at best. Snow was used instead of showers, yet was too time consuming to melt. Access to water for washing was therefore almost nonexistent. The troops

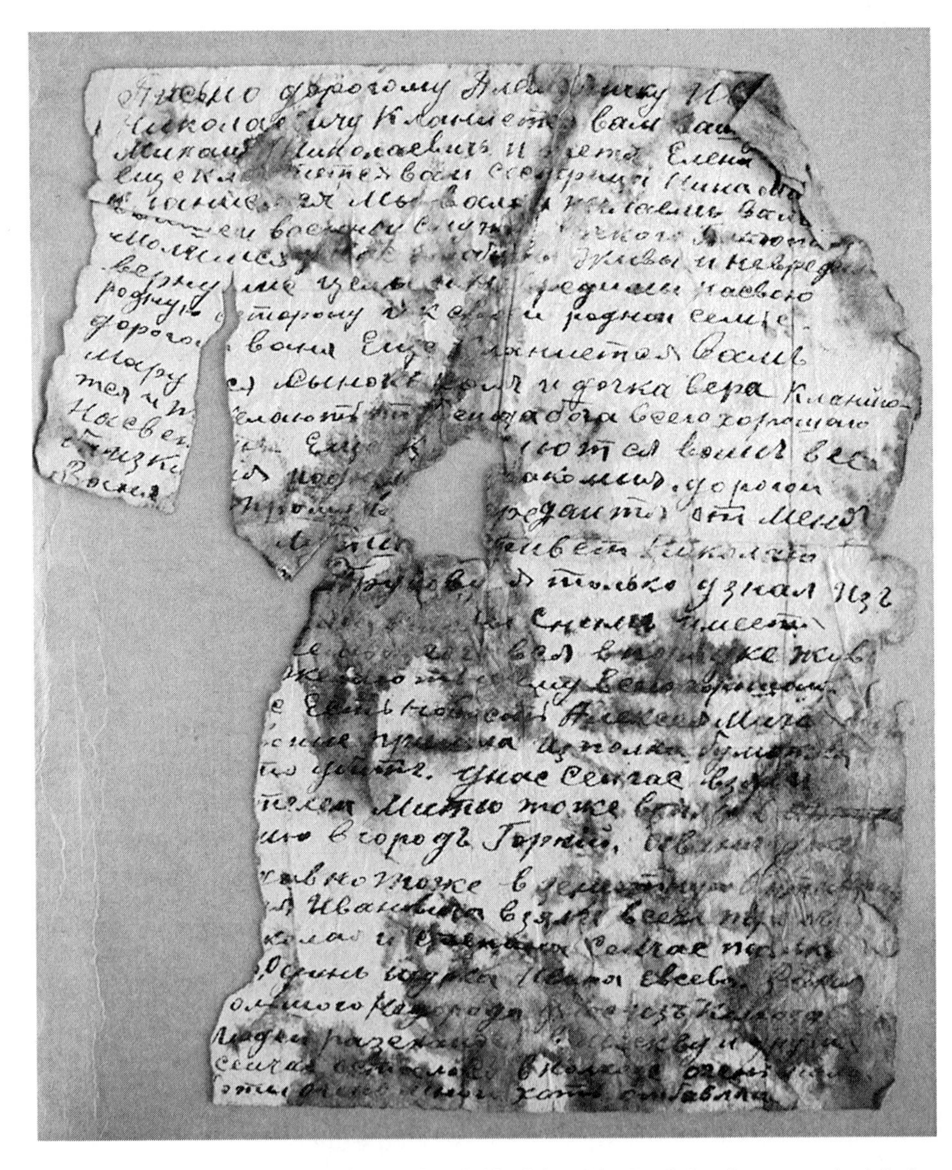

Letter damaged by snow and stained with blood found by Swedish volunteer on dead Red Army troop Ivan Nikolajevitj. The letter speaks of the cold winter and the high prices of food and other necessities at home in Russia (source: Krigsarkivet, Svenska Frivilligkåren, Kriget 1939–1940).

washed their faces at the most once a day. An opportunity to visit a Finnish sauna was equivalent to an hour in paradise.[175] Although some were lucky to have access to a "bathhouse" drawn by car, most volunteers had little opportunity to bathe or change underwear even once during the entire time spent in the ski march to the front and in subsequent combat operations.[176]

Although clothing and personal effects were shipped to the volunteers as soon as the Committee for Finland managed to do so, they did not necessarily arrive in the order they were needed. Shoes, for example, arrived before socks. Moreover, the boots issued by the Swedish government were not meant for the extreme temperatures and proved inferior to the Finnish boots. Not only were they too tight, the grease used to cover the leather trapped perspiration and made the boot damp on the inside. In extremely cold temperatures, particles of rime ice would form in the soldiers' socks.[177] One volunteer recalled how his socks had frozen to ice and came off with the boots when he removed them. Keeping the feet clean proved important in order to guard against frost injury.[178] Once they reached the front, the volunteers lived in protective dugouts in the ground, using tree branches, dirt, and rocks as roofs.[179] Magnus Dyrssen noted in his diary on February 21 that the primitive conditions allowed for too little sleep: "[R]ise early, have much to do, can shave twice a week, wash possibly every other week."[180] The tents used at Märkäjärvi, however, proved decent even in low temperatures. The fire in the stove kept the soldiers warm — wood chopping became a daily routine — and snow piled up around the edges of the floor kept out drafts.[181]

The food consisted mainly of macaroni, sausage, and pork; a diet that seemed a bit too fat and heavy at first, but which proved essential for keeping warm. Vegetables and potatoes could not be eaten in the extreme temperatures. Melted snow was used to brew coffee, which was available around the clock. Coffee rationing took place among the heavy coffee-drinking Swedes first when World War II was in full swing.[182] Care packages sent from Sweden reached the volunteers on an almost daily basis, often containing coffee and a variety of knitted clothing such as gloves and ear warmers. Soon the volunteers could no longer be recognized by their uniforms, but walked around in all kinds of knitted wool in order to stay warm.[183] The support from home proved essential for maintaining morale. Young girls and adult women, affectionately called "godmothers," wrote letters to soldiers they would never meet. One volunteer remembered receiving a letter written by a girl only half his age.[184]

The problems were not limited to logistics but included also weapons, horses, and other equipment that had to be cared for. All firearms parts had to be kept absolutely dry to prevent grease and oil residue from freezing to ice and jamming the weapons.[185] Difficulties associated with evacuation of the wounded became clear first when the volunteers discovered that their sleds were too heavy for the long distances. Some lighter models, by contrast, rode so low that they got stuck between tree stumps in the forest.[186] Medical help for the wounded consisted of first aid followed by transport to the main road,

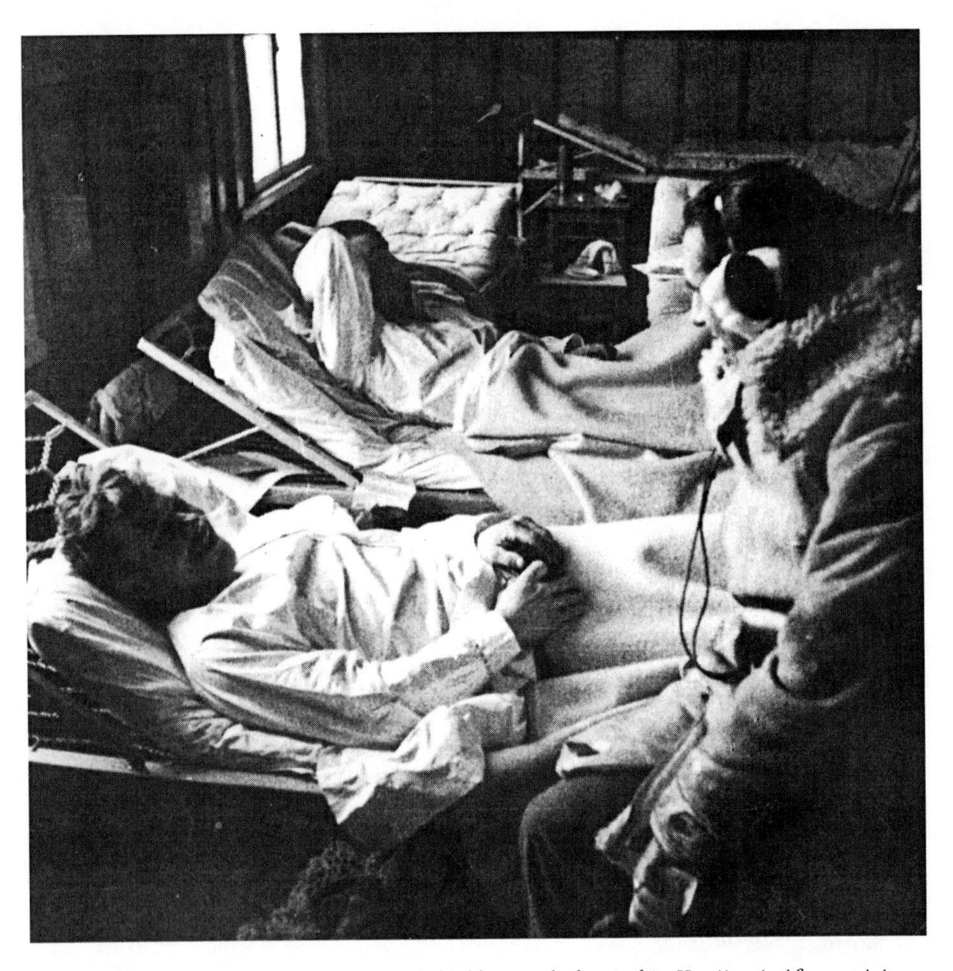

The military leadership visiting wounded soldiers at the hospital in Kemijärvi. After receiving first aid, the wounded would be transported to the main road, from where he would be transferred to horse, car, or bus for further transport to the hospital (source: Krigsarkivet, Förbundet Svenska Finlandsfrivilliga, Vol. 29).

from where the soldier would be transferred to horse, car, or bus for further transport to the hospital in Kemijärvi.[187]

Additionally, the veterinarians complained that the volunteers had utterly little understanding of how to care for the horses, despite the fact that horses were still widely used in the Swedish military at the time. The real problem was that many of the caretakers had been placed in these positions because they had failed to qualify for direct combat duty, yet were not specifically trained in veterinary services.[188] They were lucky that the type of warfare they waged did not require greater mobility. During the march from Kemi to Rovaniemi alone, fifty-two of three hundred horses were unable to complete the distance.[189] Pressure wounds from the harness were the most common causes of concern. Few actual combat injuries occurred, however, and the horses generally tolerated the extreme temperatures well.[190] Practical problems also emerged with respect to language whenever personnel had to move from a Swedish-speaking group to a Finnish-speaking group, or vice versa, although many Finns had studied Swedish in public school and spoke the language reasonably well.[191]

The volunteer army at the front was small, but to those involved it represented a cross section of Swedish culture and social class. After a few weeks, men had divided into groups of similar interests. Some were religious; others were not. Some were adventurers; others had academic backgrounds. Some smoked and used rough language in speech; others did not tolerate tobacco

Cavalry at Rovaniemi in northern Finland (source: Krigsarkivet, Förbundet Svenska Finlandsfrivilliga, Vol. 29).

use or cussing in their tents.[192] The division into groups eased the difficulties associated with the primitive living conditions the soldiers endured, and brought familiarity and stability to chaos.

Overview of the Volunteer Flight Squadron

In the late 1930s, the Finns still did not know what type of air force would serve them best, and whether they would need primarily bombers or fighters. They imported several bombers of the twin-engine type Bristol Blenheim from Great Britain, and also fighters from Holland of the type Fokker D-XXI, which they later manufactured under license in Finland. At the start of the Winter War, Finland possessed 82 fairly modern warplanes (36 fighters, 17 bombers, and 29 reconnaissance aircraft) in addition to a number of older models. The fleet was thus relatively small and two divisions lacked airplanes altogether. By comparison, the Soviets employed nearly one thousand aircraft against Finland at the start of the war; an almost ten to one ratio to Finland's meager fleet. The Finns who did not have one single aircraft to spare for the northern half of the country thus appreciated assistance from Sweden. The Swedish volunteer flight squadron, termed F19, that arrived in Kemi in the beginning of January 1940 consisted of twelve Gloster Gladiator fighter planes and four outdated Hawker Hart reconnaissance and bomb planes.[193] The Gloster Gladiator proved particularly suited for winter warfare because of its air-cooled engine.[194]

The reason why Sweden sent so few aircraft and no newer models to Finland was largely because of the downsizing of the military in the years leading up to World War II. In 1936, the goal of the Swedish Air Force was purely domestic: to defend Sweden, and primarily the capital, Stockholm. Since Sweden did not anticipate fighting a modern air war with an enemy state, the country relied mainly on a defensive fleet of attack and bomber aircraft rather than fighter planes designed for air-to-air combat. The deficiencies in equipment became painfully clear after Germany's invasion of Poland. Of Sweden's 200 military aircraft, only 150 were in good enough condition to participate in immediate military action.[195] The twelve Gloster Gladiator that Sweden transferred to Finland constituted one-third of the country's total force of fighter aircraft.[196]

Opposite top: *Field chaplain Hans Åkerhielm, who would also serve at the volunteer Hangö battalion during the Continuation War in 1941 (source: Krigsarkivet, Förbundet Svenska Finlandsfrivilliga, Vol. 29).* Opposite bottom: *Hawker Hart bomber biplane belonging to the F19 flight squadron. The Swedish Hawker Hart were powered by radial engines which made them appear more stub-nosed than their British counterparts (source: Krigsarkivet, Svenska Frivilligkåren, Kriget 1939–1940).*

The Gladiator biplane, or J8 (J for *jakt* or fighter, as opposed to A for attack and S for *spaning* or reconnaissance), was shipped semi-assembled from England to Sweden, test flown from Swedish airports, and then flown to Finland.[197] The Gladiator proved practical because it could be equipped with machineguns and/or bombs, and could also be outfitted with skis for winter operations. The planes that went to Finland were repainted with the swastika (not a sign of Nazism in Finland) in blue on a white background (the colors of the Finnish flag), as official indication of their service to Finland.[198] The swastika, which often appears on runes and pottery from Scandinavia, had impressed Swedish Count Eric von Rosen twenty years earlier when he adopted it as a symbol of good luck, and gave Finland its first military aircraft. The swastika became the national emblem of Finland's air force.[199]

The creation of F19 allowed the volunteers to break the Soviet Union's dominance of the airspace. When the flight squadron reached northern Finland, airplanes painted in Finland's colors were finally dashing across the sky and contributed to strengthening the morale among Finnish troops and civilians alike.[200] The pilots were warned not to overfly Finnish farms at low altitude, however, because the local population was prone to think it was the enemy and start firing with rifles at the airplanes. It did not take long until the civilians learned to distinguish between friend and foe and waved welcomingly at the volunteer pilots.[201]

In contrast to the largely civilian composition of the ground troops, the volunteer flight squadron was comprised primarily of men who already served in the Swedish military. They supported Finland's defensive forces through reconnaissance flights to the east of the Soviet lines, attacked enemy communications and bases preferably without making their activities known to the Soviet leadership, and provided intelligence about enemy activities to the Finnish headquarters, particularly on the Salla front.[202] Their foremost task was to guard the railway, which was responsible for delivering war materiel from Sweden to Finland, primarily in winter when the frozen water lanes prevented shipping by sea.[203] Finnish children sent to Swedish foster care likewise

Opposite top: *Volunteer pilot in cockpit ready for takeoff. Note the swastika on the side of the fuselage. The swastika was not related to Nazi Germany but was a sign of good luck, and was portrayed in blue on a white background, the colors of the Finnish flag (source: Krigsarkivet, Svenska Frivilligkåren, Kriget 1939–1940).* Opposite bottom: *Finland's* Frihetskors, *Cross of Liberty 4th class, a decoration awarded in war. The Order of the Cross of Liberty was founded on the initiative of Carl Gustaf Mannerheim in 1918. The Mannerheim Cross, a similar decoration awarded for the highest achievement in war, is also associated with the Order of the Cross of Liberty. Note the swastika that was commonly used in Finland as a sign of good luck (source: Krigsarkivet, Finlandskommitten, 1939–1940).*

Gloster Gladiator taking off in snowy conditions in northern Finland (source: Krigsarkivet, Svenska Frivilligkåren, Kriget 1939–1940).

depended on the railway for transport.[204] The flight squadron would also protect the northernmost cities of Torneå, Kemi, and Uleåborg while assisting ground personnel and interfering with enemy attacks on the flanks of the Finnish defensive line to the south.[205] The pilots were prepared to take the initiative and go to direct attack if need be. Their outdated and numerically inferior fleet, they reasoned, would allow them to succeed only if they first forced the enemy to retreat.

The total area of operations initially included almost half of Finland's territory. Reaching efficiency in such a large area would prove impossible with the few airplanes and resources available, which was why operations were eventually restricted to the northernmost parts of the country. Meanwhile, Finland's tiny air force focused on defending the Karelian Isthmus and the area north of Lake Ladoga, in addition to Helsinki. All volunteer activity in Finland had to take place under Finnish flag in order to protect Sweden's noncombatant status. Although directly subordinated to the volunteer corps and its leader General Ernst Linder, in order to improve teamwork between units the squadron accepted directions from the chief of the Finnish air defense and communicated with the chief for the ground troops stationed in Lapland. F19 received all ammunition and supply directly from Sweden, which made it self-reliant and allowed it to operate without draining resources from Finland. According to Finnish air force historian Kuno Waldemar Janarmo, F19 prevented at least thirty-five bomb attacks against northern Finland.[206] Still, the Swedish pilots had never actively engaged an enemy in warfare prior to their volunteer service. Naturally, they were a bit anxious.

A Volunteer Air Base Is Setup

When given the clear sign to depart for the war in early January 1940, the pilots flew their airplanes from Barkarby airport just north of Stockholm to northern Finland. But bad weather shifting between snowstorm, fog, and thaw would complicate the mission from the outset, forcing unplanned landings on the ice of the several lakes in the region. Some of the pilots spent up to eight days at nearby villages making phone calls to station masters along the railway in an attempt to receive at least semi-accurate weather reports or warnings of impending dangers.[207]

By the time the volunteers arrived in Finland, Soviet troops had marched across the border 120 kilometers into Finnish territory. The situation proved critical.[208] The sparsely populated area consisted mainly of forests and a few 500–600 meter high mountaintops, with water supplied by the Kemi River. Normally, the high latitudes (the Arctic Circle dissects the region) caused much of the area to be covered in snow by mid–October. Later in the season the snow cover could easily measure one to two meters in depth, making many roads completely unsuitable for motorized travel. The volunteers understood that the situation would not be eased much in spring when the snow would melt and the surroundings would turn to slush and mud. The winter of 1939–40 was exceptionally cold, however, with a snow cover measuring fifteen to thirty centimeters by early December. The hard frozen lakes made transport by heavy motorized equipment on the ice possible; thus, the climatic conditions initially favored the Red Army, who relied on tank-based warfare.[209]

The F19 flight squadron established its main base just south of Kemi approximately 300–400 kilometers from the Soviet bomber bases in Karelia, using the ice on the frozen fjord nearby for takeoff and landing. Should the war drag into spring and summer, however, it would be necessary to find land-based runways.[210] Much work went into organizing the base. Aircraft had to be hidden when not in use, yet fuel and oil, bombs and ammunition had to be easily accessible. Shops were needed for aircraft repair, as were shelters for pilots and other personnel. A paper factory nearby agreed to provide the volunteers with quarters as well as a kitchen and eating facilities, in addition to building material for airplane shelters. In order to prevent ice buildup when not in use, the aircraft wings were covered with tarps. Wheels were

Aircraft camouflaged among the trees. Note the tarps on the wings to prevent ice buildup during the night (source: Krigsarkivet, Svenska Frivilligkåren, Kriget 1939–1940).

exchanged for skis to ease takeoff and landing on the ice. Evergreen twigs placed underneath the skis prevented the airplanes from freezing stuck in the ground, and were also used as camouflage around the fuselage.[211]

Although the many frozen lakes in the area ensured that there was always a place to land should one run out of fuel or get struck by enemy fire, several difficulties emerged. Not only did the pilots lack detailed maps, the snow-covered forests complicated navigation by air, as did the far north latitude that made the compass unreliable. The smokestacks at the paper factory by the base proved a good navigational mark, but could also be treacherous to low-flying aircraft in poor visibility. The rough weather conditions and the terrain necessitated carrying skis in the airplane. In case of bailout or emergency landing, the pilots would at least have a chance to escape a pursuing enemy on skis through the forest. Covering long distances by foot would have proven almost impossible and would likely have led to death by prolonged exposure to the elements. The pilots received daily prognostic weather briefings from meteorologists in Stockholm by telephone for northern Finland and the Soviet Union. Still, the extreme cold proved problematic even during successful flight operations. A perfectly good

Opposite: *Weapon repair and maintenance for the F19 flight squadron, conducted by ground personnel in northern Finland. The extreme cold required careful inspection of the weapons that were carried along in air battles (source: Krigsarkivet, Svenska Frivilligkåren, Kriget 1939–1940).*

The terrain as seen from the cockpit during a bombing raid at Märkäjärvi on January 12, 1940. Note the forests, few well maintained roads, and lack of landmarks that could serve as good navigational aids (source: Krigsarkivet, Svenska Frivilligkåren, Kriget 1939–1940).

flight day could quickly be downgraded to no-go conditions because of treacherous ice buildup, which was true even on clear days if the temperatures fell low enough.[212]

The long distance between the main base and Karelia meant that a new doctrine had to be tested for the first time in the history of Swedish military aviation. Since the airplanes lacked the range to fly the two hundred kilometers to the front at Salla while carrying a 20 percent fuel reserve, additional refueling bases had to be established along the way. The search thus started for frozen lakes located near a decent road were aircraft could land. Some fuel and supplies could be transported through the forest by horse and sled. Preferably, however, these satellite bases should be near a village where the pilots could be fed and rested. Each base also had to have telephone access and house a team of mechanics, a weapon smith or engineer, and a meteorologist or other person who could assist with weather prognoses. Additionally, two plowed runways, 700 and 1,200 meters long respectively, had to be prepared to permit the landing of aircraft with wheels, mainly the Junkers Ju 86 and Fiat CR 42 that were expected to arrive later and strengthen the squadron.[213]

The area of operation thus came to measure five hundred kilometers in a north-south direction and nearly three hundred kilometers in a west-east direction. With only sixteen aircraft available for use, some of which would undoubtedly be lost to enemy fire, protecting such a large area would prove challenging at best and disastrous at worst. The opposing force, led by the notorious Pablo Palancar, a name that the Soviet commanding officer Pavel Vasiljevitj Rytsjagov had acquired during his earlier service in the Spanish Civil War, was comprised of nearly 250 aircraft.[214]

The airplanes had to be ready for takeoff at first light and maintained to continue flying until dark. The high latitudes and the time of year gave the flight squadron only approximately four hours of daylight in each twenty-four hour period. The pilots wore their heavy winter overalls and stayed close to the aircraft at all times, in order that they could take their seats in the cockpit and be in the air within minutes of news of enemy activity. Life was perhaps even tougher for the mechanics who had to get up long before sunrise and prepare the airplanes, warm the engines, and load the machine guns in temperatures consistently ranging between -20 and -30 degrees C.[215] Aircraft mechanic Rune Eriksson, who started his military service in September 1939, reported that he had followed the war in Europe with interest. When applying to volunteer in Finland, and in

F19 flight squadron landing on the ice at the former Russian base at Märkäjärvi two weeks after the war (source: Krigsarkivet, Svenska Frivilligkåren, Kriget 1939–1940).

F19 flight squadron pilots and ground personnel preparing an aircraft for takeoff in snowy surroundings (source: Krigsarkivet, Svenska Frivilligkåren, Kriget 1939–1940).

order to avoid confrontation with his family, he simply told them that his flight division would be moved further north. He had left by train on December 30. Throughout the war, he wore his civilian felt shoes, placed newspapers in the bottoms, and thus managed to escape the frost injuries that many of his peers wearing military boots came to suffer. The greatest difficulty was warming the aircraft engines prior to takeoff. The mechanics built small wooden shacks, two by five meters, which they isolated with asbestos socks and placed over the aircraft engines.[216] These shacks became lifesavers not only to the pilots by enabling them to start the engines at the spur of the moment, but to the mechanics who worked on the aircraft in the cold temperatures, often in the early morning before sunrise. Although most repairs took place by certified mechanics on base, spark plugs and a few tools were kept in the airplanes so that the pilots could do minor repairs if forced to land in the wilderness.[217]

When returning from a bombing mission to land at the front base in the dark, the pilots would first fly to a waiting area twelve to fifteen kilometers from the base and circle at different altitudes. At an agreed upon time, a strong flashlight would be directed at the waiting area and blink several times.

Opposite: *Major Hugo Beckhammar and Captain Björn Bjuggren of the F19 flight squadron prior to a reconnaissance flight. Note the heavy winter overalls (source: Krigsarkivet, Svenska Frivilligkåren, Kriget 1939–1940).*

Opposite and above: *Temporary wooden shack placed around aircraft nose for engine repair and maintenance. The shack allowed the mechanics to have the aircraft ready for takeoff at the spur of the moment (source: Krigsarkivet, Svenska Frivilligkåren, Kriget 1939–1940).*

Repeated long signals meant clear to land and repeated short signals meant danger and would prompt the pilots to fly to another base. After landing, due to a shortage of personnel, approximately an hour and a half of ground time was needed before the aircraft was ready to fly again. Sometimes things went dangerously wrong. For example, one day when two airplanes returned for landing at the front base, somebody on the base opened fire in the belief that it was the enemy. It was later determined that the mistake was a result of the Swedish-Finnish interpreter being absent that day, and the base not receiving the message that friendly aircraft were returning for landing.[218]

The time spent in northern Finland thus became a test of physical and mental strength. The relative calm and lack of enemy bombings at the home base was not a total blessing but came with some negative psychological consequences. The ground personnel had volunteered for service in the belief that they would experience the war firsthand.[219] They learned instead that war is not constant action, but requires patience. The feeling that "nothing happens" took a toll on the nerves.[220] Downtime between missions was spent learning Finnish phrases and first aid for treating minor injuries. There were also competitions in shooting, skiing, and other military activities. For rest and relaxation, the pilots and personnel would sing songs, tell stories, or engage in parodies. The two

women — a secretary and a nurse — who had accompanied the flight squadron to Finland might offer the pilots a dance on some suitable evening.[221]

Volunteer Air Combat Missions

On January 10, as soon as the pilots and ground personnel had settled at their respective bases, it became clear that if F19 did not launch an attack against the numerically superior Soviet forces, these might break through the defensive lines and take Kemijärvi. The pilots at the satellite base nearest the front thus prepared to fly their first true combat mission. In the hours before takeoff, they focused on tactics suitable for air-to-air battle with the Russian fighters. They studied the maps, finalized the equipment, and memorized important Finnish phrases such as "don't shoot," and "I am a volunteer Swedish pilot for the Finnish air force." Should they be forced to bail out, they would need to inform the Finns of their identity. These phrases were then written on a piece of paper and carried in the flight suit. The pilots were as prepared as they could be. Yet, at breakfast in the morning, they could not help wondering what their Russian counterparts might know about them, what they might be saying or thinking about the day that lay ahead.[222]

Pilot Åke Söderberg and Gloster Gladiator biplane on the ice immediately before takeoff. Note the skis in lieu of wheels (source: Krigsarkivet, Svenska Frivilligkåren, Kriget 1939–1940).

Light bomber squadron, January 12, 1940. From left to right: Roland Sahlberg, Thord Medalen, Gunnar Färnström, Åke Mörne, Matti Sundsten, Thure Hansson. Anders Zachau who was also part of this squadron died during the devastating baptism by fire on January 12, 1940. Per Sterner and Arne Jung bailed out after a mid-air collision, were taken prisoners by the Soviets, and later released (source: Krigsarkivet, Svenska Frivilligkåren, Kriget 1939–1940).

The mission would proceed as follows: Two groups would be formed, each consisting of two Hart and four Gladiator aircraft. Both groups would be responsible for reconnaissance and attack against the Soviet ground troops and bases. The Gladiators would escort the Harts, who would then dive toward the targets: either troops sighted on the roads or enemy aircraft parked on the ice. They would drop their bombs or fire their machine guns first when they were almost at the top of the trees, then pull out of the dive, level the airplane near the ground and escape among the nearby hills. If the attack proved successful, the tightly packed Russian columns would likely lose their cohesion and disperse into smaller groups of men and vehicles. These tactics were not without danger, however. Not only would one need to dodge anti-aircraft fire, one must also drop the bombs dead-on target in order to prevent the thick and soft snow cover from dampening the effect. By dividing into groups and flying across the desolate terrain from the south, the pilots hoped to avoid detection and fire from anti-aircraft artillery. But things would not go as planned. Warnings of incoming fire, ice buildup, and problems with attaching the bombs to the aircraft delayed the mission. Meanwhile, the sun began to set.[223] The pilots were now stuck with an alternative: Wait another day and risk discovery, or take off and attack even though only two hours of daylight remained. They chose the latter.[224]

They faced a daunting task. When finally taking to the air, it was amidst considerable loss. On January 12, three Swedish airplanes went down in the Salla area. Two bombers collided in midair while attempting to outmaneuver Soviet anti-aircraft artillery, and Russian fighter planes shot down a third aircraft. Three of the six crewmembers survived the crashes and managed to reach Finnish lines by marching on skis through the forests. Two more saved their lives by parachute.[225] A volunteer who observed the bailout later relayed seeing two airplanes crashing toward the ground and an explosion on impact, then two parachutes. He thought the Russians had one heck of a gunner to shoot down both aircraft, before realizing that a midair collision had taken place. One of the pilots involved in the incident later described it as a forceful bump against the bottom of the fuselage followed by violent shaking, as the engine was torn apart by the propeller of the aircraft with which he had collided.[226] At first he thought he had been hit by anti-aircraft artillery. The cause of the collision was likely a broken wire leading to the rudder, however.[227] Although fortunate to touch down with his parachute in the high evergreen trees and then in soft half-meter deep snow, time in Soviet prison camps would follow.[228] Crewmember Anders Zachau was unable to jump and went down with his aircraft. His body was recovered first in 1942 during the Continuation War, fifteen kilometers from Märkäjärvi.[229]

There were also some near misses the first day of air battle, and some triumphs. For example, a Russian plane attempting to get behind a Swedish fighter was shot down at the last moment by another Swedish fighter pilot, and rolled burning toward the forest.[230] Major Hugo Beckhammar, the chief for F19, wrote a report to General Linder in the evening of January 12, detailing the successes of the first day of the air war. One Soviet aircraft of the type I-15 had been totally destroyed on the ground through a direct bomb hit. (The Soviets relied heavily on the Polikarpov I-15 fighter biplane, which was brought into service in 1933.) Another aircraft had been destroyed on the ground by machinegun fire. Several bombs had struck a collection of Soviet vehicles and barracks, resulting in large numbers of dead or wounded including horses on the road by Märkäjärvi. One Soviet aircraft shot down in air-to-air combat crashed in the forest four to five kilometers to the north of Märkäjärvi, and one more enemy aircraft was shot down with unknown results. More painful was to note the losses that F19 had suffered. Three aircraft of the type Hawker Hart had failed to return to base.[231] A week and a half later, pilot John Sjöqvist would go down with his aircraft in a burning ball of fire when attacked by a

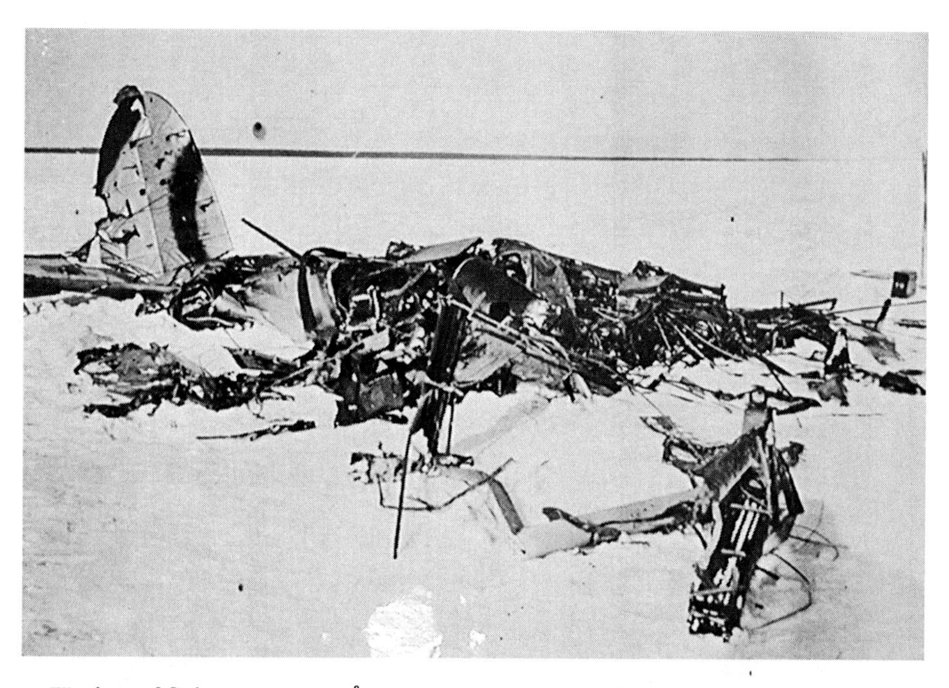

Wreckage of flight engineer Sten Åke Hildinger's aircraft. Hildinger died when test flying a Gladiator which had recently had an engine exchanged. He encountered problems with the airplane, was struck by a part that came loose, and lost consciousness. He was unable to save himself with parachute (source: Krigsarkivet, Svenska Frivilligkåren, Kriget 1939–1940).

Russian fighter. A Soviet document later described Sjöqvist's last flight: A group of fighters "led by Lieutenant Konkin shot down an enemy plane at 1300 hours by Mjatijärvi. The airplane — a biplane reconnaissance aircraft — caught on fire and crashed three to four kilometers south of Mjatijärvi."[232]

The tragic losses of the first day made the F19 pilots realize that their Hart aircraft were ill suited for bombing during daytime hours when the swift Soviet fighter planes became potent weapons. Some drastic measures had to be implemented. It was decided that bomb attacks would take place only after dark and against predetermined and precise targets such as enemy bases. Flying in dark, cold, or poor visibility proved challenging, but to do so while undertaking a military mission was doubly hazardous. Two test missions were flown to determine the extent to which navigation and the location of targets could be undertaken at night. Was it possible to navigate in the wilderness in the dark? Could one find enemy targets? What was a safe altitude? How would one avoid alerting the enemy with noise? Navigating by the light of the moon proved no problem. Although the cities and towns practiced blackouts, on a clear night the moon alone provided the pilots with a horizontal visibility of at least fifty kilometers.[233]

Grave of John Magnus Sjöqvist, who was shot down by enemy aircraft on January 23, 1940. The stone reads: "Fallen in Finland for Sweden's honor and Nordic independence." The grave can be found at Solna North Cemetery in Stockholm. Several memorials have been raised in different places in Sweden to honor those who lost their lives in the Winter War and the Continuation War, and those whose bodies could not be recovered for a proper funeral (photograph: Martina Sprague).

Lighted objects such as bivouacs seemed fully possible to target, particularly during moonlit nights. Attacks would take place by approaching the enemy from an altitude of 4,000 meters, and thereafter diving to 900–700 meters while releasing a series of bombs over the target. The first such attack was to be done against the Soviet air base located on the lake Kuolajärvi, approximately forty kilometers east-north-east of Märkäjärvi. The Soviet troops were poorly outfitted and generally did not have tents where they could spend the nights, and were therefore more or less forced to light fires in order to stay warm.[234] The night attacks prompted the Russians to extinguish their fires. The Red Army was amazingly good at blacking out their positions, according to the volunteer pilots. When unable to approach the targets during glide with the engine on idle, noise would alert the Soviets of the impending attack. They would then extinguish all lights simultaneously as if somebody had suddenly flipped a switch, after which they would open fire against the Swedish pilots, although seldom with much effect.[235]

Yet, to spend a single night without a heating source proved a dreadful experience for both men and horses and would render the Soviet troops practically useless the next day. Additionally, motorized equipment would be almost impossible to start in the morning after a full night without heat. The difficulties the Swedes had with heating single-engine aircraft and oil had made the Russians seem exceptionally skilled, who could frequently start their multi-engine aircraft with seemingly few problems.[236] As reported by Russia after the war, "[t]here was not a single technical engine failure in the six regiments, although technicians worked in very cold weather and at night." The Russian pilots and navigators also lived up to their task. Nobody refused to fly, and there was not a single report of a sudden "unsubstantiated" illness, despite the negative effects the polar nights with only a few hours of daylight could have on a pilot's psyche.[237] A reconnaissance report on January 20, however, noted the inability of a Russian flight squadron to take off due to failure to provide more than one heating apparatus per three DB-3 aircraft.[238]

Although skilled at flying, the Swedish pilots lacked equipment that could compete with the enemy aircraft. The engines on the Gladiators were overworked and needed to be exchanged. But shipping new engines to Finland required uninterrupted transport from England via Sweden.[239] Additionally, the Russian twin-engine bombers were superior for the climate and could obtain airspeeds of 350 kilometers per hour.[240] The skis used for takeoff and landing could be retracted through a simple yet elegant construction, and could glide easily even on slush.[241] According to information obtained from Russian prisoners, the skis on the Russian aircraft could be used in a snow depth of forty centimeters. Tight turns could easily be made due to a special coating on the skis which made them effective on all kinds of surfaces.[242] The retractable gear made it possible for the pilots to make an emergency belly landing on a very short field without sustaining hardly any damage to the aircraft.[243] A drawback was that the landing gear with skis had on occasion frozen in the retracted position, so that it could not be extended.[244]

The Soviet fighter planes likewise proved superior, and could reach airspeeds of 430 kilometers per hour.[245] The only way to catch one of these modern aircraft was from a position of excess altitude. Not only did the Swedish aircraft fail to catch up with a climbing or fleeing enemy even when operating with full throttle, captured armor from a downed aircraft confirmed during a test shoot that the Swedes' ammunition was not powerful enough to penetrate the armor.[246] Although the Gladiator had better maneuverability than the Russian I-15, Ian Iacobi, one of the foremost Swedish fighter pilots, noted in his journal that he had fired a thousand shots from a distance less than a hundred meters straight behind a Soviet fighter, with no notable effect.[247]

Thus, if one could not attain a superior position or attack the enemy directly through an opening in the armor, air-to-air battle should be avoided because it would lead to few positive results, and focus should be placed

Visual signs indicating the direction and altitude of enemy aircraft were placed on the ice when other means of communication with the F19 pilots failed (source: Krigsarkivet, Svenska Frivilligkåren, Kriget 1939–1940).

instead on downing Soviet bombers whose engines and fuel tanks were not armored.[248] A drawback for the Russian pilots was that their modern fighters could only carry enough fuel for half an hour flight, and were therefore less valuable for protecting bomber aircraft during longer raids. This problem resulted in Swedish and Finnish forces managing to shoot down several Russian bombers. For example, one Finnish fighter pilot completely decimated an enemy formation by shooting down six out of nine aircraft.[249]

Many of the problems encountered were not directly related to the performance of the aircraft, however. For example, the information the volunteers received about enemy actions and whereabouts through telephone reports often proved unreliable. Long distances, disturbances on the line, and hours of nonuse during bombing raids made it difficult to transmit messages successfully. Messages delayed more than twenty minutes often proved useless. Since some of the air bases were located only sixty to eighty kilometers away from enemy lines, there was often not enough time to warn of an impending attack. Pilots and ground personnel had to resort to a primitive system of relaying messages by placing visual signals on the ice. A tarp in the shape of an arrow represented the direction of the enemy, and several perpendicular lines represented the altitude in thousands of meters.[250] For example, the sign | | | → indicated that the enemy was coming from the east at an altitude of three thousand meters. The signals had to be visible from an altitude of five thousand meters in order to serve the intended function, and thus had to be large in size. Since successful attacks depended on approaching the enemy aircraft from above, correct estimates of altitude proved important. In the end of February and beginning of March, the volunteers managed to shoot down several Ilyushin DB-3 and Tupolev SB-2 bombers, some of which landed without considerable damage. The Finns took the pilots prisoners and salvaged the planes for use by their own forces.[251]

As the days were getting longer, and with the expectation that the war would be ongoing, the small flight squadron with its few members started worrying about how to maintain operations during the summer months which, at this latitude, would see virtually no darkness at all. Conditions would then begin to favor the Russians who were largely untrained in night operations.[252] In order to gain an edge through the remainder of the war, the volunteers realized that they had to undermine Soviet intelligence. For example, the Soviet fighters frequently turned around before coming within eyesight of the Swedish fighters, which indicated that they had good intelligence gathering capability.[253] The volunteers thus started using codenames and a mixture of dialects that were commonly spoken around Stockholm, Skåne in southern Sweden, and in the areas of northern Sweden in order to mislead the enemy.[254] They would

Volunteers inspecting a downed Russian Tupolev SB-2 bomber aircraft (source: Krigsarkivet, Svenska Frivilligkåren, Kriget 1939–1940).

also drop propaganda flyers telling the Red Army to surrender to the Finns with the promise that they would not get shot, would get well fed, and would have their wounds looked after by professional nurses: "Sling your weapons — show us your hands — surrender to the Finnish forces — they will not shoot you — they will give you food and warm lodgings, and 150 rubles for your rifle and will bind your wounds — the politruk are lying when they say that the Finns torture their prisoners — let us end this maniacal war."[255]

Although the F19 pilots clearly succeeded at interfering with enemy operations, the question might be asked how successful the flight squadron really was with respect to affecting the outcome of the war. The volunteers most certainly had a psychological effect on the Soviet pilots who had been the sole owners of the sky over northern Finland. The Soviet ground troops had been decimated by the Finns and their *motti* tactics, but had not counted on additional threat from the air. Many of the flights also took place after dark, when the enemy was unable to move and the bitter cold temperatures contributed to breaking their morale. Despite the tragic losses of the first day, F19's successes lifted the spirits of the Finnish people and forced the enemy to retreat some thirty kilometers further east. The Soviets thus failed to secure their goal of reaching the Swedish border and cutting off Finland's communications with Sweden. Although F19 did not produce a lasting victory for

FINLANDSKOMMITTEN
Militärbyrån
Ink. 2/3 1940 638
Avg. / 19 . nr.

Militärbyrån

Drottninggatan 10

Stockholm.

Härmed har jag äran anmäla mig som frivillig till Finland. Jag är löjtnant i A2 reserv och tjänstgör sedan den 2. sept. 1939 som chef för stationärt lvbatt m/36 inom Göteborgs F. O. Tidigare har jag sedan den 13. april 1939 tjänstgjort i samma befattning å lv-div A2. Då min tidigare erfarenhet beträffande lv sålunda inskränker sig till tjänsten å stationärt förband, skulle jag helst önska tjänst-göra å dylikt.

Beträffande de formaliteter, som är att iakttaga för erhållande av avsked m.m., vore jag tacksam för upplysning härom.

Göteborg den 1. mars 1940

Löjtnant

Adress: Hvitfeldtsskolan,
Göteborg.

FINLANDSKOMMITTEN
Militärbyrån
Adolf Fredriks Kyrkogata 12
Stockholm

Letter of application to volunteer at the Swedish anti-aircraft artillery in Turku, dated March 1, 1940 (source: Krigsarkivet, Luftvärnsdivisionen i Åbo, 1939–1940, Vol. 1).

Finland, the flight squadron halted the enemy advance and induced a two-month stalemate at the front.[256]

Of the sixty-two days that the squadron was in operation, sixty proved suitable for flying, often several sorties per night. From January 12 to March 13 when the war ended, the F19 pilots flew 560 sorties totaling approximately 600 flight hours. Although starting with sixteen aircraft (twelve Gladiator and four Hart), losses and shortage of spare parts led to only eight Gladiator and two Hart able to fly toward the end of the war. The squadron dropped 185 bombs and fired 61,000 rounds of ammunition. Twelve enemy aircraft were brought down or destroyed on the ground.[257] The relatively few rounds that were fired has been attributed to the fact that enemy bomber squadrons often turned around before fire was opened, or avoided areas they knew were defended by Swedish fighter planes.[258]

The Volunteer Anti-Aircraft Artillery at Turku

In addition to the ground troops and flight squadron, the Swedish navy organized a volunteer force for the defense of Turku by placing anti-aircraft artillery at the outskirts of the city. The idea had roots in Germany's invasion of Poland on September 1, 1939. In order to ensure that the warring nations would keep their activities outside of Swedish territorial waters (thirty kilometer limit) and that regular traffic could operate unhindered, students at the noncommissioned officer school in the Swedish navy were asked to man the warships and guard Sweden's neutrality and coastlines.[259] Eighty volunteers would come to work together with Finnish personnel at the batteries set up at Turku and surrounding areas.[260] The positions at the batteries were highly sought after by experienced military personnel. For example, one of the applicants considered himself a good candidate for the job because his rank as lieutenant, and his education and experience serving at an anti-aircraft battery in the Göteborg area in southern Sweden made him familiar with most of the required duties.[261]

The artillery in Pargas approximately fifteen kilometers south of Turku employed two cannons from Bofors, capable of firing 120 shots per minute to a height of 3,600 meters.[262] Clear days with good visibility, or so-called Molotov weather, meant that the risk for bombing attacks was high.[263] The Russian bombers were frequently overflying Turku at low altitudes and dropping their bombs until entire city blocks were burnt to ashes. Now they would meet a formidable defense. Warning of an approaching enemy normally came via telephone about five to ten minutes prior to the attack. Observers reporting enemy sightings were also stationed on the islands in the archipelago.[264] When the telephone operators at the battery received warning of incoming fire, they would notify the battery of the enemy's whereabouts while continuing monitoring the telephones for additional details.[265]

In the event no enemy activity was expected — for example, when the weather proved too poor for flying — up to one-fourth of the volunteers were granted leave, although anyone leaving the battery would generally be expected to return no later than 10:30 P.M. Any misuse of alcoholic beverages while on leave was harshly punished with deportation back to Sweden. The volunteers were instructed to leave the battery in pairs with at least one person carrying a weapon, which he was expected to use should they come under attack by a stranger. Conversations with strangers that might reveal information about the battery's position or personnel and jeopardize Finland's safety should be avoided. Soldiers on leave were also instructed to maintain good manners to avoid soiling the good name of Sweden and the volunteer corps.[266]

On February 26, the artillery in Turku was notified via telegram from Stockholm that their request for additional materiel had been fulfilled and sent by air.[267] The weeks ahead would be busy. March 3 saw little enemy activity due to poor weather, as reported in the daily log. This would soon change. Two days later, nine enemy bombers and twelve fighters were sighted

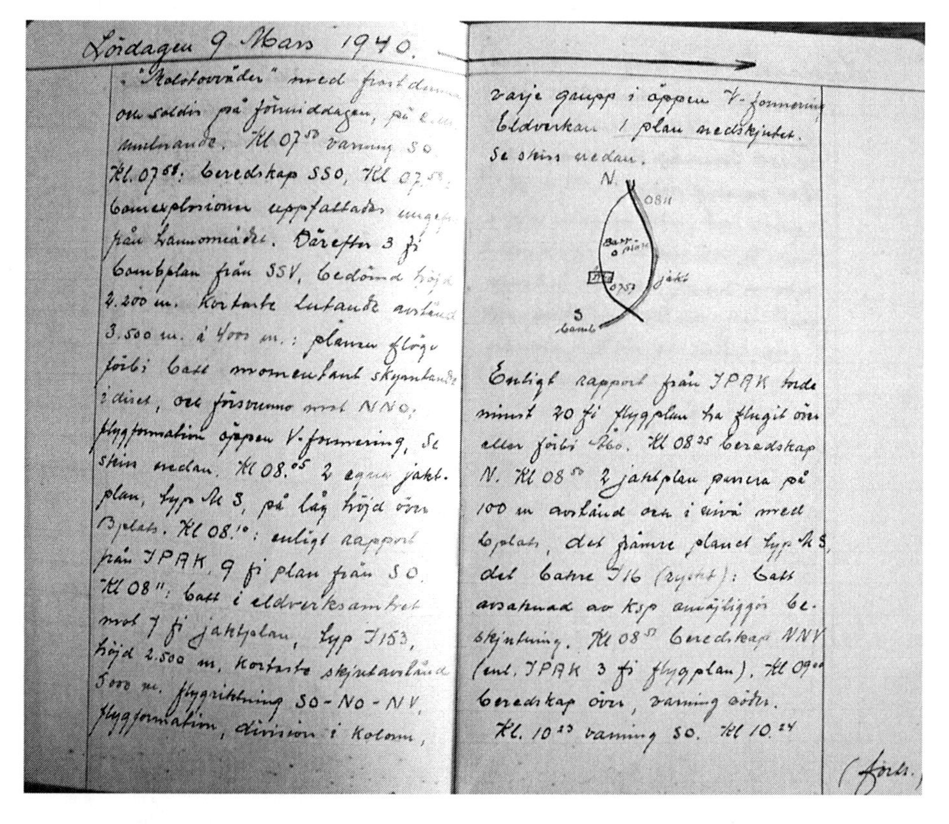

Lördagen 9 Mars 1940.

"Molotoväder" med frostdimma om solen på förmiddagen, på e.m. mulnande. Kl 07.53 varning SO Kl. 07.54. beredskap SSO, Kl 07.5[illegible] bombexplosioner uppfattades [illegible] från [illegible]. Därefter 3 fi bombplan från SSV, bedömd höjd 4.200 m. Kortaste lutande avstånd 3.500 m. à 4000 m.: planen flögo förbi batt momentant [illegible] i diset, och försvunno mot NNO, flygformation öppen V-formering, se skiss nedan. Kl 08.05 2 egna jaktplan, typ [illegible], på låg höjd över B-plats. Kl 08.10: enligt rapport från IPAK 9 fi plan från SO. Kl 08.11: batt i eldverksamhet mot 7 fi jaktplan, typ I153, höjd 2.500 m, kortaste skjutavstånd 500 m. flygriktning SO-NO-NV, flygformation, division i kolonn,

varje grupp i öppen V-formering. Eldverkan 1 plan nedskjutet. Se skiss nedan.

Enligt rapport från IPAK fanns minst 40 fi flygplan ha flugit över eller förbi Åbo. Kl 08.25 beredskap N. Kl 08.50 2 jaktplan passera på 100 m avstånd [illegible] B-plats, det främre planet typ [illegible], det bakre I16 [illegible]: batt [illegible] av ksp omöjliggör beskjutning. Kl 08.57 beredskap NNV (ev. IPAK 3 fi flygplan). Kl 09.00 beredskap över, [illegible]. Kl. 10.33 varning SO. Kl 10.24

(forts.)

Daily log with drawing of recent enemy activity, from the anti-aircraft artillery in Turku, March 9, 1940 (source: Krigsarkivet, Luftvärnsdivisionen i Åbo, 1939–1940, Vol. 1).

overflying Turku at high altitude. On March 9, the daily log noted "Molotov weather" with frost, fog, and haze in the morning, and increasing cloudiness toward afternoon. Three enemy bombers intermittently visible through the haze were sighted in the morning to the south-southwest from the battery flying at an altitude of 4,200 meters. At 8:00 A.M., nine enemy fighters flying at an altitude of 2,500 meters approached in open V-formation. The battery opened fire and managed to down one aircraft. According to reports, at least twenty hostile aircraft passed over or near Turku that morning, and two passed within a hundred meters of the anti-aircraft battery.[268]

Firing at the enemy from a distance proved preferable or, if that were not possible, then right before they dropped their bombs to cause confusion and interference with precision maneuvering. When scoring a hit, the volunteers would go out on skis and attempt to retrieve the pilot had he been lucky enough to save himself with a parachute. One volunteer recalled a downed Russian pilot taking cover behind a bush and firing at the patrol as they neared his position on skis. When he understood that he would be taken prisoner, he pointed the pistol to his own head and pulled the trigger. When searching his airplane, the volunteers found a map of Turku, with the Swedish anti-aircraft artillery positions circled. It was a chilling experience, recalled one volunteer. Had a battery been hit, they would all have died young.[269]

4

Peace Negotiations and Armistice

Political Struggles and Mediation for Peace

Although the diplomatic support that Sweden offered Finland in the autumn of 1939 failed to stop the Soviet invasion, the negotiations between Russia and Finland, with Sweden acting as mediator, contributed to the belief that the Finnish people were not alone and could count on assistance from foreign states in their struggle against the superpower. Bitterness grew as mediation attempts fell apart, and hopes that Sweden would step in as an active ally faded. The fact that the Soviet Union recognized only the puppet government it had established in Terijoki under Otto Vilhelm Kuusinen made further mediation in the conflict difficult.[1] Although a neutral country is often in position to act as peace mediator precisely because it cannot side officially with either belligerent, the situation between Russia and Finland proved extraordinarily complex. Swedish diplomats would have seen even less success, however, had Sweden entered the war in support of Finland. On December 23, 1939, the Swedish publication *Den Svenske Folksocialisten* came out with harsh criticism against the government. Sending government sanctioned troops to Finland was not only the ethical thing to do, the paper argued, but a duty which Sweden had refused. The consequences for all of the Nordic countries would be catastrophic should the Soviet Union be given free rein in the region. The only remaining hope was that Hitler would to step up and help Finland.[2]

On December 29, Madame Alexandra Kollontay, Stalin's envoy in Stockholm who maintained communications with Sweden throughout the war, explained to Christian Günther that Stalin was in favor of ending the war but saw little logical reason for discussing a peace treaty.[3] A month later, the talks took a different turn when Günther warned Madame Kollontay that the conflict between Finland and Russia could prompt the Western Powers to enter the war.[4] Kollontay then revealed that Stalin was prepared to scrap the Kuusinen puppet government and, with Sweden acting as mediator, take up the peace negotiations with Finland. But before proceeding, he asked for absolute clarity on which territories Finland was willing to give up in return for peace. Using attractive but misleading promises when Sweden asked Finland to come to the negotiating table would yield few results. Although agreeing to negotiate with the intent of reaching an agreement that would ultimately satisfy both parties, Stalin was highly unlikely, for example, to give up his request for Hangö.[5] Simultaneously, he considered it particularly important that Sweden and no other country act as peace mediator. If negotiations failed to reach a satisfying outcome for Finland, he could lay part of the blame on Sweden and thus avoid carrying the full burden of the failure. He also hoped that Sweden would recognize that time was of the essence and pressure Finland into agreeing to concessions.[6]

The tough Finnish resistance and the great losses the Red Army had suffered in the first month of combat operations had likely contributed to Stalin's desire to end the war. Although he did not agree to concessions that strayed too far from his initial plan, the fact that he had softened his position and was willing to talk was viewed as a positive change that may also have come as a result of recent saber rattling from the Western Allies. The French government, in particular, had indicated a desire to enter the war and fight in northern Finland. If a compromise were reached that allowed Finland to keep its independence, Stalin might avoid a war with the Allies. He was thus willing to consider options as long as he could acquire the territories he needed for the defense of Leningrad. Other evidence suggests that a Russian messenger in Berlin had received an ultimatum from Hitler through Hermann Göring: If the Soviet Union failed to end its military operations in Finland, Germany would officially enter the war on the side of the Finns despite the nonaggression pact between Germany and Russia.[7] With lingering threats from the Western Allies and Germany, the security of Leningrad had to be taken seriously, and Stalin had little choice but to forfeit plans he might have had of making Finland a province of Russia.[8]

Despite the relative silence from Germany, Hitler had no doubt followed the political developments with interest. As early as December 18, 1939, Wipert von Blücher, the German minister in Finland, in conversation with the State Secretary in the German Foreign Ministry, noted that in three weeks of fighting the Russians had achieved no victories that indicated that a decision might be near. Reaching a resolution, whether by force or diplomacy, would likely take much longer than anticipated. Blücher also expressed concern for the safety of German interests in the Baltic Sea where Finland, not Sweden, held all key positions including the Åland Islands. If Stalin did indeed acquire the territories he wished for, his forces would be spread across the Baltic and gain footholds in all important ports. The mere idea that Russia would possess rights to these territories and, coupled with modern weapons, could barricade Germany's access to the iron ore mines in northern Sweden proved enough to warrant serious consideration.[9] Germany imported approximately 50 percent of its iron ore from Sweden, with shipping going through the Gulf of Bothnia and the port of Luleå. Germany's Supreme Naval Commander, Admiral Erich Johann Albert Raeder, remarked that it would be "utterly impossible to make war should the navy not be able to secure the supplies of iron ore from Sweden."[10]

By January 1940, when it became evident that the war between Russia and Finland would not be resolved any time soon, Molotov warned the German ambassador in the Soviet Union about the dangers associated with a possible French-British invasion of the Scandinavian peninsula. Again, it was the Swedish iron ore that was the focus of the discussion. The Soviet government expected Germany to use her influence and prior friendship with Finland to mediate between the countries for an end to the conflict. Or, if this were not possible, persuade Sweden to act as mediator. Moreover, if Hitler could show that he had a hand in successfully ending the war to the satisfaction of both parties, not only would Germany's prestige on the world scene skyrocket, Hitler would be able to count on continued and uninterrupted delivery of iron ore for the duration of the war. But questions remained. Even if Germany or Sweden made serious efforts to meet with Soviet and Finnish diplomats, would Stalin be open to a settlement? Or, would he find any Soviet concessions too hard a blow to his image in light of the heavy losses he had already suffered on the battlefield?[11]

It might be noted that Günther, in a speech on March 13, 1940, denied that Sweden had engaged in any coordination with a foreign power. Although it has been implied that Germany had pressured Sweden to act as an impartial party in the conflict, the truth, according to Günther, was that not a word had been exchanged regarding the matter between the Swedish and German governments, and that no other government had even tried to influence Sweden regarding the country's role as mediator.[12] According to the Soviet Union, the decision to involve Sweden in the negotiations was based entirely on practicality. Stalin believed that Sweden would be the most suitable mediator, more so than Germany or the United States (yet a country that had been considered), because Sweden was in the better position to assist Finland with war materiel and manpower and thus also had the power to cut all supplies in an effort to halt hostilities.[13] In the event any other country acted as mediator, Sweden might choose to continue supplying Finland with weapons and voluntary troops.

Stalin's decision to attack Petsamo in the northernmost part of Finland in an attempt to cut Finland's communications with Sweden was thus a direct result of the delicate balance of power and the silent threat from Germany, France, and Great Britain. He reasoned that a foreign power, most likely Great Britain, might come by sea to Petsamo or use the railway between Sweden and Finland to gain access to Russia. The Petsamo region was also rich in natural resources and of strategic importance to Russia and the other belligerents, particularly Great Britain who had contracted with Finland for use of these resources.[14] According to a report issued by the Soviet leadership twenty-five years later, the bloody ground battles fought in Petsamo and the fact that the Russian 5 Bomber Flight Squadron flew 567 missions primarily against military targets on the Petsamo front and Rovaniemi in 1940 are testimony to the important role the region played.[15]

In the morning of February 5, Väinö Tanner met with Christian Günther in Sweden to further discuss the possibility of Finland reaching an agreement with Russia, and how Sweden might perceive a coming peace resulting in Finnish concessions such as Russian military bases on Hangö at the mouth of the Gulf of Finland. Günther informed Tanner that Sweden would warmly welcome peace and would agree to act as mediator to the extent Finland agreed to such, and would not have any particular objections to a Russian base by the Gulf of Finland. They also discussed the planned Allied intervention and a possible French campaign in Murmansk. Madame Kollontay reemphasized the Soviet Union's demands for territory if a peace agreement were to be struck. Not only must Finland give up Hangö, but also the Isthmus and the eastern shore of Lake Ladoga. Stalin was no longer satisfied with a few islands on which to build bases. Since Finland was unwilling to agree to the new demands, however, peace was not yet on the horizon.[16]

On February 21, Finland's Minister of Defense turned to his Swedish counterpart and officially asked for mediation in the conflict.[17] Meanwhile, the troops fighting to save Finland's independence had no knowledge of that Stalin had been looking for a way to end the two-week "walkover," which had now dragged into three months of heavy fighting. Furthermore, negotiations were near a stalemate as Stalin, through his Swedish contacts in Moscow, reaffirmed and notified Finland of his demands for a larger part of Hangö to be leased to the Soviet Union for a period of thirty years. In return, he offered to release the occupied regions in the most northern part of Finland.[18] He also desired to move the border to coincide with that of Peter the Great, as established in the Treaty of Nystad in 1721. This meant that the largest parts of Karelia, including the city of Viborg, would go to Russia. Additionally, he asked that Finland agree to a joint defense of the Gulf of Finland, but Moscow later decided not to press for this defense alliance.[19]

Although Stalin was careful to avoid provoking Sweden needlessly, and despite strict orders not to violate Sweden's airspace, the situation proved serious. As noted previously, as the political difficulties continued, Soviet airplanes bombed the city of Pajala in northern Sweden on the Finnish border. When caught and questioned after a forced emergency landing, the crew denied any knowledge of having bombed Swedish territory and insisted that it was Rovaniemi in Finland they had bombed. The Soviet government likewise denied the incident but admitted later, when Sweden examined some duds that were clearly of Russian make, that the bombing had occurred due to an error in navigation and agreed to pay Sweden forty thousand crowns in reparations.[20] Pajala at the time housed a population of approximately three thousand people. Fortunately, the seven Soviet bombers dropping 134 "explosive and incendiary bombs" caused no human casualties beyond slight injuries to two persons. The raid still resulted in considerable material damage. Several buildings were burned and telephone lines cut, and "43 big bomb holes [were formed] in Pajala's streets."[21] The Russians also dropped bombs on Swedish territory outside of Luleå. It has been speculated that this raid was meant for F19's rear base, but the Russian pilots became disoriented in the poor weather and got the two streams in the area, Kemi and Torne River, mixed up.[22]

The bombings so angered the Swedes that many activists again took up the fight to pressure the government into entering the war officially on the side of Finland. The fear that Sweden would be forced to break its noncombatant status prompted the foreign ministers of the Nordic countries to schedule a meeting in Copenhagen.[23] Although collective safety proved important and was always kept in the background, Swedish politicians also realized that they might have to undertake isolationist policies in order to keep the country outside the war. As early as May 1938, Prime Minister Per Albin Hansson had expressed his position on the matter by stating that it was unacceptable for Sweden to support military action simply because the Great Powers mandated it. Simultaneously, absolute neutrality seemed unwise because of the strong bond that Sweden shared with Finland. Should Sweden be forced to take action, it would be crucial at the very least to continue promoting Western democratic values. In order to drive home the point, some Swedish politicians referenced the volunteers who had fought in the Spanish Civil War, claiming that noncombatant or noninterventionist politics did not mean indifference to the difficulties other countries suffered, but should be used to bring stability to a war-torn region.[24]

But it was not only pacifist policies that drove Sweden's decisions. The government's resistance to sending part of its armed forces to Finland was motivated by a need for large numbers of troops at home should the war between Germany and the Allies escalate and also threaten Sweden.[25] Meanwhile, the Nazi press took advantage of the opportunity by criticizing Sweden for claiming neutrality while shipping war materiel to Great Britain. As the foreign ministers of the Nordic countries concluded that mediation between Finland and Russia was crucial if peace were to be reached any time soon, Bofors, Sweden's developer of defense systems, started increasing the production of anti-aircraft weapons and bombs in preparation for a full-blown war at home.[26]

The Iron Ore Mines

As has been demonstrated, the Allies' attempt to intervene in the Winter War was closely tied to Sweden's export of iron ore to Germany for Hitler's weapons production. According to Édouard Daladier, Prime Minister of France, if the Finnish army were annihilated, not only the ore fields but the entire Scandinavian peninsula would be in danger of falling to Soviet control and could be handed over to Hitler at will.[27] British statesman Winston Churchill was informed on the morning of Hitler's attack on Poland in 1939 that it would be impossible to avert a war with Germany.[28] Britain must therefore consider how to undermine German strength, and one way was by cutting the supplies of Swedish iron ore. Control of Scandinavian waters proved crucial. Without command of the Baltic, Hitler could not further his war aims. Although Churchill "sympathized ardently with the Finns and supported all proposals for their aid; [he] welcomed this new and favourable breeze as a means of achieving the major strategic advantage of cutting off the vital iron ore supplies of Germany."[29]

In order to shed proper light on how the political situation affected Sweden, several factors must be considered, however; foremost the fact that Germany had served as a role model to Sweden since the late nineteenth century. Germany's industrial development had leant inspiration to Swedish politicians, students, and the artist elite alike. The sympathy that many Swedish officers had displayed for the German cause in World War I contributed to the fact that Swedish politics at the outbreak of World War II was German-friendly, and further led to certain blindness with respect to the negative aspects of Germany's foreign and domestic policies during the war. It is interesting to note, however, that although a handful of Swedes, mainly officers searching for ways to further their education, were looking to Germany for military opportunities, the Swedish people at large did not admire Germany so much that they were willing to enter the war or develop an organized volunteer force to the benefit of Hitler. Sweden also expressed sympathy toward France, perhaps in part because the Swedish royal family was directly descended from the French Marshal Jean-Baptiste Bernadotte of Napoleon's army.[30] Note that as German power began to decline after Hitler's defeat in Stalingrad in 1943, favorable opinions would shift away from Germany and become oriented toward the Allies.

Although commerce between Sweden and Germany remained strong during the war, Sweden exercised neutrality with respect to trade; it did not give Germany monopoly on the iron ore but shipped also to Britain. One reason why history has failed to emphasize this fact may be because Britain's economy was weak at the time and restricted the amount of iron ore the country could afford to buy. Britain was thus unable to take full advantage of Sweden's willingness to engage in commerce with foreign states and had to rethink its strategy.[31] Britain's economic and military weakness in the 1930s was due in part to a fear of communists coupled with a sympathetic position toward the military uprising in Spain against the left-wing government in 1936, and in part to a downsizing of the military and the belief that the League of Nations had established a collective safety net for the European countries.[32] Rather than trying to keep up with Hitler by importing even more iron ore, Britain thus looked for ways to completely halt the exports.[33] Britain also entertained the idea of coercing Sweden into accepting coal or other goods in exchange for iron ore, in order to prevent Germany from getting the ore. As stated in a memorandum by Churchill on September 29, 1939:

> Our relations with Sweden require careful consideration. Germany acts upon Sweden by threats. Our sea-power gives us also powerful weapons, which, if need be, we must use to ration Sweden. Nevertheless, it should be proposed, as part of the policy outlined in paragraph 2, to assist the Swedes so far as possible to dispose of their ore in exchange for our coal; and, should this not suffice, to indemnify them, partly at least, by other means.[34]

The purpose, of course, was to secure control of shipping and regulate it to the benefit of those nations who were acting according to the will of the Allies.

The Swedish iron ore fields were located north of the Gulf of Bothnia. In summer, Sweden sent ore to Germany via rail to the Gulf and then by ship through the Baltic Sea. In winter when the Gulf of Bothnia froze over, ore was sent via rail to Narvik in Norway and then by ship through Norwegian coastal waters. The Swedish town of Malmberget, situated roughly halfway between Narvik and Luleå, contained vast amounts of ore that could be shipped to either port. Controlling the transports thus required control of both Swedish and Norwegian territories, as well as suitable harbors and water lanes used for shipping.[35] The Russo-Finnish Winter War came along just in time to provide Britain with an opportunity to interfere with the transports without formally invading Sweden. It did so by offering to send Finland a strong military force comprised of 50,000 British and French soldiers.

The Allies recognized the need to proceed cautiously through diplomatic means, however, and simply requested that Sweden allow transit of the French-British troops through Swedish territory on their way to Finland. The hope was that Sweden would find the request morally impossible to turn down. A Finnish victory was crucial to Sweden, who had given

Finland enormous support in the form of material assistance, weapons, humanitarian help, and volunteers. To allow this huge investment to go to waste this far into the game would surely be a blow too hard to take for the Swedish people. Secretly, however, the Allies hoped to catch two birds with one stone. Once they had access to Sweden, they could redirect part of their forces to the iron ore fields, while sending a much smaller force than initially promised to Finland.[36]

Sweden's geographical location proved both a blessing and a curse to the Allies. Germany controlled the southern part of the Baltic and the Soviet Union had conquered the Petsamo region in northern Finland.[37] Although a direct attack against Russia through Petsamo and Murmansk might have seemed the better alternative if the goal were to assist the Finns, it would also have foiled a simultaneous attempt to secure the iron ore fields in Sweden. Moreover, the only viable way to proceed through the wilderness from Petsamo to the front was on skis. Not only did the British forces lack sufficient training on skis, fighting a war simultaneously would have proven nearly impossible. This idea was therefore scrapped.[38] The only way that Britain and France could gain access to Finland was thus through Norway via rail to northern Sweden.[39]

But the Swedish government proved hardnosed about the proposition. Transporting troops through Sweden would not only be a neutrality breach — as stated by the Hague Convention of 1907, "belligerents are forbidden to move troops or convoys of either munitions of war or supplies across the territory of a neutral Power"[40] — Swedish politicians suspected Britain's true intent. Honoring the request would surely rouse Germany to action. Hitler might then well decide to invade Skåne in southern Sweden in order to gain a foothold for retaking control of the iron ore mines. Sweden considered few things as important as preventing the country from becoming a battleground for the World War II belligerents. A German occupation of Swedish harbors would have cleared the way for Hitler to undertake direct battle against Britain and France from Swedish soil. The results would have been disastrous to both Sweden and Finland.[41] Wedged between Allied and German forces, Sweden would have had no choice but to recall all volunteers currently serving in Finland and redeploy them within the borders of Sweden in order to defend the country's sovereignty. Curiously, both the Allies and Germany claimed that the only reason why they might interfere in the region was to secure the safety of the Nordic countries. The Allies insisted that their motive was to help Finland by sending troops through Swedish territory via Narvik-Haparanda. Germany, by contrast, asserted that its presence in the area (if it came to that) would be to protect Denmark and Norway, and thus indirectly protect Sweden against an Allied invasion.[42]

The prospect of the Western Allies sending troops to Finland and occupying the Swedish iron ore fields in the process also proved worrisome to Stalin, not so much because of the additional troops that might stand against him in the Winter War, but because this engagement would violate Swedish neutrality, force Germany into action, and make a major battle zone out of the Scandinavian peninsula. Stalin might then have to split his focus and be forced into joint operations alongside of Hitler against Britain and France. Molotov voiced concern that the Winter War had acted as a starting point for "British and French imperialists" to make war against Russia by using the Scandinavian countries, and later stated that, "what was going on in Finland was not merely our collision with Finnish troops. It was a collision with the combined forces of a number of imperialist states."[43]

The Allies Move Forward

Time was of the essence. To prevent German expansion to the east, the Allies had to gain control of the iron ore fields before the ice broke in the Gulf of Bothnia, or by March 20 at the latest. One Finnish officer who had been sworn to secrecy later reported that he had received information pertaining to England's and France's desire to land three divisions in the Petsamo region by February 19, 1940.[44] Churchill, however, had offered his opinion to the War Cabinet as early as December 11, 1939, and believed that it would be to Britain's advantage if Norway and Sweden found themselves at war with Russia: "We would then be able to gain a foothold in Scandinavia with the object of helping them but without having to go to the extent of ourselves declaring war on Russia."[45] General Edmund Ironside reported to his diary a week later that Churchill was "pushing for us to occupy Narvik in Norway."[46] As Churchill confirmed, "If Germany can be cut from all Swedish ore supplies from now onwards till the end of 1940 a blow will have been struck at her war-making capacity equal to a first-class victory in the field or from the air, and without any serious sacrifice of life. It might indeed be immediately decisive."[47] Simultaneously, he realized that to every blow there is a counter, and that it was therefore imperative to prepare for the retaliation that would undoubtedly come from Germany. If it meant a German invasion of Sweden, then Sweden must naturally be defended, or the Allies would completely lose the good will of the Swedes. To Finland, the threat of an Allied intervention, on the one hand, was a diplomatic weapon to be used against further Russian aggression. On the other, it summoned Sweden and Norway to put forth a clear effort to end the war before the neutrality of the Scandinavian peninsula was threatened.[48]

Should the English and French actually fulfill their promise and send troops to Finland, however, it would be in Finland's interest to keep its forces in good enough shape to stave off the Russian advance until help arrived, even if it meant that the country had to give up some territory while saving the capital and vital areas. If it were determined that help from foreign states was unlikely, no credible plan existed other than to seek peace with the enemy as soon as possible and save what could be saved. Even then, it would be of utmost importance to defend Finland vigorously, lest Stalin might get the idea that Finland was ready to give him more than he legitimately needed for the defense of Leningrad. Only after the war was over did the Finnish troops learn that the political and military leadership had considered the possibility of foreign assistance virtually nil. Although the Finnish officers received information about negotiations for an end to the war, the details of this correspondence remained confidential, and the troops were encouraged to continue fighting with vigor. If they could demonstrate their military capacity by halting the Russian attacks on their flanks, they might preserve at least some leverage in coming negotiations.[49]

Soon talks of an Allied intervention would take a more serious turn. Operation Royal Marine, designed to destroy shipping of enemy supplies from the Scandinavian countries, stipulated that an Allied force would invade Norway on March 15, 1940 and intercept the iron ore transports. The French-British troops would also fully prepare to fight against Norwegian or Swedish opposition. Should Hitler decide to get involved, the Allies promised to assist Sweden and defend the country against German occupation.[50] The question might be asked why Hitler did not preempt an Allied entry into the region and simply seize the ore from Sweden. Part of the problem rested with the fact that Germany and Sweden had good prewar relations, including trade agreements that were mutually beneficial, which Hitler wished to maintain. Hitler also realized that if he ordered his army into Sweden, Sweden would likely do everything in its power to destroy the iron ore mines.[51] If Britain and France took control of the mines, however, it would leave Hitler little choice. The question might also be asked, if Britain and France had preempted the war by attacking Germany before Hitler invaded Poland in September 1939, would they still have been as eager to assist Finland in 1940?

Although Hitler understood that the Swedes were fully prepared to defend their country, the Allies were slower reaching the same conclusion. The fact was that Sweden was ready not only to protect its borders, but pull up the railroad tracks between Narvik and the iron ore fields to ensure that no transport of troops could take place.[52] Should the Allies manage to reach Narvik and the Swedish border, they still had to secure transportation 150 miles further east. If they were met with serious resistance, what would be their next step? Opening fire upon Norwegian and Swedish troops would severely damage their reputation on the world scene and was thus a last resort.[53] As commented by Lord Halifax, the Secretary of State for Foreign Affairs in Britain, "Well, if we can't get in except at the cost of a lot of Norwegian lives, I am not for it — ore or no ore."[54] The risk also existed that Sweden would stand with Germany and not with the Allies in the unfortunate event that the war would end up on Swedish soil.[55] When these concerns had been pondered, and in order to avoid the possibility that the Allied plan would fall apart at the Swedish doorstep, the good will of the Swedes was intensely sought. But Sweden refused to budge and instead increased its reconnaissance flights over the Baltic Sea in order to validate its stand on the issue. Since no suspicious activities from Germany could be detected, the Supreme Commander of the Swedish Armed Forces recommended no buildup of troops in southern Sweden at the time, and instead focused defense preparations on a possible Allied invasion in the north.[56]

Moreover, the position of the Swedish king proved of little help to the Allies. On January 19, 1940, King Gustav V Adolf had notified the people that he could not with good conscience allow Sweden to officially assist Finland with military forces, because he could not risk that Sweden would get pulled into the war.[57] A month later, the king reinforced his earlier decision by declaring that Sweden would remain neutral while continuing to send humanitarian and volunteer help to Finland.[58] The announcement, which had come as a hard blow to Finland, meant in practicality that Finland, would be unable to defend its sovereignty for any length of time. From a Soviet perspective, however, the decision meant a decreased risk of Russia getting pulled into the war in Europe via the way of Finland. When the Allies criticized the king's position, he suggested that they might consider assisting Sweden in finding a peaceful solution to the conflict rather than trying to escalate a war that had already brought Finland and the Soviet Union thousands of casualties.[59]

Prime Minister Per Albin Hansson echoed the king's decision. He had dedicated his working life to improving social equality and economic welfare for the citizens of Sweden. Should Sweden get pulled into the war, everything he had worked for would be lost and enormous sums of money would be wasted instead on manufacturing artillery pieces, war ships, and fighter aircraft. If the war came to Sweden, Hansson, who had consistently propagated anti-militaristic policies, would have to preside over the greatest military buildup in modern times. The situation might have seemed comical had it not been so serious. Success in Finland, Hansson stressed, could have come only if Sweden had intervened militarily in the conflict from the outset, and not this far into the war. Anybody who argued to the contrary failed to see the situation with a clear eye and was likely concerned only with demonstrating a courageous face to the international community, while completely ignoring the fact that thousands of Swedish soldiers would perish alongside their Finnish brothers on the frozen battlefields of the Karelian Isthmus. The risk that Sweden would end up a player in World War II was grave enough as it was, Hansson meant, and the government should not deliberately force the issue.[60]

The situation proved even more complex. Sweden was noncombatant with respect to the "little" war between Finland and Russia, yet clearly stood on the side of Finland emotionally. Simultaneously, Sweden was neutral with respect to the "big" war between the Western Allies and Germany, and therefore had little choice but to take military action if push came to shove and the Allies insisted on violating the country's borders. The Swedish people clearly understood that the war might become reality on their home turf, and took several measures to prepare for such an event. For example, in February 1940, blackouts were practiced in Stockholm for three evenings and nights, while reconnaissance airplanes flew over the capital and took photos to determine the extent to which the city had been darkened.[61]

Admitting that it was better to make peace than continue beating "the drums of war" required ability to confront fear.[62] It took courage to stand steady in the political storm against the pressing forces of the Western Allies, but Hansson firmly believed that keeping Sweden outside the war was best for the country and the citizens in the long run. Sweden's national interests were indeed threatened by the war, not so much by hostile military forces as by "friendly" nations desiring to make Sweden a battleground for their own gain. Even if Sweden's national interests were not directly threatened, what would be the long-term consequences if Sweden joined the war and exasperated the conflict rather than acting as a stabilizing force in the region? Letters and telegrams from the populace, from workers and labor unions, flooded Hansson's office as a result of his decision not to commit troops to the war or allow the Allies transit. The letters did not express unanimous agreement in either direction; although approximately two-thirds of the people applauded him, and female writers in particular begged Hansson to find the strength to continue opposing official involvement.[63]

How did the military leadership directly engaged in the conflict react? Magnus Dyrssen, commander of Combat Group I, noted in his diary on January 26, 1940, that the border between Finland and the Soviet Union was a cultural rather than geographic boundary. Finland was recognized as a novel and capable modern nation whose people were striving for Western ideals and freedom from oppression. The Soviet Union, by contrast, was a despotic, barbarous regime who did not use honorable methods in war. Although foreign states openly sympathized with the Finns, the lack of direct action made their views nearly useless. Sweden had done all it could within the restrictions of neutrality. The question was, would it be enough? How long could Finland stand against the offensive if the Red Army continued to feed its masses of troops across the border? If Finland were defeated, the consequences ought to be utterly clear to Sweden, who would lose its strategic position with Finland as a buffer state against the eastern armies. According to Dyrssen, preserving the border between Finland and Russia was necessary for Sweden's survival. This was "not a common war," he said, "but one that was aimed at the extinction of Finnish culture."[64]

Moreover, if the borders gave way to the hordes of Soviet troops, the main part of Finland's population would be forced to seek refuge in Sweden, which would result in a huge human tragedy with starvation likely in the north. If Russia managed to overrun Finland, it would only be a matter of time before Sweden's borders would be violated. Although it proved crucial to guard against threats from the west, Sweden could not afford to ignore the fact that the Red Army was advancing into Finland and could cause the country's downfall. The Soviet advance *must* be halted, even if the troops and materiel Sweden sent to Finland would ultimately weaken Sweden's defensive capabilities against a possible German or Allied invasion. The security of the Scandinavian peninsula was at stake. In Dyrssen's view, Norway was at least as threatened as Sweden should Finland fall and the Red Army manage to advance to the Swedish border. Although Finland had long acted as a shield for all of the Nordic countries, Sweden was now responsible for the future safety of the entire Scandinavian peninsula, particularly if economic growth and social equality were to be preserved during the formation of the "New Europe." Changes were coming quickly and the situation was steadily worsening. It would be better to act sooner than later, Dyrssen meant, yet the Swedish people had become complacent after two hundred years of peace and considered their military endeavors a thing of the past.[65]

Väinö Tanner continued to press Hansson. If Finland agreed to peace negotiations but the peace terms proved too barbarous, would Sweden then be prepared to support Finland with military help? Impossible, Hansson answered, as it would be the same as officially taking part in the war. Would Sweden offer Finland continued diplomatic support? Tanner asked next. "Within the limits of our power," Hansson answered. Tanner considered Hansson's refusal to officially join Finland a combination of unwillingness to make sacrifices and fear of German retaliation. Note that although Hitler had warned Sweden about taking sides in the conflict, contradictory evidence indicated that he was bothered by the war and would rather have seen a quick end to hostilities, which jeopardized his trade agreements with other countries. Hitler's true fear was the Western Allies. He was not concerned with the welfare of Russia.[66] He had signed the nonaggression treaty with Stalin in order to bring about a favorable division of the Baltic states, and did not care to join Russia in the current conflict and fight on two fronts.

Although the Finnish leadership was ready to seriously discuss peace terms and decide how the new border should be drawn, they continued asking for assistance from the Western Powers. If 50,000 Allied troops could arrive by the end of March, in addition to a hundred bomber aircraft with crews, the harsh peace terms might be eased. The hope was also that Sweden would do a better job mediating in the conflict if facing a simultaneous threat of an Allied invasion.[67] Discussions with General C. G. Ling, the British military attaché in Finland, and Colonel Jean Ganeval of France made it clear that the Western Powers not only intended to block the Swedish iron ore exports to Germany, but also ask Finland to assist in the process. When Finland's renewed request for armed forces from Sweden was denied, as was expected, Finland could with good conscience request help from the Allies. By then, the Allies would have forces stationed off the coast of Norway ready to land and advance across northern Norway and into Sweden. Britain and France believed that if the process could be brought this far along, Sweden would give in and grant them transit rights. To Per Albin Hansson, it appeared as though the Allies were simply attempting to transfer the responsibility for the war to neutral Sweden, however. When Sweden denied Finland help, Finland would be forced to request assistance from Britain and France, who could then disclaim responsibility for future developments. But Hansson would not accept such hogwash and warned that if the Allies forced their way through neutral territory, Sweden might have to join the war on the side of Russia against Finland.[68]

By now the Finnish leadership had evaluated the situation to the extent that they doubted the effectiveness of the Allied troops. If Britain and France occupied northern Sweden, would they still have enough resources to send to Finland in order to make a true difference? The barriers that Sweden was expected to present to the Allied transit would also delay or completely prevent any help from arriving in Finland. Allied troops would likely be delayed first at the Norwegian coast, and then at the Swedish border. Finland would then no doubt be dragged into the major war in Europe, while accomplishing little with respect to securing its own independence and safety. Simultaneously, Finland realized that it had no time to waste. The Russians had advanced almost all the way to Viborg, and the city was expected to fall in a few more days. Acting in the interest of peace seemed the better alternative than escalating the war by accepting help from the Allies this late in the game.[69] It thus became clearer with each passing day that little remained for Finland other than to sue for peace.

But General Ling was not done yet. He met with Mannerheim and ensured him that the Allied forces coming through Sweden would be fully prepared to deal with a German counter-offensive. Mannerheim listened but had reservations. He recognized that if Hitler retaliated against the Allies, most of the British and French forces would have to focus on Germany rather than reinforcing the Finnish troops. Furthermore, he understood that it was not in Finland's interests that Sweden became a battleground for the Great Powers.[70] He was reluctant to accept help from the Allies for three reasons: First, Finland had to formally request the help before the Allies would move, which might worsen Finland's diplomatic relations with Sweden and Norway who had clearly stated that they did not intend to allow transit of French-British troops through neutral territory. Second, the Allies kept wavering back and forth as to the strength of the forces they were willing to send, and the effectiveness and ultimate objective of their mission thus came into question. Third, by inviting the Allies, Finland would no longer be in control of the war but might get drawn into the bigger conflict that was raging in Europe.[71] As Mannerheim had recognized twenty years earlier during the War of Independence, "A nation's liberation, if it is to have lasting effect, must come by the people's own efforts, trials, and blood."[72] He took this opportunity to discourage the Allied plan while suggesting that all efforts be focused on finding a diplomatic solution to the conflict between Finland and the Soviet Union. The time was ripe for diplomacy since the imminent threat from the Allies would likely encourage the Russians to act in favor of a quick peace.[73] Moreover, although the Soviet losses throughout the war had proven heavy, the Finnish battalions were exhausted; their weapons so worn "that many Finnish guns no longer had much rifling in their barrels."[74]

Toward the end of February, the situation stiffened further. Molotov reported to Laurence Steinhardt, United States Ambassador to the Soviet Union, that the Soviet government intended to press forward toward Helsinki after taking Viborg, and was not considering negotiating for peace unless this effort failed. The Soviet government likewise believed that neither Sweden nor Great Britain would enter the conflict on the side of Finland, and that Sweden was merely selfish in its attempts to mediate for a peace settlement.[75] Meanwhile, Mannerheim indicated that peace must be sought immediately, if they were to avoid a total military catastrophe. The fact that the Finnish army was not yet beaten and could still inflict losses on its enemy gave Finland leverage for negotiating the peace terms. Any wait would decrease Finland's chances of salvaging what could still be salvaged.[76] Per Albin Hansson indicated in a letter to Christian Günther that discussions with Väinö Tanner had revealed three alternatives for solving the Russo-Finnish conflict: official assistance from Sweden, a negotiated peace treaty, or an Allied intervention. Since Hansson had already declared that Sweden did not intend to send government sanctioned troops to Finland, the alternatives that remained were diplomatic negotiations for peace or Allied military action. Britain's Prime Minister Neville Chamberlain understood by now that he could not send Allied forces to Finland and maintain his good reputation, unless Finland explicitly asked for help. Even then, Norway and Sweden must agree to allow the troops passage. Finland was expected to reply with a final decision no later than March 5. The situation looked particularly grim because of the Finnish government's split feelings about the issue.[77]

As the situation grew more intense, Günther reemphasized that he was not willing to make Sweden a battleground for Germany and the Allies in order to save Viborg, and stressed that Finland should agree to concession so that the war could be ended. Should Finland accept help from England and France, Sweden would be forced to withdraw all support in order to prepare for a war on home turf.[78] In worst-case scenario, Germany and Russia might form a coalition against Britain and France. The front would then extend all the way from the Arctic Circle to the Mediterranean Sea. The complexity and danger of such a battlefront would clearly outweigh any benefits that could be gained by refusing to meet at the negotiating table.[79] Moreover, the fact that Stalin was willing to negotiate for peace was an indication that he feared an Allied intervention. The opportunity should be taken advantage of accordingly.[80]

The Allies continued their military buildup despite the difficult diplomatic relations. On March 2, France notified Sweden that they were ready to send 50,000 troops to Finland via Narvik and launch an offensive against the Soviet Union. Yet an attempt was made to emphasize that the situation would be eased if Sweden would at least agree to allow the troops to transit without weapons, which would be sent separately.[81] They had a moral obligation per a League of Nations resolution, the Allies argued, "to furnish Finland in the measure of their ability material and humanitarian aid and to refrain from any action which would be calculated to reduce Finland's ability to resist."[82] Finland was becoming destitute and the troop contribution came in response to a Finnish request. Note that it was not entirely clear, per the Finnish Minister of Foreign Affairs, whether or not Finland had officially asked Britain and France to send large numbers of troops. It is speculated that the idea originated with the Western Allies.[83] Edmund Ironside would state a week later that the French "have been promising far more than they can ever carry out, and doing it very deliberately in order to force the Finns to ask for help."[84]

The Finnish leadership did not want the French-British forces to land on the Scandinavian peninsula, yet they needed the threat of a landing to strengthen their bargaining position with Russia.

As the situation began to come to a head, an informant expressed that the German government was eager to see the Russo-Finnish conflict terminated, and that Finland would do well to accept a peace treaty. It was unlikely that the French-British troops would accomplish anything on Finland's behalf, as their only desire was to occupy the iron ore mines in Sweden. It was not entirely clear whether Germany would take direct action against Sweden in case of an Allied invasion. Since Germany and the Soviet Union would be allies because of the nonaggression pact, however, Hitler would likely send airplanes and submarines to Murmansk.[85]

Although the Allies promised that Sweden and Norway would be defended against a possible German retaliation, upon examination the numbers did not add up. In addition to the 200,000 troops that Finland needed in order to reach any prospects of success, Sweden estimated that an additional 300,000 troops would be needed to defend Sweden and Norway against Germany. Were the Allies really prepared to send such large forces to the Nordic countries? When Christian Günther accused Victor Mallet, the English Minister in Stockholm, of not having Finland's best interest in mind but intending only to battle Germany on Swedish soil for the purpose of stopping the exports of iron ore, Mallet waved the accusation away, declaring it unfair. Sweden also feared that France's announcement would escalate the conflict, halt the peace talks, and encourage Finland to prolong the war in the hope that Britain and France would resolve the issue with force. In order that Sweden would not lose its impartial status, the only viable alternative was to discourage Finland from asking for an Allied intervention, while continuing to encourage peace talks.[86]

On March 3, Sweden and Norway notified the Allies that they would stand by their previous decision and not permit passage of troops through neutral territories. Chamberlain scoffed at the announcement and accused Sweden of having a bigger bark than bite. Yes, from a political standpoint, Sweden was expected to voice opposition. Yet, neither Sweden nor Norway, he meant, would likely take physical action once the Allies had breached the borders. According to Chamberlain, the bigger war in Europe was of vital interest also to Sweden, who was presently riding on the Allies' coat tails and profiting off the sacrifices of others, while being unwilling to carry part of the burden.[87] Günther defended his decision and replied once more that Sweden was not willing to allow the country to become a World War II battleground simply because the Allies were irritated with Hitler. Furthermore, Sweden was a democratic country and the wishes of the people had to be heard and respected. How could he with good conscience explain to them that Sweden would be drawn into the greater war, just because Finland wanted to save Viborg and Sortavala, when "[n]either city was a matter of vital interest to Finland, and their loss did not mean Finland's ruin"? An opportunity to make peace existed, yet Finland was not prepared to take advantage of it. If the question were brought up again, Günther warned, Finland would receive the same answer that he had just given the Allies.[88] Günther was also unsure that Germany's quick defeat would be beneficial to Sweden. If the iron ore exports were halted and Hitler defeated, he could obviously no longer focus on future campaigns against Stalin. Russia, an age-old enemy of Sweden, would then gain strength and become a direct threat to the Scandinavian peninsula.[89]

The Grand Finale

With heightening danger of an Allied invasion, the goal was now to find a path that allowed Stalin to satisfy his demands for territory in order to defend Leningrad while simultaneously saving Finland's independence. Finland complained that the Swedish deliveries of war materiel had almost ceased. Of the approximately one hundred trucks that were expected to arrive, only twenty or thirty had been delivered, and in northern Sweden approximately three thousand tons of other materiel was still stored awaiting transport. Sweden's failure to ship the equipment was taken as a silent suggestion to Finland to accept the terms of the peace treaty. On March 6, Finland sent a delegation to Moscow via Sweden. During the night in Stockholm, Finland's Prime Minister Risto Ryti revealed to Christian Günther that influential people had suggested that Finland should give the Åland Islands to the Soviet Union in return for a promise that Finland would keep Hangö, but that the Finnish government had not taken the suggestion seriously.[90] The Soviet Union also reported that it was willing to negotiate for peace with Finland, but that it could not agree to a cease-fire before negotiations actually had started.[91]

Meanwhile, the Red Army was planning a circumvention of the Finnish troops stationed along the Mannerheim Line, across the frozen Gulf of Finland for the purpose of surrounding Viborg. Ice strong enough to carry the weight of the Russian tanks had finally formed on the Gulf, and the Red Army was no longer restricted to meeting the Finns in frontal assault. The highway through Viborg would likely be under Soviet control within two weeks, after which a successful march on Helsinki would be inevitable. The forts that had been erected on islands in the Gulf to protect the city against enemy warships were now manned with Finnish gunners,[92] who shattered the ice until the Russian tanks fell through and whole Russian companies were swallowed up in the waters.[93] Still, aware of the Red Army's progress and their own weaknesses, the Finns understood that the bargaining power was in Stalin's hands. The Finnish army had depleted its forces, had no more trained troops in reserve, and was expected to take heavy casualties if sending insufficiently trained men still in their teens into combat against the elite Russian forces. By the beginning of March, the daily rate of Finnish casualties was already six times higher than it had been during the preceding months of warfare.[94]

Displaying weakness was unacceptable, however, and would have placed Finland in an even more precarious situation, despite the fact that the highest in command knew about the government's decision to negotiate for peace. Mannerheim agreed and expected his army to keep fighting, even if there was no chance that Sweden would permit transit of Allied troops. In an attempt to pressure Stalin into easing his demands when meeting at the negotiating table, Mannerheim stressed in a letter to Daladier that Finland was in need of manpower and weapons; an indication that the country was not considering succumbing to Soviet requirements. Upholding a strong image proved crucial in order to ensure a better position at the bargaining table. Should the Allies march into Russia in defense of Finland, the situation would inevitably spiral out of Stalin's control. This was a risk that Stalin could not afford to take.[95]

On March 7, the Red Army, with reinforcements on the way, took control of the road that led from Viborg to the heart of Finland. It was feared that the city would fall any day.[96] On March 11, the Finnish leadership considered it impossible to hold Viborg against the Russian forces without losing a large part of the Finnish army. The situation was so grave that Finland would ultimately have to choose between saving the city and saving what was left of its decimated army.[97] Finland issued a final request to the Swedish government to grant the Allies passage. Johan Otto Söderhjelm, Minister of Justice in Risto Ryti's government, expressed in his diary his disappointment in Sweden's failure to formally stand by Finland in the war. It has since come to light that his complaints about Sweden's lack of action and refusal to grant the Allies transit might have been political strategy used to dampen opposition to the impending peace treaty. Finland had accepted the peace accords by March 11, yet continued to request that Sweden open its borders and allow the Allies passage. The move proved necessary in order to gain popular support for the treaty. If Finland experienced a political split, another civil war was not out of the question.[98] Yet, it was crucial that the Winter War ended when it did. When the ice melted in spring and the extreme cold would no longer be a factor, a Russian breakthrough on the Karelian Isthmus would have caused

40-millimeter anti-aircraft artillery cannon. Approximately 2,500 rounds were fired with this type cannon, with eight confirmed hits against enemy aircraft (source: Krigsarkivet, Förbundet Svenska Finlandsfrivilliga, Vol. 29).

the Finnish defense to suffer enormously.[99] The fitness of the troops that remained was not what it had been when the war started, and it was crucial that an agreement be reached before all bargaining power was lost.[100] If Finland had not sued for peace, the only alternative was to continue the war until the last Finnish troop had fallen.[101]

During the night between March 12 and 13, a Swedish patrol set out to destroy a Russian stronghold where the enemy had taken cover behind thick walls and fired with automatic rifles at the volunteers. When returning to camp around 2:00 A.M., the volunteers were informed through a message intercepted over the radio that a peace agreement had been signed. Although rumors of peace negotiations had been circulating for some time, nobody was willing to believe that a resolution had actually been reached. At 5:20

A.M. on March 13, it became official. A report from the Finnish headquarters confirmed the announcement and stated that all military activities were to cease at 11:00 A.M. Heavy fighting continued throughout the morning. Around 6:00 A.M., a violent firefight that included Soviet attack and bomber aircraft erupted along the entire front and continued without interruption for five hours. Rovaniemi and Kemijärvi were bombed, although the damage was not severe and resulted only in slight injuries to one person. The Swedish anti-aircraft artillery fired at the Russian fighters and bombers but was unable to down a single enemy aircraft.[102] The last shot was reported fired from afar at 11:04 A.M. The Finnish flag at Viborg fortress was lowered to half pole as a signal of defeat, and then raised one final time before permanently lowered while saluted by the Finnish army.[103] Yet, the defense of Viborg never broke. When the war ended, Viborg was still in Finnish hands and was ceded only as a condition of the peace treaty.[104]

The heavy bombardment of artillery, mortar, and machinegun fire in the war's final hours resulted in ten dead volunteers and thirty other casualties.[105] One volunteer recalled how he had been awakened by someone shouting that

SVENSKA FRIVILLIGKÅREN
2 BILKOMP.
Rovaniemi 13/3 1940

Fred har slutits mellan Finland och Ryssland.
Fientligheterna inställas 13/3 kl 1100.
På befallning

(Ernst Linder)
Chef SFr

(Richard Åkerman).

Message from General Ernst Linder indicating that peace has been negotiated between Finland and Russia, and orders to cease fire at 11:00 A.M. on March 13, 1940 (source: Krigsarkivet, Svenska Frivilligkåren, Kriget 1939–1940).

the Russians were attacking. Seconds later an airplane could be heard flying overhead and a bomb struck close to the tent. The volunteer remembered how the pressure from the bomb had carried him some distance through the air before he lost consciousness. When he came to, he was lying in the snow approximately ten meters from the tent, which now hung limp over the stove. Another bomb had hit the neighboring tent, which housed three volunteers, all of whom were killed. Low-flying attack planes swept over the treetops firing automatic rifles. Several grenades were thrown into the volunteer camp, but the deep snow dampened their effect and many were duds.[106] Soviet airplanes flew over Finnish territory as late as 12:41 and 1:15 ., as reported from Rovaniemi.[107]

When the firing ended a few minutes past 11:00 A.M., the pristine snow-covered landscape was no longer white. One might ask why the Russians launched such a massive campaign in the hours before the war ended. The answer to this question is not totally clear. It has been speculated that Stalin had been preparing a large offensive when peace came and wanted to make a final impression on the Finnish and Swedish troops. His march toward Helsinki and failure to occupy the city would have jeopardized the prestige of the Red Army had he not taken further action. Conversations with the Russians in the days following the armistice revealed that the firefight that took place in the last hours of the war was meant as a "final salute"; a sign that the Soviets had "greased their weapons" and were ready to resume the conquest in the near future.[108]

Bivouac after bombing raid on March 10, 1940 (source: Krigsarkivet, Förbundet Svenska Finlandsfrivilliga, Vol. 29).

Through the territories he acquired, Stalin had after all created a good starting point for a new war, as he would demonstrate through renewed military preparedness and deployment of a well-equipped army to Soviet Karelia during the rest of the year and into 1941.

Finland's Concessions

The Moscow Peace Treaty was signed between Finland and the Soviet Union on March 12, 1940. The war had lasted roughly a hundred days and the peace came as a great relief to Sweden. Now, the Allies had no further reason to send troops to Finland through Swedish territory. Finland would escape the destiny of the Baltic states and would remain a free and sovereign nation.[109] Yet Finland's losses proved painful. The Soviet Union and Finland agreed that the border between the countries should be moved to coincide with the border of 1721, from the time of Peter the Great. In addition to certain areas in northern Finland, the treasured Viborg would fall under Soviet rule. Approximately 10 percent of Finland's territory would befall the Russians. Parts of these areas were of economic significance. For example, Finland would lose 10 percent of its farming land, 30 percent of its fishing waters, and 20 percent of its industrial capacity.[110] Finland's President Kyösti Kallio, when signing the treaty with the Soviet Union, supposedly uttered, "This is the most awful document I have ever had to sign. May the hand wither, which is forced to sign such a paper."[111]

The Swedish publication *Den Frivillige* (The Volunteer) estimated that approximately 650,000 Finns would be forced to leave their homes, 42 percent of Finland's production of wood materiel would be lost, the country's export industry would decrease by 2.6 billion Finnish marks per year, Finnish industry production would decrease by 22 percent, Saima Channel, the longest channel in Finland, would be lost, Trångsund, the world's largest port for the export of forest products would befall the Russians, and the fortresses meant to protect the country would now end up on Russian soil. The loss of territory and industry meant that Finland would be deprived of much of its unique culture. Additionally, Finland's defense capabilities would be severely hampered and would also affect Sweden. That the border would be moved in line with Salla and Kuusamo meant that Russia would acquire two bridges over which the Red Army could march to Uleåborg and Torneå for further transport to northern Sweden. As noted previously, some people feared that Stalin planned to turn northern Sweden into a north–Scandinavian communist state. The fact that the Finns had to cede their part of the Fisherman Peninsula at the northernmost coast of the country

Detonation of Russian mines (source: Krigsarkivet, Förbundet Svenska Finlandsfrivilliga, Vol. 29).

meant that the road would be open for a Russian advance to the west.[112] Other speculations that Finland would be forced to give up its fleet and air-power, and be allowed to raise a limited army of only fifteen thousand men, were later proven false.[113] Mannerheim, who was in favor of reaching a settlement, still argued that Finland could not agree to the demands unless the country could keep an effective army.[114]

With the new border closer to Helsinki, the Finnish capital was no longer as secure as it once had been. Stalin also gained permission to lease Hangö and surrounding waters for a period of thirty years in order to establish a base for his air defense.[115] The ceding of Hangö and a twenty kilometer wide coastal stretch meant that Finland's coastal defense would be damaged and would lay the rest of the country open to invasion. It also meant that the Russians could close off the Gulf of Finland and Helsinki harbor at will. *Den Frivillige* considered Finland mutilated with Sweden next in line.[116] Finland's independence had been secured for the moment, but few people believed that the war was truly over. Although not all shared this viewpoint, and at least one volunteer admitted that he was jubilant that the war had ended and his life had been spared, several others promised that should Finland need their help again, they would stand ready to serve.[117]

There were several reasons why Finland was forced to agree to the hard terms of the treaty. The shipments from Sweden had nearly come to a halt, and not enough artillery pieces and ammunition existed in order to continue the war. The country did no longer have the troops it needed to stop the Soviet advance, and would not have lasted long without assistance from the Allies. In contrast to the huge Russian army who had been able to rotate its troops regularly, the Finnish soldiers were exhausted from having fought continuously without relief. Many soldiers were also of middle age and lacked the physical stamina to fight day after day without letup. Moreover, the intelligence service had functioned poorly, and casualties continued to increase until they amounted to approximately a thousand men per day.[118] The country would have been unable to hold its position militarily even a few days longer. Although Finland had little choice but to succumb to the demands and sign the treaty, the bitterness the Finns felt at the hard peace was understandable.[119]

When the tally was taken, the war had cost Finland 24,923 killed or missing in action and 43,557 wounded, in addition to 420,000 civilians losing their homes. These numbers proved considerable in view of Finland's small population of not even four million people.[120] Although the Soviet Union ultimately got its demands for territory fulfilled, the Red Army's road had also been difficult and full of losses. "They are so many and our land is so small," the Finns joked. "Where shall we find the land to bury them all?"[121] One Russian lady reminiscing about her country's experiences declared, "The Finns were the worst; even the Germans were afraid of them."[122] The Soviet outlook had been glum from the outset. One of Stalin's generals is said to have remarked that the Soviet Union would win "just about enough ground to bury our dead." Although the final count is unknown, Molotov reported 48,745 killed and 159,000 wounded. The Finns estimated the Soviet losses to four times that many, and modern estimates are closer to 230,000 killed and nearly 300,000 wounded.[123] A report presented in 1993, however, declared that the total losses of the Soviet Union amounted to 126,874 dead and 268,908 other casualties.[124] The Swedish losses amounted to 37 dead and 45 men wounded in combat, in

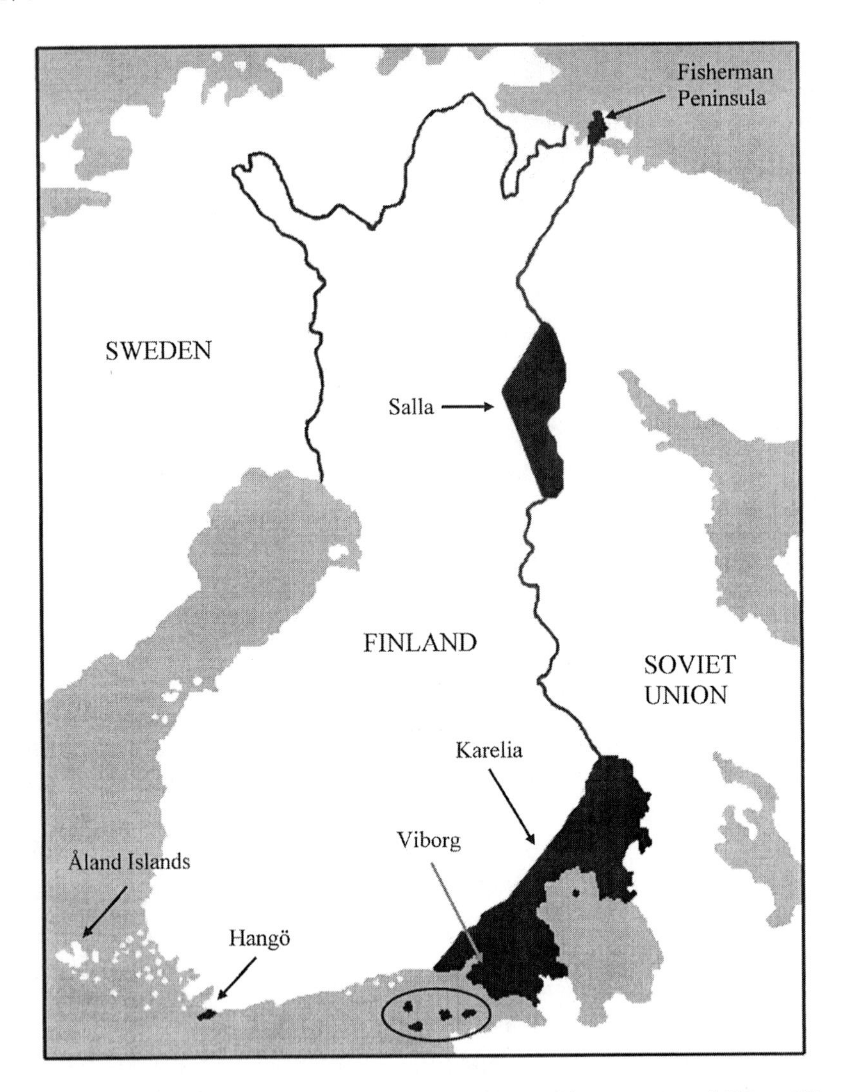

Areas ceded by Finland to the Soviet Union at the conclusion of the Russo-Finnish Winter War. Most notably, Finland lost the city of Viborg on the Karelian Isthmus, Hangö at the mouth of the Gulf of Finland, and several smaller islands in the Gulf (circled). Finland also ceded the Salla area and the western part of the Fisherman Peninsula in the north. Note that the Åland Islands remained a part of Finland (source: Martina Sprague).

addition to 140 other casualties, many of whom had serious frost injuries. The Soviets also captured five volunteers but released them to Sweden in the summer of 1940.[125]

Although the Finnish and Swedish soldiers had fought heroically against the numerically superior Red Army, a correspondent for the *Dagens*

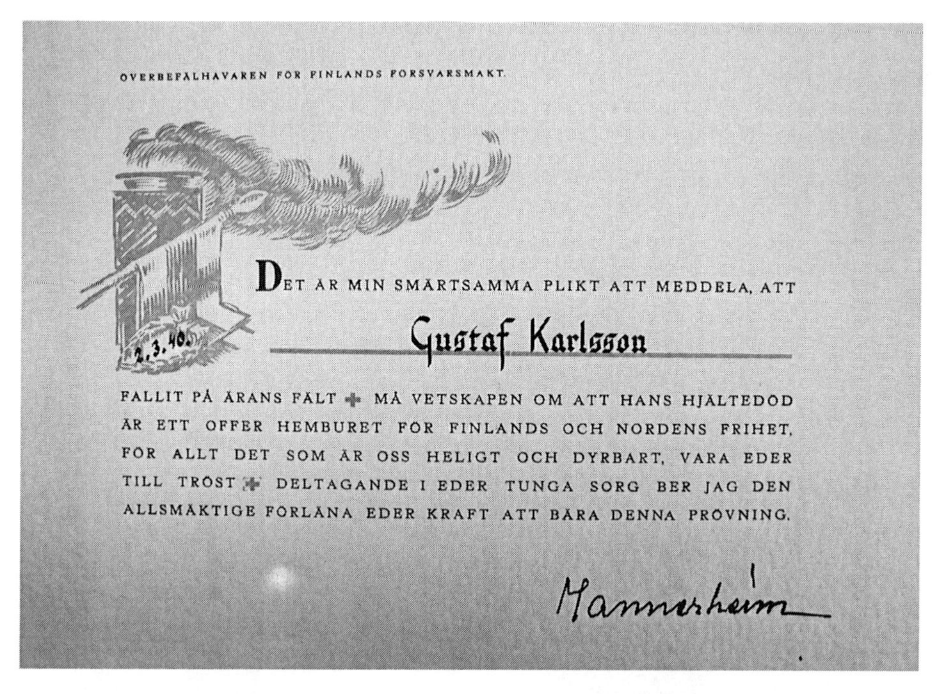

ÖVERBEFÄLHAVAREN FÖR FINLANDS FÖRSVARSMAKT.

2.3.40.

DET ÄR MIN SMÄRTSAMMA PLIKT ATT MEDDELA, ATT

Gustaf Karlsson

FALLIT PÅ ÄRANS FÄLT ✚ MÅ VETSKAPEN OM ATT HANS HJÄLTEDÖD ÄR ETT OFFER HEMBURET FÖR FINLANDS OCH NORDENS FRIHET, FÖR ALLT DET SOM ÄR OSS HELIGT OCH DYRBART, VARA EDER TILL TRÖST ✚ DELTAGANDE I EDER TUNGA SORG BER JAG DEN ALLSMÄKTIGE FÖRLÄNA EDER KRAFT ATT BÄRA DENNA PRÖVNING.

Mannerheim

Notice of combat casualty dated March 2, 1940, and issued by Carl Gustaf Mannerheim: "It is my painful duty to inform you that Gustaf Karlsson has fallen on the field of honor. May the knowledge that his death occurred as a result of his heroic struggle for Finnish and Nordic independence, for all that which is dear to our hearts, be of some consolation. As a participant in your sorrow, I ask that the Almighty will grant you the strength to carry this burden" (source: Krigsarkivet, Finlandskommitten, 1939–1940).

Nyheter (a Swedish daily newspaper) noted that Finland's losses far outweighed the benefits brought by the peace treaty.[126] The media and government had also painted a grander picture of the war than reality portrayed; they had positively stated that Finland could win.[127] The Swedes believed that their contribution had come too late, and the big offensive they had anticipated participating in never materialized. The Finns and Swedes shared the bitterness of their experiences and blamed the Swedish government for its unwillingness to send government sanctioned troops to Finland. Some meant that had the government allowed open advertisement in the early stages of the war, as many as thirty thousand volunteers might have been recruited.[128] As noted in *Den Frivillige* on March 15: "Finland's cause was not ours."[129] The publication continued to criticize the government so heavily that Sweden was forced to stop its distribution. (*Den Frivillige* was printed in ten issues between February 28 and April 1, 1940. The first four issues were printed in Haparanda in northern Sweden. The paper then moved to Rovaniemi where it could follow the activities of the volunteers as they moved further east.[130])

The day the guns fell silent was a day of national mourning. Sweden's leadership had known fully well that Finland could not sustain a lengthy fight against Russia without help, yet they had refused to act. The heroism that the world had witnessed in the Finnish soldiers had become merely a stage play with a predetermined outcome. As noted by one volunteer, the sudden silence felt surreal, as if the war had been but a military rehearsal for things yet to come.[131] Many of the volunteers had missed the chance to fight at the front and therefore felt that their efforts and good will had made little difference. Per Albin Hansson was bombarded with phone calls and letters from people accusing him of having "betrayed all of the Nordic countries," and asking for his resignation. Many did not yet understand the bigger forces at play at the start of World War II. Finland had no reason to blame Sweden for the hard peace, Hansson alleged, since the Swedish government had clearly stated from the beginning that Finland should not count on government sanctioned troops from Sweden and had done all in its power to mediate in the conflict.[132] When the waves had settled and the disappointment faded, many people recognized that Sweden's leadership had acted wisely. Had Sweden assisted Finland militarily, Sweden would have been pulled into World War II, and likely on the side of the Nazis.[133] Hansson became a celebrated statesman. He was applauded for his foresight, for staying true to his beliefs, and for remaining an "anchor" in the storm.[134]

As soon as the war was over, Hitler was quick to note the consequences of the sudden peace, and what it might mean for the future of Germany. An urgent message sent from the German minister in Finland to the German Foreign Ministry indicated that Russia would likely improve her strategic position through the domination of the Baltic Sea and the territories she had gained. The expansion into the Karelian Isthmus would also give Russia access to southern and northern Finland and to the railroad between Karelia and Kiruna in northern Sweden, where the iron ore mines were located. Although a British occupation of the mines had been deterred through the peace treaty, Germany and Russia were the true superpowers as demonstrated by the French-British failure to breach Swedish neutrality. Should the current good relations between Germany and Russia deteriorate, Russia might gain full control of the iron ore fields. Furthermore, Hitler had lost much of his good reputation in the eyes of the Finns because of his failure to defend Finland against the Soviet invasion, and he feared that Finland might assist Russia in its pursuit of the ore fields.[135] Nikita Khrushchev, however, took a different stand. When the peace treaty was signed, he noted how the

Soviet Union "sensed in our victory a defeat by the Finns. It was a dangerous defeat because it encouraged our enemies' conviction that the Soviet Union was a colossus with feet of clay."[136] Had Stalin succeeded at controlling Finland, it would have communicated the power of the Soviet Union to the rest of the world. Instead, the severe setbacks the Red Army had suffered indicated that the country was vulnerable to attack and even takeover, which prompted Hitler to move forward with Operation Barbarossa.[137]

Mannerheim's Speech to the Troops

Despite the shared bitterness felt by the Finns and Swedes at the disappointing outcome of the war, Johan Otto Söderhjelm, the Finnish Minister of Justice, reminded the people that, rather than discussing what Sweden had failed to do, it should be remembered what Sweden had done for Finland in the form of volunteer help, peace negotiations, and humanitarian efforts.[138] On March 26, Mannerheim officially thanked the Swedish troops:

> My Swedish friends, after more than a hundred days of hard fighting, Finland has negotiated peace. United and ready to suffer any hardship, our people took up arms in order to defend our highest ideals: honor, freedom, and Western cultural values. We are now forced to cede parts of our beloved country; whose villages and cities are burnt and deserted, but whose courage has not been quelled and who stands with head held high under the protection of our army, which has bled for us in many battles but refused to succumb to the superior strength of the enemy forces. Volunteers, I greet you, who came to our assistance, who left your home and country ready to offer your lives here in the Finnish wilderness. In my own name and in the name of our army, I wish to extend to you my sincerest thanks. Your proud spirits and honorable intention have made you our brothers in our struggle against the Eastern armies.... I greet you, Swedes, who for centuries have shared our many victories but also the bitterness of defeat. In honor of the Swedish name, thousands of you have stood by our side.... Finland's appreciation for what you have done shall never pale. God save Finland, God save Sweden. Long live the Swedish volunteers and their chief General Linder.[139]

The volunteers who had offered their lives for Finland had not done so in vain. Sweden had proven that its youth was courageous and willing to make a sacrifice of standing value. Simultaneously, the Swedish government had demonstrated integrity by focusing on diplomacy and refusing to sway under international pressure to send military help to Finland, which would certainly have escalated the war and brought devastating consequences to all of the Nordic countries. In the end, the war tightened the bonds between the Finns and the Swedes. Finnish soldiers invited Swedish soldiers as their guests, and vice versa. Stories were exchanged and friendships reaffirmed.[140] Finland

HÖGKVARTERET. 24. 3. 1940.

ÖVERBEFÄLHAVARENS DAGORDER

N:o 38.

Efter mer än hundra dagars hårda strider har Finland slutit fred. Enigt och redo till alla offer grep vårt folk till vapen för att värna sitt högsta goda: ära, frihet och västerländsk kultur. Nu har det sett sig tvunget att till övermakten utlämna delar av ett älskat fosterland; dess byar och städer ha bränts och ödelagts, men dess mod har ej kuvats och det står med högburet huvud i skyddet av sin armé, som blött i många strider, men som fiendens väldiga övermakt ej förmått besegra.

Frivilliga, till Eder, vilka över land och hav ilat till vår hjälp, lämnande hem och fosterland, redo att offra Ert liv här på den finska drivan, vill jag i arméns och mitt eget namn uttala mitt varma tack. Edra stolta hjärtan ha gjort Eder till våra vapenbröder i striden mot österns härar. Att av Er endast en del hann med i vapenleken, förringar ej värdet av Edert ädla uppsåt.

Jag hälsar Eder, svenskar, med vilka vi på många slagfält under sekler delat segrars ära, men också nederlagets bitterhet. Värdiga det svenska namnet ha tusenden av Eder ställt sig vid vår sida. Att hjälpen för Sverige varit en hjärtesak, därom vittnar det bistånd i många former, som med öppen hand givits oss, kanske till och med på bekostnad av egen trygghet.

Jag hälsar Eder, norrmän, vilka från de höga fjällens land skyndat hit för att värna Nordens frihet.

Jag hälsar Eder, danskar, som, besjälade av samma anda, trotsat köld och snö för att sluta Eder till den nordiska brödraskaran.

Ni, våra blodsförvanter från Donaus stränder, ha även hört den fjärran klangen av våra stridslurar, och efter tusen år har madjarens sabel åter höjts bredvid den finske broderns svärd.

Jag hälsar Eder, belgier och fransmän, och Eder, Storbritanniens söner, vilka trots hotet vid egen dörr, velat komma oss till hjälp.

Jag uttalar även mitt tack till alla övriga nationers söner, vilka samlats under våra fanor, redo att rycka ut. Av hjärtat tackar jag finnarna från Nya Världen och stamfränderna från Fjärr-Karelen.

I denna tid, då våldet hotar de svagas frihet än värre än fordomtima, trampande under tunga stövlar frukterna av generationers arbete på kulturens och framåtskridandets fält, då de små nationernas existens är i fara, hava Ni alla bevisat, att det ännu finnes män, vilka sporras av ädla ideal och tron på livets högsta värden.

Må det vapenbrödraskap vi här knutit vara ägnat att stärka samförståndet och varaktigt närma våra folk till varandra. Finlands känslor av tacksamhet och aktning skola aldrig förblekna.

MANNERHEIM.

Carl Gustaf Mannerheim's speech to the volunteers following the end of hostilities in March, 1940 (source: Krigsarkivet, Förbundet Svenska Finlandsfrivilliga, Vol. 29).

The remains of a Russian bunker after the war (source: Krigsarkivet, Förbundet Svenska Finlandsfrivilliga, Vol. 29).

had won morally if not territorially. The Finnish people retained their government and their autonomy.

Wrap-Up

Although the war was over, much work remained to be done. Personnel, materiel, and aircraft had to be returned to Sweden as soon as possible in preparation for a potential conflict with Germany. On April 9, 1940, as reported in German radio, Hitler had taken upon himself to "protect" Norway and Denmark, which in practicality meant an invasion and occupation of these countries. The Swedish people could not help but wonder what lay in wait for them.[141] Immediate transport of the troops back to Sweden was not possible, however, because the Finnish railways were overloaded with Finnish citizens departing Karelia. The volunteers were promised that they would return home no later than April 30, although those desiring to stay and serve in specialty positions in the Finnish army were granted an opportunity to do so, and were allowed to keep their uniforms and issued clothing. All other equipment was to be stored in Rovaniemi, Kemi, and the area surrounding Torneå.[142]

The Russians recovered their dead, as did the volunteers, although some of the bodies could not be found and recovered until August 1940. Many men also used this time of rest to revisit the battlefields at the front, and made several discoveries about the Red Army's strongholds. For example, the Russian

Volunteers inspecting a Russian barbed wire barricade (source: Krigsarkivet, Förbundet Svenska Finlandsfrivilliga, Vol. 29).

General Linders avskedshälsning till de frivilliga.

Soldater, krigskamrater!

Då jag kanske ej får tillfälle att råka Eder före Svenska frivilligkårens upplösning sänder jag Eder härmed min hälsning. Jag lyckönskar Eder till den heder, som bevisats Eder genom Fältmarskalkens besök och erkännande ord. I min utnämning till general av kavalleriet i Finlands tappra här ser jag främst en hedersbevisning åt kåren och därmed åt Eder.

Den plötsligt slutna freden — hård för Finland och olycksbådande för Sverige — avbröt i förtid Eder verksamhet. Om svenska regeringen från början underlättat frivilligkårens rekrytering i lika hög grad som den gjorde då freden stod för dörren, hade Överbefälhavaren tidigare och med större resultat kunnat insätta våra förband.

Kårens flygstyrka har trots materiell underlägsenhet uträttat ett gott arbete och vid upprepade tillfällen — liksom luftvärnet — nedkämpat sina motståndare. Vid fronten löste kårens huvuddel, stridsgruppen, sin uppgift, varvid särskilt spaningsförbanden utmärkte sig. De bakre förbanden arbetade väl, ehuru även deras verksamhet försvårades av fiendens överlägsna flyg och den stränga vintern. Genom Svenska frivilligkårens insättande frigjordes finska förband för användning vid Viborg.

Jag tackar Eder, officerare, underofficerare och manskap, för plikttroget arbete och föredömlig tapperhet. Fastän målet icke nåddes, kunna Ni med rätta känna stolthet och tillfredsställelse över att ha vågat Edra liv i kamp för Nordens frihet och fosterlandets ära.

Stockholm, Sophiahemmet, den 29. mars 1940.

ERNST LINDER
Kårchef.

General Ernst Linder's thank you address to the volunteers after the end of hostilities in March, 1940 (source: Krigsarkivet, Förbundet Svenska Finlandsfrivilliga, Vol. 29).

troops had "resided" in two-story buildings made of tree trunks, with the capacity to hold approximately twenty men each. An outer and inner wall with a "filling" of gravel and rock added extra protection. The bottom story was under ground. The top story contained eight openings through which firearms could be extended. The strongholds were very well built and were further protected with barbed wire, automatic artillery, and infantry positions.

The Russians had done a good clean-up job before departing, however, so not much evidence of their lives at the front existed for further study.[143]

When Viking Tamm, the commander of Combat Group II, held his final speech before the volunteers parted for travel back to Sweden, he noted that although Finland left the war with an unsmirched reputation, the country was weaker now than when it had entered the war. One-sixth of Finland's population was forced to move from their homes, and the country's defensive capabilities were so deficient that a renewed attack from Russia would likely lead to Finland's downfall. That the Soviet Union had started the war purely for the purpose of securing Leningrad was difficult to believe. More likely was that Stalin would pursue Finland anew in the near future. Tamm finished his speech in the hope that, should destiny call, the volunteers would once again join in the fight and honor the emblem of the four hands representing Nordic independence.[144]

5

Analysis and Conclusions

Combat Operations in the Finnish Army

Not only did Finland encounter an enemy many times superior in numbers and resources; the complex terrain and extreme temperatures required imagination and use of primitive equipment such as skis rather than modern tanks. The Finns were "[c]itizen soldiers and reservists led by well-trained professionals.... They knew the ground and were used to living in the forest."[1] Not only were they nearly invisible in the snow in their white camouflage suits, they were dressed to withstand extremely cold temperatures. Superior knowledge of the terrain, stamina, and extensive use of captured enemy weapons allowed them to maintain morale and delay the Red Army's advance toward Helsinki, while their Soviet counterparts nearly froze to death in their insufficient autumn uniforms. Although in need of product imports from other countries, if living conservatively and rationing coffee, sugar, certain fruits, and tobacco, the Finns estimated that they could survive for several years on their own food resources. An enemy could not force Finland to its knees through starvation.[2] Although the economic setbacks that Finland suffered during the Great Depression had left the country at a severe disadvantage at the start of the war, the Finns' ability to function in the combat environment, and their spirit, made them by average better soldiers than the masses of Red Army troops.

Two factors in particular would prove crucial to Finland's success: the mobility of the troops and their firing power. The terrain did not lend itself to mass firing and hampered the ability of the Red Army to fully utilize its resources. Individual Russian troops firing from a distance of 100 to 250 meters risked firing into the trees and endangering their own. Firing from a greater distance complicated the accuracy of the aim against an enemy who could easily hide in the forest. Moreover, the Soviet troops were trained to fight a conventional war in open terrain with motorized equipment, but tanks could only travel along well-maintained roads. Although the skis and light sleds issued to the Finns enhanced their ability to fight from a numerically inferior position, one Finn bragged how they would have proven superior even if the Russians had been good skiers.[3] The infantry in particular had the nerves to operate for weeks at a time in the snow-covered forests, and the patience to sit quietly and observe the enemy's movements even after dark. They generally maintained their cool and shot accurately, while the Russians were more apt to fire blindly in close combat. If a Finnish patrol unexpectedly encountered a Russian patrol, the Finns tended to draw the long straw. Additionally, they were skilled at handling common tools such as saws and axes from childhood. These improvised weapons came in handy in close encounters with the enemy.[4]

The Finns thus used economy of force and unconventional battlefield tactics to compensate for their inferior numbers and technology. Tactical doctrine dictated individual initiative and small-unit operations along the nearly impenetrable — except for a handful of unpaved roads — Finnish frontier with Russia. They attacked the enemy's main force as a distraction, simultaneously launching an offensive against the flanks or rear. The fast-moving ski troops and *motti* tactics of splitting and encircling the enemy led to several smaller victories.[5] The Finns also placed mines under the ice of the newly frozen lakes and shattered the ice as the Soviets tried to cross.[6] They had little to be ashamed of. As a people, they had participated actively in combat since Sweden's time as a superpower in the seventeenth century. They valued their independence and were mentally prepared to fight and die for their country.[7]

Several weaknesses became apparent in the Finnish army as the war progressed, however. Although Finland was generally blessed with experienced military personnel — the older officers had prior combat experience and had received military education in Finland and other countries, and the younger generation had completed mandatory military training in the army and noncommissioned officer schools[8] — Mannerheim believed that the education of officers and soldiers was not as good as had been propagated. At the start of the war, the Finnish officer school had been in operation approximately fifteen years, but, as a result of cutbacks in military spending, the number of students at the school never matched the actual need for officers. Likewise, the number of troops that officers had at their disposal in training exercises proved too few to meet the requirements for modern combat operations. When corrections had been made for the numerous frictions the army would encounter in war, the actual need proved much higher than what had been estimated on paper. Moreover, it soon became evident that not all officers had the mental strength to lead their subordinates through the hostilities, particularly at the start of the war when the Russian forces managed to move deeply into the main defensive line. Two officers were reported suffering nervous breakdown and a third requested to be relieved of his duties as this was his fifth major campaign — he had also served in Finland's War of Independence and in East Karelia — and expressed concern that his nerves might fail him in the deciding moment. Because of failing discipline among the officers, orders were often sent too late to have the desired effect, and some problems were solved in impractical ways while others were ignored altogether.[9]

Military education also remained theoretical in nature. Winston Churchill recalled, "All the resentment felt against the Soviet government for the Ribbentrop-Molotov pact was fanned into flame by this latest exhibition of brutal bullying and aggression. With this was also mingled scorn for the inefficiency displayed by the Soviet troops and enthusiasm for the gallant Finns."[10] Yet, although the officers were reminded that the world was rooting for Finland and betting on how long the Finnish *sisu* would last, and no amount of propaganda was needed to motivate the Finns to fight for their country and families, or convince them about the righteousness of their position, Harald Öhquist, a Finnish officer in the Winter War, held the opinion that the spirit of the Finns had been exaggerated. Most were ready to fight to the death against the Red Army, yet were not quite as exemplary as portrayed in the numerous publications discussing the history of the war. For example, contrary to the belief that the military leadership displayed a particularly aggressive mentality and encouraged the troops to attack without regard for their own safety, Finnish officers focused largely on an analytical approach to warfare rooted in the study of military history and examination of different strategic approaches to war. Another problem was insubordination to authority. Officers and troops enjoyed near social equality, which made it difficult for the former to exercise authority over the latter.[11]

Additionally, the obligatory military service for a Finn was only one year to the two to four years required of his Russian counterpart.[12] Although Finland could draw from a large pool of uneducated men who were physically fit to participate in combat, a substantial amount of the training had been used for civilian work that was not even remotely related to warfare, and not enough focus had been placed on firing discipline, guard duty, and firearms care. These men would now get thrown into combat on a sink or swim basis, which would undoubtedly lead to heavy losses.[13] The Finnish leadership later determined that it was wrong to send newly educated troops to the northern front where the Russians proved stronger than expected. Although the railway communications from Torneå undoubtedly needed protection, the distance from every part of the border between Lake Ladoga and the Arctic Ocean was longer than the distance from the border on the Karelian Isthmus to the vital parts of Finland, and the troops in the north were spread much too thin.[14] The 1,300 kilometer long border that Finland shared with the Soviet Union had remained one of the main defense problems. Since the Finns could only guess where the main attack would come, it was necessary to defend the entire stretch of the border, which proved exceptionally difficult in light of the small army that Finland possessed. Maneuvers held in the area around Viborg in the late summer of 1939 indicated that the Finnish army lacked the experience and technical routine that a modern war demanded.[15] In the end, it was not possible to win against an enemy as numerically superior as the Soviet Union, no matter how great the spirit of the Finnish troops.

Thus, despite their resourcefulness and the beneficial forested terrain, the Finns proved ill prepared to meet the "Russian Bear" in battle. Whatever advantages Finland possessed in ingenuity and fighting spirit were overshadowed by the numerical superiority of the Russian war machine. Artillery played an absolutely crucial role in defending the border for any length of time, even in the forested terrain, or perhaps even more so than in Central Europe where tanks and airpower could establish dominance over the battlefield. The Russians had rightfully spoken of artillery as the "god of warfare." One Finnish officer admitted that, although it was troublesome that anti-aircraft and antitank weapons were in short supply, these limitations did not have a decisive effect on the outcome of the war. Rather, it was the Finns' lack of artillery against ground forces that proved decisive.[16]

Toward the end of the war, Finland's resources of ammunition were down to approximately twenty thousand rounds. The Finnish army required at the minimum between six and eight thousand rounds per day in order to defend the front. Thus, no matter how skilled the forces were, they could not have stood against the Russian army for more than a few days in defensive positions, and probably only for one more day if going on the counter-offensive and attempting to retake ground that had already been taken. When the ammunition was depleted, the victory could not have been secured even if Finland had had access to great troop reinforcements in the battle areas that required it the most. For comparison purposes, during a six-hour offensive in February, the Russians had thrown more than 200,000 grenades into Finnish lines.[17]

The few firing arms available forced the Finns to rely on improvised explosives and dangerous close-combat missions. As they began to take casualties, the weakness of their numerical inferiority became more evident with each passing day of fighting against the seemingly endless supply of Red Army troops. The Swedish forces that arrived in northern Finland could relieve only a few of the Finnish battalions for reassignment to Karelia, and the artillery pieces that Sweden sent to Finland were too few to cover the entire front.[18] The small numbers of soldiers also forced the Finns to fight from defensive positions, giving the enemy the initiative and ability to decide the time and place of battle. The Finnish troops had to be transported from all parts of Finland to the theater of operation, while the Russians were already positioned in Leningrad ready to attack. The Finns knew that if they failed to halt the Russian advance at the Isthmus, they would likely be unable to halt a further advance toward Helsinki.[19]

From the middle of February 1940, the part of the front where the Russians focused their main attacks became severely difficult to defend. As long as the troops remained in their stationary positions, the losses proved relatively small. But as soon as their retreat was forced, losses escalated until the situation became destitute. Although Finland did not need to defeat the Soviet Union per se, only keep the Red Army at bay long enough for international help to arrive, the country's isolation, sandwiched between the Soviet Union and neutral Sweden, prevented foreign military aid from arriving. Moreover, the nonaggression pact between Germany and Russia resulted in Finland's inability to count on Hitler to step forward, despite the good relations that Finland had enjoyed with Germany during the War of Independence. Better preparations and a greater defense budget during the prewar years might have helped Finland turn the tables on the Soviet Union. Although Stalin had falsely believed that he could conquer Finland in two weeks, in the end, the Soviet Union's numerical superiority allowed him to claim the victory.

Several years after the war, Mannerheim stated that he was convinced that if Finland's armed forces had been properly prepared with access to better equipment, the Winter War could have been avoided. The total number of Finnish troops on the Karelian Isthmus reached approximately 120,000. The ability to compensate for casualties and other losses proved relatively good at first. The main problem was that large numbers of fully educated troops were not called upon to serve, because there were not enough weapons and equipment available to supply them. Losses in manpower could thus be compensated for but not losses in equipment.[20]

What did the Winter War accomplish for Finland? Many questions remain unanswered and are left to speculation. Had Stalin believed that Finland was capable of offering such tough resistance, he might have been less motivated to instigate the war. And, had the Winter War been avoided, the rest of World War II would likely have taken a much different turn.[21] Likewise, had the Finns agreed to Stalin's requests for territory in the autumn of 1939, they might have been able to avoid the war and still preserve the country's independence. But such concessions early in the game could also have been an invitation to subject Finland to the same fate that befell the Baltic states. One might be tempted to ask why Finland but not the Baltic states put up a fight against the Soviet Union. Part of the answer to this question likely rests with the fact that Finland, due to the country's geographical location and historically strong bonds with Sweden, was counting on full support from Sweden. It is unlikely that Stalin knew how close to the breaking point the Finnish forces were. Had the Finns had access to the artillery pieces and ammunition that they would come to enjoy during the Continuation War, they might have been able to stave off the Russian advance along the Mannerheim Line, which could have led to more satisfying peace terms even if Finland had ultimately lost the war.[22]

It is uncertain to what extent the combat experiences the soldiers gained in the relatively short duration of the Winter War contributed to the security of the Nordic countries. Although the answer to this and other questions will never become entirely clear, some conclusions can be drawn. Since the War of Independence in 1918, the people of Finland comprised a mix of economic and political classes and ideologies. The Winter War united the Finns nationally. Fighting for political independence, for what it meant to be a Finn, gave them common ground, and their sacrifices and tough resistance gained them international acclaim.[23] The Finns were fortunate that twenty years and not ten had passed since their last war. Had Russia attacked a decade earlier, many Finns would likely have sympathized with the communists.[24] It can thus be surmised that Finland's defensive forces managed to fulfill the role in which they had been placed. Had they not displayed such tenacity and fought so well, Russia would likely have conquered all of Finland, placing the Red Army uncomfortably close to the Swedish border. The Finns preserved their independence and won a moral victory, even as country and troops "bled from a thousand wounds."[25] The courageous fighting of the Finnish soldiers will no doubt be celebrated in Scandinavia and remembered with pride for generations to come.

Combat Operations in the Soviet Army

Through flights over Finnish territory in the weeks preceding the war, the Russians determined that the Finns only had approximately 160 antiquated airplanes and hardly any tanks at all. The massive numbers of tanks and soldiers and several thousand bombers and fighters that the Russians possessed reinforced their belief that they were more than prepared to take out the Finnish nation before Christmas 1939.[26] Yet, the Soviet invasion of Finland has historically been deemed a severe failure. Few periods in Russian history may be viewed as more embarrassing than the enormous difficulties and losses the Red Army suffered in the Russo-Finnish Winter War.

When Stalin came to power, he focused on industrializing the country and building a highly modern and mechanized army. He looked forward to using tanks, aircraft, and artillery pieces with great success in a coming war. According to Nikita Khrushchev, however, the question of acquiring territory from Finland did not emerge until it became evident that the Soviet Union might have to protect against an attack from the west. The country did indeed view Finland as a threat to Leningrad. Finland had a history of friendly relations with Germany and in general followed policies that the Soviet Union perceived as hostile. In other words, Khrushchev saw it fully possible that Finland might ally itself with a Western European power, or allow a foreign state such as Germany access to Finnish territory where it would gain a foothold dangerously close to Leningrad. Mannerheim was also a strong political influence in Finland and his background as a tsarist general had turned him against the Soviet Union and Marxist-Leninist ideology. When Finland refused to budge in the early negotiations, Stalin had no choice but to go to war. As stated by Khrushchev later, none of the Soviet political leaders thought that the war would actually materialize, but were sure that the Finns would accept the terms once an ultimatum was put forth.[27]

Stalin had prepared for war with Finland for the greater part of the decade preceding the Winter War, and exercised several attempts at destabilizing Finnish society, which, had they succeeded, might well have made Finland ripe for takeover and ultimately annexation. For example, he encouraged labor strikes within Finland's metal industry in the 1920s to weaken Finland's ability to develop armaments, and further influenced public opinion in the 1930s. He sent out spies to map out roads and bridges and determine the strength of the fortifications on the Karelian Isthmus. Otto Vilhelm Kuusinen suspected as early as 1935 that the Soviet Union would soon be in war with Finland, and even told this to his wife; although, the idea then was that it was crucial to make war preparations not to start a war, but to counter a Finnish offensive against Russia aided by Germany, Great Britain, and Norway.[28] The fears were linked to the erection of the Mannerheim Line several years earlier.[29] Maps in a scale of 1:20,000,[30] confiscated from Russian prisoners, have verified that the Red Army had precise knowledge of the location of the Finnish fortifications.[31]

The Red Army soldiers had had plenty of opportunities to practice their tactics in conditions closely resembling those of the Karelian Isthmus. But neither the leadership nor the soldiers knew their enemy.[32] They misjudged the Finns' capability because of the casual approach they took to organizing a combat plan, coupled with unrealistic confidence in their technology.[33] For example, the difficulty of breaking the Mannerheim Line was attributed to the fact that Russia had underestimated the strength of the structures. Had good engineering reconnaissance taken place during the pre-war preparations, the line might have been broken more easily.[34]

Moreover, the originally proposed plan of attacking north of Lake Ladoga and encircling the Finnish forces was ignored by General Kirill Meretskov, who instead focused on concentrating the troops for a quick breakthrough on the Karelian Isthmus where the Finns were relatively strong.[35] Since Leningrad with its masses of people and large industrial areas was located only a few miles from the border, the Karelian Isthmus became the most convenient place for an offensive against Finland.[36] But it was an error in judgment that had catastrophic consequences and assisted the Finns in delaying the Soviet advance. The barbed wire along the Mannerheim Line forced the Russians to cross an open field, where they became easy targets for Finnish shooters. Worse, it was only the beginning of the difficulties they would come to suffer. In order to attack the flank or rear of the Finnish army on the Isthmus, it was necessary to maneuver around Lake Ladoga. The lake prevented the Red Army from focusing all forces at the decisive point. Thus, the war did not go as planned. The assumption that the Finns would be split with respect to their political and cultural ambitions, which further prompted the transmission of propaganda encouraging them to shoot their own officers and defect to the Soviet Union, had, needless to say, little effect.[37] Instead, the Finns' counterattacks during the month of December 1939 decimated the Soviet infantry. Stalin's generals had promised him Finland as a gift on his sixtieth birthday on December 21. Instead, they sent back loads of dead and wounded.[38] As reported by Laurence Steinhardt, United States Ambassador to the Soviet Union:

> Although military information in the Soviet press has been confined to the daily communique which gives few details of the fighting, even accepting these communiques at their face value, it is clear that far from achieving a speedy victory, the Soviet forces, after 19 days on the offensive, have made very little progress against Finland. Reports have reached Moscow from numerous sources that the large number of wounded arriving in Leningrad have necessitated the conversion of schools and other public buildings into temporary hospitals. Up to the present, no indication as to Soviet losses has appeared in the Soviet press. Swedish sources estimate the Soviet dead at 25,000.[39]

Stalin misjudged the conditions in part because he had gained confidence from his earlier campaign in Poland, where the Red Army's victories had convinced him that the "class antagonism that had made those victories possible also existed in Finland," and based his strategy on the assumption that the war would be short-lived.[40] But the natural obstacles on the Karelian Isthmus, the forests and swamps, should have been an indication that Finland could not be conquered without a long, expensive, and brutish war that would last several months at best, or even years, and would likely involve other countries offering to come to Finland's assistance. The monetary cost would be astronomical, and the cost in human lives would amount to hundreds of thousands of soldiers killed by enemy fire or external factors related to weather, shelter, and availability of clothing and food.[41] The roads used by the Red Army were one-lane roads of solid ice, which slowed progress. According to one Russian commander, the terrain in the theater of operation consisted of "50 per cent forests, 25 per cent water, a percentage of swamps, and some 10 per cent of land where tanks could operate."[42] Huge numbers of soldiers and equipment had to be stretched over distances of thirty to fifty kilometers, which prevented the troops from utilizing their numerical superiority in massed attack against the Finns.[43] Later analysis revealed that the leadership was determined to use tanks even though they were aware of the difficulties.[44]

A revealing example of how little the leadership knew about their enemy, the occasional confusion that existed among the Finnish leadership, and the conditions under which they must fight, might be Khrushchev's visit to a tire factory in Yaroslavl northeast of Moscow prior to the outbreak of war. He had been tasked with visiting the factory and finding out why tires that were almost new were easily blown out. The problem needed to be addressed and resolved quickly since Russia was heading for war, and "the mobility of the army depends on the quality of the transport industry."[45] Khrushchev was not aware that their first major engagement was a conflict that had to be fought using unconventional tactics and primitive methods of transport. When the Red Army assaulted the Finns, it was so cold that their rifles jammed and could not be fired. The troops could not utilize their high quality tanks and weapons, but had to resort to fighting with bayonets against the Finnish bunkers on the Mannerheim Line.[46]

Communication issues brought further difficulties. Commanders tended to use lies in order to glorify combat and mislead the troops to believe that the war would be easily won,[47] yet did not understand how to fight effectively in small units. Regimental commanders went before the troops to lead the charge and took unusually high numbers of casualties. A few weeks into the war, there remained only inexperienced junior commanders unprepared to lead. After one commander received two bullet wounds, was cut by a Finnish knife, and had his decorations, tabs, and documents carried off by the enemy, an order was issued that commanders had to travel with an escort of armored vehicles. The extreme "shortage of army communications facilities," as well as "skilled telegraphists"[48] further complicated the ability to keep the soldiers informed. One commander admitted after the war that he "lost 60 per cent of [his] battery commanders and 70 per cent of [his] control platoon commanders in two days of fighting—7 and 9 March—owing to the wrong understanding of communication."[49]

Part of the problem lay in improper organization and lack of cooperation between infantry and tank units. Although the gunners shot well and the tanks cleared the way for the infantry, "the infantry's performance was poor." Cooperation was also missing between ground troops and aviation, and aviation mostly stayed in the rear.[50] The Russian pilots flew a lot but accomplished little. The long and dark nights, coupled with the forested terrain along the front, made it difficult to target the Finnish troops successfully from the air.[51] According to Russian captives, the bomber pilots navigated by map and compass until reaching an easily identifiable point, such as a lake, located 60–80 kilometers from their target. They would then follow an identifiable line, such as a river, leading from the lake to the target. They would approach the target from 4,000–7,000 meters and maintain this altitude during bombing raids. Sometimes they would drop down a few thousand meters to ensure greater accuracy or to mislead the Swedish fighters that were waiting to interfere in the attack. Since the bombs were generally dropped from high altitude at a rate of a few seconds between each bomb, however, the accuracy was often poor.[52] The lack of good dive bombers also forced the Russian pilots to use horizontal flight when bombing targets such as bridges, which severely affected the accuracy of their aims. One Soviet commander disclosed that eighty bombers sent to destroy a bridge overflew the target horizontally in a long line at an altitude of 1,200 meters, yet only one bomb actually struck the target.[53] The pilots seldom used clouds as cover. The weather was for the most part clear and, according to Soviet captives, most pilots did not possess the knowledge to fly through clouds safely.[54]

By bombing the cities at the start of the campaign, Stalin hoped to break the Finnish will to resist. But it soon became evident that the attacks had the opposite effect and only strengthened Finnish resolve. With the exception of the surprise bombing of Helsinki, which resulted in ninety-one civilian casualties, the Finnish losses proved minimal.[55] Not until the pilots had gained some experience in night operations toward the end of the war, did their courage and skill begin to take a toll on the Finnish army.[56]

Other problems relating to geography quickly became apparent. Since Russia's border with Finland was long and uneven, it was necessary to operate in several theaters simultaneously, and the predominantly north-south orientation of the border generally prevented the Red Army from engaging in surprise attacks. The sparsely populated areas close to the border would in any case have made it impossible to control the citizens of Finland. The logistical difficulties were a nightmare and restricted the number of troops that could actually be utilized. The soldiers and animals needed a steady supply of food, and the vehicles needed fuel, oil, and spare parts, all of which had to be transported through a system of roads which was nearly nonexistent. Not even horses could get through. Provisions therefore had to be unloaded and hand carried to the troops. Because of these limitations, the Red Army was unable to bring overwhelming force at the decisive point. Along one narrow road, there was such a traffic jam "that it took several days for many senior officials to relieve it."[57] Living off the land or taking what one needed from nearby farmers was not possible, since the season did not allow it and farms were few and far between. As stated in an article in *Life* magazine, "The forests and tundras of northern Finland allow of no living off the country. Any invading force must bring its supplies with it and the numbers that can be used are strictly limited by the availability of roads and of motor transport."[58]

Simultaneously, wounded soldiers and animals along with materiel in need of repair had to be transported in the opposite direction back to Russia. If the needs of the army exceeded the number of transports that could be conducted at a time, delays would occur that would inevitably prevent the soldiers from functioning.[59] In times like these, the lack of coordination between combat arms became particularly apparent. When discussing with the chiefs of the artillery why the infantry would not move forward, one commander was told that the roads were clogged with guns. When suggesting that the guns be taken to the woods, he was told that it was not possible because there were no roads in the woods. Thus, neither the artillery with the big guns, nor the infantry, which was barricaded by their own artillery on the roads, could move.[60]

The difficulties naturally led to low morale. Although at least one commander of the Finnish Army considered the Russians generally well-trained and ferocious fighters displaying contempt for death,[61] analysis of the war revealed that the troops could not fall back on their superior numbers and were overly afraid of encirclement. "As soon as they saw a dozen of Finns on a flank, they shouted out that they were encircled,"[62] which was particularly detrimental since the Finns' main tactic was the divide and encircle *motti*. The firing seemed to come out of nowhere. Even when courageous and refusing to retreat, the Russians could often not see the enemy hiding in the forest. Troops operating in forested conditions also tended to lose their bearings, split from their group or drop behind their peers, or even fire by mistake at their own comrades.[63] Khrushchev complained that the Red Army had proven unsuccessful in the most rudimentary tasks. For example, the Soviets failed to sink a Swedish merchant vessel they had mistaken for a Finnish ship; an incident which Hitler mocked by asking Stalin if he needed the assistance of the well-trained German troops: "You can't even sink an unarmed ship? Maybe you need some help from us?"[64] It was a horrible time, recalled Khrushchev. Not only did the Soviet Union suffer enormous losses, Hitler insisted on standing back and gleefully observing the beatings the Russians took.[65]

In April 1940, shortly after the Winter War had ended, the Soviet leadership joined Stalin to analyze their accomplishments, or lack thereof, in a meeting "convened on the initiative of the Chief Military Council for summing up the results and taking account of the experience gained by the command personnel in the war with Finland." The focus was particularly the shortcomings of the army organization, leadership, and command.[66] It was determined that the Finnish troops were well trained in defensive tactics and had made good use of the terrain and camouflage suits. Moreover, their firing was well planned and coordinated for maximum effect.[67] The Soviet infantry, by contrast, was utterly unprepared for fighting in rough terrain and cold weather. They could not maneuver well "because they were overloaded and wore bulky outfits," and their shoes failed to protect against frostbite in the cold temperatures.[68] Soviet tactics in all larger offensives focused on attrition by wearing down the Finnish forces, rather than on reaching a decisive victory as quickly as possible. The Russians surely knew that the Finns lacked manpower and could not relieve their frontline troops. Yet, the Red Army's systematic and ordered way of attacking, without making an effort to properly camouflage the troops or use any form of surprise, gave the Finnish artillery an opportunity to capitalize on their skill, particularly the ability to concentrate all fire in unison against a detected enemy target. A Russian prisoner is said to have uttered, "Since your artillery is so phenomenally precise, why don't you shoot more often?" The problem, of course, lay in the Finns' scarcity of ammunition.[69]

Stalin's generals also informed him that bayonet fighting on skis had proven nearly impossible, and the skis the troops were issued were too long and narrow. An airborne party could not be dropped into the combat zone because the terrain demanded the use of skis, which were either not available or completely unsuitable. Although the Finns relied on their small *puukko* knives in hand-to-hand fighting in the trenches, the Soviet troops had no good weapons for such encounters. They could not use rifles at very close range, and the bayonets proved too long. It was suggested after the war that bayonets be shortened, made sharper, and shaped to resemble a dagger, and that knives be issued to individual soldiers. The generals thus acknowledged the weaknesses of modern technology. Many of the troops had also failed to use the weapons they were provided and tended to fall back on more primitive techniques, because the Finns proved so efficient.[70]

After the war, several recommendations were made and measures taken to strengthen the Red Army in preparation for meeting coming hostilities with confidence. The 1936 field service manual and the 1938 draft manual, for example, were revised with respect to winter operations in "woody and swampy terrain." The current sections were outdated. Not only were they very short but directions ran "counter to modern warfare." The suggestion that "in snowy winter the troops normally advance along roads" rather than to the sides had been exceptionally treacherous to the Red Army. Many of the setbacks they had suffered were a direct result of commanders insisting on following the manuals to the letter. It was also the opinion of the Russian commanders that most troops were severely lacking in physical endurance, likely because the manuals did not emphasize physical training as part of the soldier's basic education. One commander noted how his own training from 1917, in a "very tough regiment," had instilled some good habits and made him "keen on sports" even now at the age of forty-five.[71]

Stalin, who had succeeded in expanding into the Baltic states and Poland, failed in Finland because he failed to recognize the impact of the geographical location and the season, and because he did not understand the Finnish mentality despite the close relationship that Russia had enjoyed with Finland through much of its history. The war cost Russia so dearly not only because of faulty intelligence with respect to Finland's defensive capabilities, but because the region had not been studied and the intelligence officers had not been consulted before the war began.[72] To many of the troops, this was also their first experience of warfare. Even those who had fought in the Polish campaign had seen no serious battles. The tough Finnish resistance naturally caused some tense nerves. As stated by one senior sergeant, when the enemy guns fired a salvo, "[w]e all fell on each other! I remember that our cook was so scared that he put a pot on his head."[73] The Winter War was also Stalin's first test of a major full-scale invasion. When he marched into Poland, the Polish state had already been weakened by the Germans. This was not the case with Finland, whose citizens had not experienced conflict since the War of Independence twenty years earlier.[74]

Why did Stalin attack at the start of winter instead of waiting a few months for spring and more favorable weather? As noted previously, one reason was because he believed that the war would last only two weeks and Finland would be delivered to him by his birthday. Another reason was because he needed to secure Leningrad while the circumstances in Europe were still favorable. If the war between the Great Powers shifted toward the eastern front before he had secured Finland, he would have to focus all his forces on preventing an invasion.[75] It was also easier to move troops with motorized equipment at the start of winter when the ground and lakes were frozen but the snow cover so thin that skis and sleds could not yet be used efficiently.[76] Hitler, who had laid low during the conflict but followed it with interest, took a different view, however. In a letter to Mussolini on March 8, 1940, he stated that "Russia, I am convinced, never intended to take up this fight, for otherwise she would have chosen a different season of the year."[77]

Although Stalin failed to control Helsinki or acquire any larger parts of Finland, and despite the terrible losses the Red Army suffered in a war that lasted much longer than the predicted two-week "walkover," modern research indicates that the Red Army may not have been quite as ineffective as generally professed. Although seriously challenged, the troops continued to display unit cohesion, good morale for the most part, and a desire to win the war. Morale suffered mainly because the soldiers expected the war to be over by Christmas as they had been promised.[78] Stalin had also misled the troops by stating that the Finns would welcome them with open arms and view the Red Army's march into Finland as a war of liberation from an oppressive capitalist regime.[79] It is theorized that it was not merely the inefficiency of the Red Army that prevented Stalin from reaching his original goal. Rather, it was foreign support for Finland, international pressure, and poor publicity that contributed to his decision to end the war at a time when he might still have had a chance to take Helsinki by force.[80] All other factors remaining constant, a different time and place of battle and more candid communication with his soldiers might well have shifted the war in Stalin's favor.

What did the war accomplish for the Soviet Union? Although it is possible that the invasion of Finland was part of a greater plan of imperialism and expansion into Sweden, Khrushchev insisted that Stalin's only goal was to protect Leningrad. Since Finland had little to offer with respect to natural resources, making Finland a protectorate of Russia was not considered.[81] Regardless of whether or not this was true, and despite the course that history took, it is interesting to speculate. Had Stalin succeeded at advancing all the way to Helsinki, what would have happened to Sweden? When the Continuation War started, was the Red Army tougher and better equipped than it would have been had it not learned from the tremendous losses it had suffered in the Winter War? One soldier admitted that the trials he lived through in Finland were of great value to him in the Great Patriotic War (the part of World War II that was fought on the Eastern front) and taught him to "support the rifle units in battle and co-ordinate with them."[82] Although the formidable

Finnish resistance might have reinforced Hitler's belief that Russia could be beaten, the war acted as a catalyst for Stalin to modernize his forces and prepare for future conflicts with Germany. Another soldier considered the Winter War of no value at all. It had been "a political failure and a military defeat.... Our dead comrades remained buried in foreign soil."[83]

Combat Operations in the Swedish Army

World War II prompted the greatest military buildup in modern Swedish history. The defense budged, paid for through an increase in taxes and defense loans, increased from 234 million crowns in 1938–39 to 2,010 million crowns in 1940–41. Every new day of Finland's struggle against Russia was considered a reprieve used to strengthen Sweden's armed forces.[84] The focus was on keeping the country outside the war in Europe. Despite the neutrality declaration, the leadership was concerned that Sweden would get attacked as soon as the warring powers found it in their interest to do so. The Winter War had created a conscience among Swedish politicians about Finland's value to Sweden, and reinforced the need for organized cooperation between the Nordic countries.[85] Prime Minister Per Albin Hansson, fully realizing the importance of protecting Sweden from foreign aggression, formed a coalition government comprised of left and right parties, who could hopefully work together and preserve Swedish neutrality. Yet, the government was at odds with the people, who blamed the leadership for being overly cautious.

To make matters worse, Stalin's request for territory in Finland in the autumn of 1939 fell on deaf ears. Finland rejected the proposal in part because the country counted on military assistance from Sweden.[86] But Sweden was militarily weak from years of cutbacks in defense spending, and therefore took great care to avoid angering Stalin. The recruitment and training of volunteers for Finland was initially kept a secret and certain newspapers, mainly those with a communistic bent, were censored. It was not a matter of morality but of surviving as unaffected by the war as possible.[87] If Sweden did not lie low, Stalin might stage an offensive to justify an invasion, much as he had done in Finland with the shots fired at Mainila. Moreover, even if Finland agreed to concessions, it was not clear what Stalin ultimately had in mind. Would the initial requests for territory satisfy him, or would he ask for more until the Soviet Union would completely engulf Finland and also threaten Sweden? When the Swedish cabinet minister Herman Erikson visited the Soviet Union in September 1940, Molotov uttered that the Winter War was really Sweden's and not Finland's war.[88]

Although Hansson expressed hope of growing cooperation between Finland and Sweden, he was unwilling to say how far Sweden would go in Finland's true hour of need.[89] It soon became clear that some form of active participation was necessary in order to ease the suffering of the Finnish people and prevent the war from spreading to Swedish soil. Although the winter that followed Hitler's invasion of Poland was so cold that it drove the Swedes to stay indoors by the fire, the war made them feel morally obliged to fight in the Finnish wilderness for the sake of preserving Nordic independence.[90] Success in recruiting volunteers was directly tied to the amount of moral support from home. Prior to the 1930s, technology that allowed the quick spread of information had been largely nonexistent. By World War II, newspapers and radio broadcasts reached millions of households and contributed to heated debates that roused sympathy for the Finns and motivated large numbers of Swedes to volunteer in Finland. The Soviet invasion of their friendly neighbor was clearly viewed as a David and Goliath type scenario.[91]

Despite Sweden's refusal to send government sanctioned troops to Finland, the two countries cooperated regarding the defense of the Åland Islands by placing mines in the waters. Swedish volunteer battalions relieved Finnish battalions for redeployment elsewhere. (It is believed that the Soviets never realized that the Finns at the front at Märkäjärvi had been replaced with Swedes. All Soviet propaganda transmitted through the radio was in Finnish.[92]) The volunteers encountered several problems upon their arrival in the combat zone, however. Since 1926, only half of those obligated to serve in the military had received training in the use of weapons, and very few had been trained in winter warfare.[93] Some of the more important work may have been done by the F19 volunteer flight squadron, which managed to keep the railway open for continued shipments of supplies to Finland. Through its presence in the region, it signaled that the enemy was no longer safe against air attacks, and likely contributed to the Red Army's retreat back to Märkäjärvi in the middle of January 1940.[94]

Although the experiences during the two months of air battles between the Swedish and Russian pilots must be viewed against the particular conditions that shaped the war, some general conclusions can be drawn. The activities of the F19 flight squadron were limited by the few airplanes available and the great distances that had to be flown (the main base was more than 150 kilometers from the areas that were defended). The poor maps and snow-covered forests in northern Finland caused difficulties with navigation. Navigational marks consisted mainly of a few roads and railroads, or lakes that were easily identifiable. The Soviet bombers were faster than the Swedish fighters. Since a chase and catch-up did not prove possible, attacks must be undertaken from a position of superior altitude. After the initial losses the first day, it was determined that it was too dangerous to attack enemy targets during daytime hours with the slow bombers the Swedes utilized, and that subsequent attacks were to be conducted after dark. The Russian fighters of type I-15 and I-16 were also difficult to combat due to their superior armor and performance. Much of the volunteer activity therefore had to take a defensive form. Rather than meeting the enemy actively in air battle, the pilots focused on defending cities and villages. The enemy's fighter bases were located on lakes to the north and northeast of Märkäjärvi and by Kairala, approximately forty-five kilometers to the rear of the foremost infantry lines. Their bomber bases were located in a sector that stretched from the north to the southeast. Thus, even if the weather did not permit air activity in the northern part of Finland, incoming attacks by air could still be expected from the east and southeast.[95]

Of particular interest might be the trials of the two Swedish pilots, Per Sterner and Arne Jung, who were taken prisoners by the Soviets after a midair collision and bailout on January 12, 1940. Reports of their experiences upon their release in May 1940 revealed that Sterner had lost rudder control of his aircraft and gone into a 90-degree dive toward the left. After giving his reconnaissance pilot the sign to jump, he prepared to follow. Although getting out of the aircraft had proven difficult in the strong wind that pressed his upper body against the seatback, the touchdown in the forest was soft thanks to the deep snow cover. Shortly after landing with his parachute, Sterner was able to make contact with Jung, the pilot from the aircraft with which he had collided. The two pilots escaped the collision and bailout uninjured, and started a search for their downed airplanes to recover skis and provisions, but to no avail. After spending two uneventful nights in the wilderness sleeping under the pine trees with the parachutes rigged up as a tent, they decided by dusk on January 14 to seek shelter in an abandoned barn nearby. With provisions down to one can of food and a few crackers, it was crucial that they made their way back to friendly lines. Although many cottages stood empty in the Finnish wilderness, and a whiff of smoke from a chimney or the lack of frost on an outside wall could easily give one away, Sterner and Jung were in desperate need to warm their frozen fingers and toes. After entering the barn and building a fire, they received a few hours of rest. Shortly thereafter, human voices along the road outside disturbed the silence. Somebody shouted in Finnish for them to come out. Their immediate impression was that a Finnish patrol had found them, but it soon became clear that the voices belonged to the enemy.[96]

Sterner and Jung were brought to the Russian base approximately one kilometer away. They were treated well at first, and were allowed to keep personal effects such as watches. The Russian commander gave them warm tea and canned meat to eat. As reported by Sterner, their captors were poor skiers, but well dressed and disciplined. Communicating mainly through sign language, the Russians indicated that they had found one of the downed aircraft and a crewmember who unfortunately was "asleep." (Anders Zachau lost his life as a result of the incident. His body was not recovered until in 1942. Three others made their way back to friendly lines on skis through the forest. It is not entirely clear which crewmember the Russians were referring to.) Continued interrogations in German focused on the location of the Finnish bases. The Russians also took turns bragging about their skill in air-to-air battle. Soon, the prisoners were on their way to Moscow. Part of the trip went by train and part by open truck. The horribly cold temperatures did not help their frost injuries. They continued to be well fed, however, and were even given a shave by a beautiful female barber.[97]

When arriving in Uhta in Russia, the interrogations took a different turn. Sterner and Jung were locked inside a wooden non-insulated single story structure, with a snowdrift slowly building in the corner of their cell. The temperature reached only a degree or two above freezing. They were fed three meals of cabbage or macaroni soup and Russian bread a day. On rare occasions, they received warm water or a sugar cube for their tea. The lack of fat in their diet made it impossible to stay warm in the drafty cell. Most of the guards were quite humane, however, offering the prisoners gifts of tobacco and newspaper for rolling cigarettes, and even allowed them to visit the hospital a couple of times a week to get their wounds looked after.[98]

Much time was spent feeding the prisoners propaganda, and coercing them into writing and signing letters favorable to the Soviet Union. It was the "hawk" Mannerheim, supported by the French-English bloc, who was responsible for starting the war, right? His purpose was to help the "whites" oppress the Finnish proletarian working class, right? Or, why else were they fighting against the Soviet Union? How much did Mannerheim pay them? Could they describe the location of the aircraft bases the volunteers used? It was the Swedish government that was behind the volunteer fighter squadron, right? Would Sweden officially join Finland in the war? What would they like to write as their last words to their families? Or, if they wanted to live, all they had to do was speak the truth and apply for citizenship within the Soviet Union. With time, they could work themselves into respected positions in society. Some interrogation sessions, conducted by a translator speaking broken English, lasted up to twenty hours and took Sterner and Jung to the breaking point. Their future was uncertain. In a few days they might be executed, they were told, or sent to Siberia. Escape was unthinkable in light of the cold weather, the long distances, and the deteriorating conditions of their bodies. Not only did they go without sufficient food and exercise, their frostbitten hands and feet prevented them from undertaking long marches.[99]

On May 10, nearly two months after the war ended, Sterner and Jung were released and returned to Sweden in exchange for Soviet prisoners of war.[100] Concerned that it might harm Swedish-Soviet relations, the Swedish government forbade them to speak openly about their experiences in Russian captivity. Hitler had by then occupied Norway and Denmark, and good relations between Sweden and Russia proved crucial. Should Sweden end up in conflict with Germany, the country might no longer be able to secure basic necessities from the Western world.[101]

What did the war accomplish for Sweden? Sweden was fortunate that the war ended when it did. Had the volunteers continued in serious and prolonged combat, they would likely have suffered great numbers of casualties due to their lack of training and combat experience. Although they benefited from the relatively poor training of the Red Army, the sheer numbers of Soviet soldiers, their firepower and access to modern equipment would likely have annihilated the Swedish volunteer force come spring.[102] Success in war required weapons and equipment, but foremost men on the ground. The Soviet army was so exceptionally large that no matter how many volunteers or how much materiel Sweden sent to Finland, the final outcome would likely have favored the Soviet Union. Although the volunteers' presence in northern Finland freed up several Finnish battalions to fight on the Karelian Isthmus where the heaviest action took place, and Finland valued the assistance so highly that they entrusted the volunteers with defending the whole part of northern Finland, it is doubtful if it had a lasting effect on the outcome of the war.[103] It would also be naïve to think that Sweden's enthusiasm for the volunteer corps and humanitarian efforts would have been never ending. Stalin's numerical superiority finally enabled him to claim the victory. Thus, despite the emotional support and the large volunteer force that Sweden sent to Finland, for all practical purposes, Finland had stood alone in its fight against the giant enemy to the east. The only consolation to the hard-won peace may have been the fact that had Finland received no help at all, the outcome could have been even more severe.

Other factors relating to the war in Finland might have contributed to the security of the smaller European nations. For example, the "russification" of the Baltic states was delayed by several months, which gave Rumania breathing room and time to prepare its army for coming hostilities. One of the more important consequences of the war may have been the degradation of the Soviet Union's military capability. The underestimation of Stalin's potential gave Germany increased motivation to attack the superpower in 1941.[104] The most important military benefit that Sweden gained through its volunteer efforts in Finland, however, might have been insight into the caliber of its troops and how well they would hold up under enemy fire. When the Continuation War started, for fear that it might spread to Sweden, Supreme Military Commander Olof Thörnell thought it a good idea for Swedish soldiers to continue gaining combat experience in the east. In cooperation with the Swedish government, he gave 5,200 volunteers permission to serve in Finland in 1941. The Swedes did not sympathize with Finland as deeply this time, however, in part because Finland was siding with Germany who had occupied Norway and Denmark and thus become the dominant power in the region, and in part because the Finns were fighting to the east of their previous territorial limits.[105] The men enlisting for the Continuation War did so mainly because they felt a need to conclude a chapter of their lives that had been left unfinished.[106] Orvar Nilsson, a veteran of the Winter War and the Continuation War recalled how everybody in officer school in 1940 wanted to go to Finland, but few were selected. Many of the men who had signed up for the Winter War never got the opportunity to participate in combat since the war had ended abruptly on March 13, 1940. They were disappointed in how the conflict was resolved and felt that they were never given a true opportunity to make a difference. The Continuation War gave them a second chance. The Swedes were not fighting for Hitler's Germany, however, but against the Russians, and insisted that they knew or cared little about Nazis.[107]

The Geopolitical Landscape

The small countries of Sweden and Finland may not be prominent political world powers, yet they constitute a corridor between Europe and Russia, and therefore a political balance point. They have historically proven economically significant because of their location by various waterways and trade routes, and thus strategically significant in the struggles between the superpowers. Although Sweden lost its superpower status in its defeat in the Battle of Poltava in 1709 and had to cede Finland to Russia in 1809, the country has nevertheless remained an influence in Europe through its central location by the Baltic Sea, and its territory has been coveted by warring powers well into the twentieth century. Sweden's geographical location proved both a blessing and a constraint to the leadership. The extensive coastline, which includes many rivers for inland travel, led to the country developing a maritime culture early in its history. The Vikings, for example, proved successful largely as a result of their ability to travel by ship on rivers, lakes, and oceans.

When Sweden held superpower status in the seventeenth century, expansion was aimed primarily at the areas to the east. Expanding to the west would have required travel over extensive bodies of open water and would have meant conflicts with other seafaring nations, such as England and Holland. Moreover, the Swedes were culturally close to the Finns, although Russia directly to the east of Finland remained a traditional enemy of both countries. Since Russia did not have access to many ports even after it acquired Finland — those by the Gulf of Finland and the Gulf of Bothnia tended to freeze over in winter — it was largely limited to land-based warfare. Defending against hostilities from the east thus became a matter of using Finland as a buffer against the large Russian armies before these reached the Swedish border.

At the start of World War II, a Russian invasion of Sweden was thought possible if coming through northern Scandinavia via the way of Finland. Any war with Russia would therefore preferably be fought on Finnish soil by the Finnish-Russian border, or if the Russian troops managed to advance across Finland, by the Swedish-Finnish border in northern Sweden. There was also a slight possibility that Russia would rely on its bases in the Baltic states of Estonia, Latvia, and Lithuania for launching an attack against Sweden. Geographical location proved particularly detrimental, because Sweden was placed very close to the center of the action, halfway between Germany and Russia. Had the country's location been more at the periphery of the region, the tug-of-war that Sweden was exposed to would likely have been less severe. The access to numerous ports and waterways made Sweden very attractive also to the Western Allies, who could find no easy way of transferring troops and supplies to Finland except through Swedish territory. Neither the Allies, Germany, or Russia may have been interested in laying claim on Swedish territory per se, had it not been for the strategic location of the country and its abundant supply of natural resources.

Finland as a buffer state faced an even more precarious social and political situation and had to count on neighboring states to go to war for its cause. Politically and socially Finland was leaning toward Sweden even in peacetime, in the hope that Sweden would come to its aid should hostilities break out. Finland had been subjected to war several times in its history whenever conflicts had developed between Sweden and Russia. Although Finland mistrusted Russia based on prior experiences as a Grand Duchy under the Russian Empire, the Finnish leadership was trying to improve the diplomatic relations with Stalin and find a favorable end to hostilities. Stalin worried not only that an enemy power might use Finland to launch an invasion against Leningrad, however, but that Finland would turn more and more toward Western ideals. Between April 1938 and April 1939, Russia and Finland had undertaken a series of negotiations, in which Stalin had made it clear that he had no doubts that Germany would eventually attempt to attack Russia.[108] The situation worsened with the development of new political relations between the Soviet Union and Germany, and with British and French interference in Germany's dealings in Poland.[109]

With heightening tension in the area, Stalin proposed that Finland agree to deny German troops access to its territory. If they came anyway, then Russia would send military and economic assistance to Finland. If Finland openly acknowledged that it did not intend to stand against a German invasion, however, then Russia would invade Finland and advance as far as possible against the German troops, but would withdraw all forces as soon as the war was over.[110] Although Sweden's interests in Finland were predominantly emotional — aside from the fact that Finland acted as a buffer to Soviet aggression, Sweden had no interest in expanding its own territories further east — Russia's interests were mainly of military strategic necessity. Control of Finland would not only allow Russia to prevent hostile forces from using Finland as a "springboard" against Leningrad, it would also allow Russia to display a strong face outward in order to deter attack and create the illusion that the country was capable of raising a strong military force that could achieve its aims successfully. Russia naturally had to be defended with or without Finnish assistance, and deserves perhaps a bit of sympathy for the precarious situation the country would face if a foreign power, indeed, laid claims on its territory. As a former general in the tsarist empire, Mannerheim understood Russia's defensive needs and had urged Finland to agree to the initial requests for territory, rather than facing the giant Red Army on the battlefield.

Although Stalin naturally needed bases in the Baltic if his primary concern was the defense of Leningrad, the same could not be said for the Western Allies. Great Britain and France did not perceive Soviet naval power in the Baltic as a threat and were not concerned with assisting Finland when offering to send troops through Swedish territory. A German fleet in the region, by contrast, would have been catastrophic. In fact, Churchill had stated in a departmental note on October 27, 1939 that it was not in the best interest of Britain to oppose Russia's attempts to establish naval bases in the Baltic, since opposition to the idea might strengthen German power in the region.[111] Simultaneously, he believed it would be detrimental to "stiffen Finnish resistance to Russian demands."[112] Because of these utterances, it might be particularly interesting to note that a few months later Churchill would be in favor of supporting Finland. Rather than joining the war on the side of the Finns, however, the Allies might have benefited from persuading Finland to make concessions to Russia and end the war as quickly as possible. The concern, of course, was not Finland, but the iron ore mines in northern Sweden. The problem was that Britain could not justify its condemnation of Germany's invasion of Poland, while ignoring the Soviet Union's invasion of Finland.[113] The peace treaty signed on March 13 degraded the prestige of Britain and France and was a diplomatic victory to Germany.[114] That an Allied invasion of Sweden was staved off at the last instant came as a tremendous relief to Sweden, and, in the end, must also have been a relief to Britain and France. Sending troops to Finland via Sweden and starting a war on a second front would likely have been a huge military blunder with grave consequences for the Allies.[115]

Swedish Neutrality

The Winter War which lasted roughly three months has often been viewed as a separate part of World War II history. It was not merely a conflict between Russia and Finland, however, but a collision between several states desiring to expand their empires and control the Baltic region. By the middle of February 1940, political tensions were at their height. The Allies had split motives of controlling the iron ore mines and opening a second front in Scandinavia; Germany was worried about the continued shipments of iron ore; and Russia was afraid of losing face if ending the war in Finland prematurely.[116] Countries cannot operate in isolation, however, but must rely on a number of political and diplomatic means in order to ensure their wellbeing. The geopolitical landscape and external environment proved crucial to Sweden's ability to exercise foreign policy. Although the Winter War may be considered a "little war" against the backdrop of World War II, it also had big consequences for the political developments in Europe and the Soviet Union. As has been demonstrated throughout this book, Finland's tough resistance and the political decisions made by the Swedish leadership influenced the strategy the Western Allies and Germany decided to pursue.

Sweden's involvement in the war was of a dual nature. The country sent a volunteer combat force approximately 8,000-men strong to Finland, while simultaneously resisting official military engagement. The extent of involvement necessary for the protection of Sweden's neutrality was heavily debated. Not only did the country have to prepare for military action against a possible invasion from a hostile power (or a formerly friendly power such as Great Britain or France), should Finland fall to Soviet dominance, Sweden could in theory face threats both from the east and west. Sweden's strategic location and access to numerous ports, and the Allies' desire to intervene in the deliveries of iron ore to Germany, proved particularly worrisome and forced Sweden to walk a diplomatic tightrope. Several events of importance might be noted prior to the outbreak of war. For example, the shift in the balance of power that came as a result of the Molotov-Ribbentrop pact of 1939, followed by Germany's invasion of Poland and the division of the Baltic states, was preceded by the Anglo-German Naval Agreement signed between Great Britain and Germany in 1935. In an attempt to improve the relations between the countries and ease the restrictions imposed on Germany by the Versailles Treaty, the agreement allowed Germany to increase the size of its navy until the total tonnage of the *Kriegsmarine* reached 35 percent of the total tonnage of the British Royal Navy. The simultaneous withdrawal of the Royal Navy from the Baltic Sea made Germany the dominant power in the area.[117] Winston Churchill worried about the potential consequences for the Scandinavian peninsula, however, and expressed his dissatisfaction with the agreement:

> Europe was astonished to learn that the British government had made a private bargain for themselves about naval strength with Nazi Germany [which] condoned the breaking of treaties about naval strength at the very moment when they were urging the smaller powers of Europe to make a combined protest against breaking of the military clauses. This was a heavy blow at all international cooperation in support of public law. They now found themselves high and dry, and the interests of Scandinavia and the Baltic were profoundly affected.[118]

Sweden's political leadership clearly understood the dangers that were brewing on the horizon. Although desiring to remain on good terms with his neighbors, Prime Minister Per Albin Hansson was quick to assure the people that Sweden was well prepared to defend its sovereignty and started a massive rearmament program in order to strengthen the country's defenses and give weight to his words. It was fully legal for a neutral state to increase its military preparedness even if it had no intention of entering the war, for example, by instituting a draft, conducting training maneuvers, or manufacturing war materiel. Some people also considered it unlikely that a simple neutrality declaration would allow Sweden to remain outside the war, since several factors, many of which were not in the hands of the Swedish government, played a part in the proceedings and ultimately in the success or failure of the warring powers.

The problem with neutrality was two-fold: It had legal ramifications as expressed by the Hague Convention. For example, a neutral country was obligated to take countermeasures against violations of its territory even if these measures required the use of armed force (which should not be interpreted to mean that the country had become a belligerent in any war). And it had emotional ramifications as expressed by the Swedish peoples' wishes to remain outside the war. Although a neutral state could not actively support a warring power or allow it to make neutral territory, including water and air space, a theater of war, it had the right to enter into trade contracts including dealings of arms and ammunition with any of the belligerents for the purpose of acquiring necessities for its own citizens, but must do so on a mutual basis. In other words, Sweden could legally sell iron ore to Germany, but only if it also offered to sell to the Western Allies. Moreover, the duty of a neutral state to adhere to a principle of impartiality applied only to the operational and not the ideological level. Thus, a neutral state could openly sympathize — verbally, for example — with either of the belligerents without violating its neutrality. The conventions further stated that if a neutral state engaged in passive internal violation of its neutrality because the circumstances required that it trade with only one of the belligerents (to ensure food for the people, for example), it should not be interpreted to mean that it had taken sides in the conflict or desired to serve the political objectives of the particular belligerent with whom it had engaged in commerce.[119]

To some extent, a country's ability to remain neutral has to do with size. Although large states, which tend to have great political and economic influences on the world scene, are more or less forced to take an official stand and enter a war, small states have limited power and are at a severe disadvantage if drawn into conflict. A large state will likely survive as a sovereign nation regardless of the outcome of a war, but a small state may lose its very existence if things do not go in its favor. Even when small states try to avoid war, they may not be successful because of the interests of the belligerent powers. If choosing to remain neutral, a large state normally has the economic and industrial means and capacity to defend its neutrality. But a small state cannot defend its territorial integrity if a warring nation decides to breach its neutrality. Additionally, as was the case with Sweden, a neutral state can become the object of a tug-of-war between the belligerents and be compelled to ward off diplomatic pressures, if not military force, on two fronts.[120] Remaining neutral is therefore a delicate balancing act, particularly for a small state, and a complex political matter.

Thus, although Sweden never failed to declare that its foreign policy focused on keeping the country outside the war as a free and independent state, neutrality became a heavy burden and came under scrutiny several times. The difficulty associated with neutrality became painfully clear as the complexity of the conflict increased. Isolation was not an option. Since Sweden could not ignore geopolitical forces or external circumstances beyond its control, it came as no surprise when difficulties developed with respect to impartiality. Some states were naturally in possession of certain goods or resources that other states lacked. The warring powers to the west, for example, had different needs with respect to export and import than the warring powers to the east. Likewise, some states had greater economic capacity than others to buy certain desirable products; thus, the "illusion" that Germany benefited the most from Swedish exports of iron ore. The Allies viewed Sweden as Germany-friendly on account of the iron ore exports and, later, because Sweden granted German troops on leave transit through Swedish territory.

Sweden also took the liberty to "tweak" several gray areas of the conventions. For example, although it was clearly stated that a warring country could not transport troops, ammunition, and other provisions through neutral territory, a neutral state had the option of allowing transportation of weapons, ammunition, and other articles that could be of benefit to a warring army or navy, *if* the sender and receiver of such articles were private firms and not government-controlled entities. Furthermore, a neutral state had the duty to ensure that no recruitment offices were opened on its territory to the benefit of a warring power. Although it can be argued that Sweden violated this principle by allowing volunteers to be recruited for Finland, the article did not apply to private individuals who chose to volunteer in another country's armed forces. Sweden further managed to circumvent this article by assuming noncombatant, or nonbelligerent, status rather than neutrality with respect to Finland.[121]

The author acknowledges that it is debatable whether or not Sweden violated its neutrality internally by appearing to side with Germany more than with the Allies. As has been demonstrated, however, neutrality is a practical issue as much as a theoretical one. Every action or lack thereof has a consequence. When critiquing a neutral state, one must ask where a certain policy will ultimately lead. Strict codes can often not be adhered to if a neutral country's population is to survive, nor if the duty of the country is to act as a stabilizing force in the region. Had Sweden halted the iron ore exports to Germany, the world situation would likely have reached even greater instability. Sweden would have been pulled into the war, and its territory would have become a theater of operations for Germany and the Western Allies.

When fortunes turned toward the end of World War II, Sweden more openly sided with the Allies and reduced the economic benefits it had earlier granted Germany. For example, "in September 1944, Sweden closed its Baltic ports to German shipping, and the Swedish firm SKF [Svenska Kullager Fabriken — Swedish Ballbearing Factory] agreed to cease supplying its products, above all ballbearings, to Germany."[122] It is also important to note that the few Swedes who enlisted as volunteers in the German army were either adventurists or officers attempting to further their education. Their service to Germany was not considered a heroic deed, and many of these volunteers were not welcomed home with open arms when the war ended. The Swedish foreign minister emphasized that the government granted Swedish citizens permission to serve in other countries' armies only with respect to the defense of Finland. The Swedes serving in the German armies and in Waffen-SS were forced to travel to Norway or Denmark and enlist at a Nazi recruitment station located outside of Sweden.[123]

Although the Swedish government needed to protect the citizens from starvation resulting from a shortage of necessities such as coal, salt, and medical supplies which were imported from Germany, had Finland (or Sweden for that matter) taken larger losses in the Winter War, it is possible that the government would have welcomed the French-British alliance rather than opposing their transit through Swedish territory.[124] As noted by Winston Churchill, however, the neutral states of Sweden and Norway, "in equal fear of Germany and Russia, had no aim but to keep out of the wars by which they were encircled and might be engulfed."[125] How might World War II have progressed had an allied force 50,000-man strong been unleashed in Sweden and taken control of the iron ore mines? The Allies would likely have ended up at war not only with the Soviet Union but also with Germany, forcing them to fight on two fronts at a time when Germany was at its strongest.[126]

That Hansson's stubborn adherence to Swedish neutrality managed to keep Sweden outside the war was likely a combination of luck and foresight guided by good statesmanship. Great statesmen have vision to look beyond immediate temptations when determining the extent to which they shall exercise neutrality, or noncombatant status in the case of the Winter War. A statesman's highest obligation is the country's continued existence and the welfare of the people. No foreign state can therefore require that the citizens of a neutral country go to their deaths for others. That fact that many countries were dissatisfied with Sweden's decision to remain outside the war, and even accused Sweden of cowardice, does not change the fact that Sweden provided enormous help in the form of humanitarian missions while simultaneously protecting the safety and future of its own citizens. As the war ended, Sweden continued to profess neutrality and refrained from allying with a Western power even in peacetime.[127] The Soviet Union has traditionally been the only real threat that Sweden has faced. Had Sweden aligned itself with NATO after the war, however, the Soviet Union might have pressed to station military forces in Finland. Sweden would then have lost its strategic advantage and would no longer have been able to rely on Finland as a buffer against aggression from the east.

The degree to which Sweden remains or should have remained neutral continues to be debated in modern day. Although the elected politicians support the idea that all citizens of Sweden should defend their nation and maintain the country's democratic values while rejecting influences and pressures from foreign states, according to former Prime Minister Olof Palme (leader of the Social Democratic Party from 1969 to 1986, when he was assassinated), neutrality does not mean isolation, and does not excuse a country from its duty to promote peace, democracy, and social equality between people in the rest of the world. Although critics of Swedish neutrality claim that Sweden tries to have it both ways — Sweden refrains from forming coalitions with allies, yet meddles in the affairs of others, for example, by sending weapons, volunteers, and humanitarian aid to countries of choice — according to Palme, Sweden alone determines what neutrality politics means to Sweden.[128] Despite the fact that Sweden has not been involved in war since 1814 and has consistently adhered to a policy of neutrality, Sweden's neutrality politics is flexible and not necessarily permanent doctrine.[129] As long as Sweden refuses to align itself with any other state, however, it can continue to serve an important function by participating in peacekeeping and humanitarian missions, and maintaining the balance of power on the Scandinavian peninsula.[130]

Afterword

The combat activities and political actions of the Winter War are important fields of study because they had a major effect on international relations and the geopolitical landscape in Europe throughout World War II. Although this book has covered the trials and tribulations of the Finnish, Soviet, and Swedish armies, the emphasis has been on the problematic political situation of neutral Sweden. Sweden's geographical location made the country the focal point in the war between the Great Powers and was instrumental in shaping foreign policy. Control of the iron ore mines in the north and the shipping

TILL DE SVENSKA FRIVILLIGA

För ett stort och ädelt mål gingo Ni ut som frivilliga till Finland för att kämpa för dess och Nordens frihet.

Ni ha därigenom i handling visat, att "Finlands sak är vår". Svenska Frivilligkårens insats blev kort men hedersam och förtjänar hela vårt folks aktning och erkänsla. Finlandskommittén, som med varmaste intresse följt kårens öde, överlämnar härmed till Eder ett minnestecken, som skall vara Eder en erinran om Edert deltagande i Finlands hjältemodiga frihetskamp 1939—40.

Stockholm i maj 1940

FINLANDSKOMMITTÉN

273

Official letter of thanks issued by the Committee for Finland in May 1940 to the Swedish volunteers for their service in Finland and willingness to fight for Nordic independence (source: Krigsarkivet, Finlandskommitten, 1939–1940).

lanes through the Baltic Sea were crucial to Germany's continued success, and the Western Allies proved relentless in their attempts to use Finland's needs for international help as an excuse for taking possession of the mines.

During the Russo-Finnish negotiations preceding the war, three factors emerged as particularly important to Sweden: material assistance for Finland, mediation in the conflict, and neutrality rights and obligations. Sweden donated enormous amounts of war materiel to Finland, including antitank cannons, airplanes, rifles, and ammunition. With the approval of the government, businesses and private individuals alike engaged in humanitarian missions, collected clothing and monetary donations, and took thousands of Finnish children into foster care. Particularly noteworthy might be the volunteer force of more than 8,000 men who went to the front and faced the Red Army in bloody battles in support of Finnish independence and Western democracy. The fact that Sweden and Finland shared a history that stretched several hundred years contributed to the decisions that Sweden made with respect to material and military assistance for Finland.

The Finnish people had continued to display loyalty to the Swedish king even after Sweden had to cede Finland to Russia in 1809. Swedish citizens in turn supported Finland during its struggle for independence in 1918. When World War II broke out twenty years later, the Finns were no longer politically split but united in their strife for Western ideals. The Soviet invasion of Finland, without an official declaration of war only three months after Hitler's invasion of Poland, came as a shock to all of Europe, who expected a quick Soviet victory. Stalin's main concern was the protection of Leningrad, the heart of the Russian Empire and a city that had controlled the Karelian Isthmus, the land bridge between Russia and Finland, since it was founded as St. Petersburg in 1703. The "secret protocol" of the Molotov-Ribbentrop pact between the Soviet Union and Germany stipulated how the Baltic States were to be divided, and proved particularly detrimental to Finland's future.

Once the invasion of Finland was under way, the Soviet Union attempted to mirror Germany's *Blitzkrieg* tactics by cutting the country in half at the narrowest place and severing communications with Sweden. But restrictions imposed by weather and terrain severely hampered the mobility of the Red Army. The Finns were well versed in surviving in the wilderness and used innovative tactics to split the Soviet forces into manageable units that could be combated separately or starved and frozen into submission. After taking enormous losses in the first month of fighting, Stalin had to rethink his strategy and decided to fight a war of attrition along the Mannerheim Line. But Carl Gustaf Mannerheim, the Finnish Commander-in-Chief, had intricate knowledge of the character of the Russian state from having served in the armed forces of tsarist Russia for thirty years. Knowing that Finland had little hope of surviving the crisis without help from the international community, he appealed to the Swedish leadership for official assistance with armed troops.

The fact that Sweden had escaped military conflict since 1814, however, may have influenced the country's decision to stay outside the war. Even as moral support for Finland increased, the people's feelings were divided with respect to active military assistance. Sweden's Prime Minister Per Albin Hansson had worked most of his life to improve social equality and economic welfare for the citizens of his country, and was not willing to jeopardize the long period of peace and prosperity that Sweden had enjoyed. Mediation for a quick end to the conflict seemed the better alternative. Constant attempts by the Allies to gain access to Swedish territory and take possession of the iron ore mines meant that a long-lasting war could turn northern Sweden into a battleground for the Great Powers.

How necessary was Russia's war with Finland, and how did it ultimately affect the balance of power in the region? That Finland, a border country between east and west, succeeded in its strife against the superpower was deemed crucial to the maintenance of Western cultural, political, and economic values, and thus to the security of the Scandinavian peninsula. When the Soviet Union invaded Finland, it was the hope of many nations that Sweden would intervene in the conflict and agree to send government-sanctioned troops to Finland. In order for a country to practice a philosophy of neutrality, however, it must refrain from laying territorial claims on other nations or forming alliances even in peacetime, while simultaneously preparing to guard its own borders with armed force. Sweden displayed a consistent willingness to defend its territorial integrity, for example, by threatening to destroy its own infrastructure (tear up the railways) to prevent an Allied occupation of the country. Particularly noteworthy may be the fact that the Allies came within three days of invading Norway and Sweden with 50,000 French and British troops.

Of even greater importance than the stubborn adherence to neutrality politics may be the moral and emotional support that Sweden furnished Finland, in the form of an accepted willingness of the volunteers to offer their lives in the Finnish wilderness. The volunteers saw action at the front in the weeks before the war ended, and the flight squadron in the north flew for two months and logged hundreds of hours in combat operations against the Soviet air force. The anti-aircraft artillery in southern Finland, manned by several hundred volunteers, played an important part in strengthening Finland's defense. The volunteer combat force of 12,705 applicants, of which 8,260 were chosen, is the largest assembly of volunteers that any country has sent to the aid of another in a modern war.

Chapter Notes

Introduction

1. Finnish is an officially recognized minority language in Sweden. Many people in Finland likewise speak Swedish with proficiency. Still, Swedish, a North Germanic language, and Finnish, which belongs to the Baltic-Finnic (or Finnic-Ugric) group of languages, differ vastly. For example, the numbers one through five in Swedish (ett, två, tre, fyra, fem) are recognizably similar to English (one, two three, four, five), but very different from Finnish (yksi, kaksi, kolme, neljä, viisi). This example demonstrates the different roots of the two languages and the difficulty Swedes would have understanding Finnish. Finnish has more in common with the languages spoken in Estonia and Hungary than with the languages spoken in Sweden and the rest of Scandinavia.

2. See Nicolas von Schmidt-Laussitz, *Svenska Frivilliga (Swedish Volunteers)*, Svenska Frivilliga, http://www.svenskafrivilliga.com.

3. Sweden held "noncombatant" status in the Russo-Finnish Winter War, although the country did not officially declare itself as such. The Swedish government concerned itself with fundamental human rights and participated in several humanitarian and peacekeeping operations throughout both World Wars. Although Sweden declared neutrality in World War II, at the same time the country desired to maintain its trade relations with other states. Sweden had to compromise on several accounts with Germany in order to avoid future conflicts. Sweden has been criticized for allowing more than two million German soldiers on leave to pass through Swedish territory. Sweden's government maintains that the country's status of "active neutrality" does not mean isolation from the rest of the world and makes allowances, for example, for economic sanctions and humanitarian efforts.

4. See Lars Ericson, *Svenska Frivilliga: Militära Uppdrag i Utlandet Under 1800- och 1900-talen (Swedish Volunteers: Foreign Military Missions During the 1800s and 1900s)* (Lund, Sweden: Historiska Media, 1996), 7–8. The Sweden-Norway union was resolved peacefully in 1905.

5. Information from the Army Museum in Stockholm, Sweden, 2000. The Swedish casualties in each of these wars numbered in the tens to a few hundreds. The Spanish Civil War claimed 164 Swedish lives; the Russo-Finnish Winter War claimed 37.

6. A total of 26 nations supplied volunteer soldiers in smaller numbers for Finland's cause; however, most of the applicants never saw combat. A 300-man Finnish-American "legion" got its baptism by fire on the last day of the war. See Carl Gustaf Mannerheim, *Marskalkens Minnen (The Marshal's Memories)* (Helsingfors, Finland: Holger Schildts Förlag, 1954), 234. For cultural reasons, 25,000 Hungarian volunteers applied to go to Finland. But since Germany denied them transit, only 350 made it. See Göran Andolf, "Svenska Frivilligkåren (The Swedish Volunteer Corps)," *Svenska Frivilliga i Finland 1939–1940 (Swedish Volunteers in Finland 1939–1940)* (Stockholm, Sweden: Militärhistoriska Förlaget, 1989), 47.

7. See William Trotter, *A Frozen Hell: The Russo-Finnish Winter War of 1939–40* (Chapel Hill, NC: Algonquin Books of Chapel Hill, 2000), 196.

8. Sweden's concerns about the iron ore mines were warranted. At the conclusion of the Winter War on March 13, 1940, British General Henry Pownall revealed that not one of the four or five Allied divisions that might have been sent to Finland actually intended to assist the Finns. Rather, their sole interest was to occupy the mine fields. See Trotter, 254.

9. See Swedish Military History Library, *Den Stora Urladdningen (The Great Discharge)*, http://www.smb.nu/pos/06/01_europa_i_krig.asp.

10. See Finlandsfrivilliga, *Svenska Finlandsfrivilligas Minnesförening (The Association for Swedish Volunteers in Finland)*, http://www.finlandsfrivilliga.se/historik.html.

Chapter 1

1. See Freds Fördrag Emellan Hans Maj:t Konungen af Swerige och Sweriges Rike å ena, samt Hans Maj:t Keisaren af Ryssland och Ryska Riket å andra sidan, Fredricshamn den 17 September, 1809 (Peace Treaty between His Majesty the King of Sweden and the Kingdom of Sweden on the one hand, and His Majesty the Emperor of Russia and the Russian Empire on the other), http://www.histdoc.net/historia/se/frhamn.html. The original Swedish text to the treaty reads as follows: Article IV: "Hans Maj:t Konungen af Swerige afstår oåterkalleligen och för altid, så för Sig som Des Efterträdare til Swenska Thronen och Riket, samt til förmån för Hans Maj:t Kejsaren af Ryssland och Des Efterträdare til Ryska Thronen och Riket, från alla Des rättigheter och titlar til de härefter upräknade Höfdingedömen, hwilka af Hans Kejserliga Maj:ts wapn under detta krig blifwit från Kronan Swerige eröfrade, nemligen: Kymmenegårds Län, Nylands och Tawastehus, Åbo och Björneborgs med de Åländska Öarne, Sawolax och Carelen, Wasa och Uleåborgs Län, samt en del af Westerbotten ända til Torneå Elf, sådan som den uti nästa Art. om Gränsornes utstakande, skal utsättas. Dessa Län, med alla deras Innewånare, Städer, Hamnar, Fästningar, Byar och Öar, med deras tilhörigheter, företräden, rättigheter och afkastningar, skola härefter under full ägande rätt och Öfwerherrskap tilhöra Ryska Riket, och med detsamma blifwa införlifwade. Til följe häraf lofwar och utfäster Sig Hans Maj:t Konungen af Swerige, på det högtidligaste och mäst bindande sätt, så för Sig, som Des Efterträdare och hela Sweriges Rike, at aldrig göra något direct eller indirect anspråk å nämnde Höfdingedömen, Landskaper, Öar och Områden, hwilkas samtelige Inwånare, i kraft af nämnde afsägelse, skola frikännas från den tro- och huldhetsed de til Swenska Kronan aflagt." Article V: "Ålandshaf, Bottniska Wiken samt Torneå och Muonio Elfwar skola hädanefter utgöra Gränsen mellan Ryska och Swenska Rikena. På lika afstånd från kusterne skola de til fasta landet af Åland och Finland närmast belägne Öar tilhöra Ryssland, samt de närmaste til Swenska kusterne, tilhöra Swerige." Article X: "De Finnar som nu befinna sig i Swerige, äfwensom de i Finland warande Swenskar, skola hafwa full frihet at til deras Fädernesland återgå.... Til yttermera wisso hafwe wi Underteknade i kraft af wåre Fullmagter underskrifwit närwarande Freds-Tractat, samt den med wåre insegels undersättande bekräftadt, som skedde i Fredricshamn den 17 (5) September, år efter Christi börd det Ettusende Åttahundrade och på det Nionde."

2. See Olli Vehviläinen, *Finland in the Second World War: Between Germany and Russia* (New York: Palgrave Macmillan, 2002), 2.

3. See Claes Skoglund, "Sverige — Finland från Vikingatågen till Andra Världskriget (Sweden — Finland from the Vikings to the Second World War)," *Svenska Frivilliga i Finland 1939–1944 (Swedish Volunteers in Finland 1939–1944)* (Stockholm, Sweden: Militärhistoriska Förlaget, 1989), 22.

4. See MastersWork Media, *Fire and Ice: The Winter War of Finland and Russia*, produced and directed by Ben Strout, 2005.

5. See Skoglund, 24.

6. Ibid.

7. See Vehviläinen, 3. Nikolai Bobrikov was assassinated by the Finnish nationalist hero Eugen Schauman in 1904.

8. Ibid., 4.

9. See Claes-Göran Isacson, *Ärans Vinter: Finska Vinterkriget 1939–40 (A Winter of Honor: The Finnish Winter War 1939–40)* (Stockholm, Sweden: Norstedts Förlag, 2007), 20.

10. See Carl Gustaf Mannerheim, *Marskalkens Minnen (The Marshal's Memories)* (Helsingfors, Finland: Holger Schildts Förlag, 1954), 50.

11. Ibid., 89–90.

12. See Lars Ericson, *Svenska Frivilliga: Militära Uppdrag i Utlandet Under 1800- och 1900-talen (Swedish Volunteers: Foreign Military Missions During the 1800s and 1900s)* (Lund, Sweden: Historiska Media, 1996), 67.

13. See MastersWork Media.

14. Mannerheim, 69.

15. Ibid., 107 & 168.

16. See Ericson, 67.

17. See Skoglund, 27.

18. See Ericson, 67.

19. See Skoglund, 27.

20. Ibid., 28–29. The islands had originally been part of Sweden and had a large Swedish-speaking population. In the end, Sweden and Finland agreed that the islands should belong to the new and independent Finnish state, despite the fact that a vote among the islanders indicated that 96 percent were in favor of the islands belonging to Sweden.

21. See Vehviläinen, 10.

22. Ibid.

23. Ibid., 14.

24. See Efraim Karsh, *Neutrality and Small States* (New York: Routledge, 1988), 86.

25. See MastersWork Media.

26. See Geoffrey Roberts, *Stalin's Wars from World War to Cold War, 1939–1953* (New Haven, CT: Yale University Press, 2006), 52.

27. See Leif Björkman, *Det Svenska Vinterkriget, 1939–1940 (The Swedish Winter War, 1939–1940)* (Stockholm, Sweden: Hjalmarson & Högberg Bokförlag, 2007), 29.

28. Ibid., 31.

29. Treaty of Non-Aggression and Pacific Settlement of Disputes between the Soviet Union and Finland, concluded on January 21, 1932, translation published in *The Major International*

Treaties 1914–1973, by J. A. S. Grenville (London: 1974).

30. See Skoglund, 33.

31. The emotional blow that Germany suffered after its loss in World War I, along with a large unemployment rate and a complex political situation, may have been contributing factors to Hitler's invasion of Poland. Since the focus of this study is Sweden's role in the Winter War, however, and the accomplishments of the Swedish volunteers in the roughly one hundred day long conflict between Finland and the Soviet Union, a detailed study of the events that preceded World War II will not be included in this book. The reader is advised to resort to the numerous books and resources that already exist on this subject.

32. Nazi-Soviet Relations 1939–1941, Documents from the Archives of the German Foreign Office (Washington, DC, 1948), 78.

33. See Evgeni Nikolaevich Kul kov, *Stalin and the Soviet-Finnish War, 1939–40* (Portland, OR: Frank Cass Publishers, 2002), xx.

34. See MastersWork Media.

35. See Isacson, 20 & 43.

36. See Mannerheim, 275.

37. See Nikita Khrushchev, *Khrushchev Remembers,* translated by Strobe Talbott (Boston, MA: Little, Brown, 1970), 105.

38. Ibid., 126–127.

39. See Robert Edwards, *The Winter War: Russia's Invasion of Finland, 1939–40* (New York: Pegasus Books, 2008), 131.

40. See Carl Nordling, *The Molotov-Ribbentrop Pact Provoked the Outbreak of World War II,* http://www.carlonordling.se/ww2/stalinevoke.html.

41. See Carl Nordling, *Stalin's Speech to the Politburo on 19 August 1939,* reconstructed from Renderings in Novyi Mir, Moscow, and Revue de Droit International, Geneva, http://www.carlonordling.se/ww2/stalin_speech_complete.html.

42. See Harry Järv, *Oavgjort i Två Krig: Finland — Sovietunionen 1939–1944 (Undecided in Two Wars: Finland — the Soviet Union 1939–1944)* (Avesta, Sweden: Samfundet Sverige-Finland, 2006), 34–37.

43. See Khrushchev, 128–129.

44. Ibid., 149.

45. See Harald Öhquist, *Vinterkriget 1939–40 Ur Min Synvinkel (The Winter War 1939–40 from My View)* (Tammerfors, Finland: Tammerfors Handelstryckeri, 1949), 67.

46. Some people held the opinion that the friendship pact between Germany and the Soviet Union meant that Sweden and Finland had little to fear in case of a war in the rest of Europe, and that a conflict between Hitler and Stalin was unlikely. See Alf W. Johansson, *Per Albin och Kriget: Samlingsregeringen och Utrikespolitiken Under Andra Världskriget (Per Albin and the War: The Coalition Government and Foreign Policy During the Second World War)* (Stockholm, Sweden: Tidens Förlag, 1984), 63.

47. Edwards, 79.

48. See Jan Nilsson, *Svensk Diplomatrapportering Under Finska Vinterkriget Oktober 1939–Mars 1940 (Swedish Diplomacy Report During the Finnish Winter War October 1939–March 1940),* Artikelbiblioteket, http://members.chello.se/akademin/artikelbiblioteket/artiklar/arngren.htm.

49. See Gene Keyes, "Stalin's Finland Fiasco: The Kuusinen Government Reconsidered," first published in *Crossroads: An International Socio-Political Journal,* No. 17 (1985).

50. See Mannerheim, 191.

51. See Douglas Clark, *Three Days to Catastrophe: Britain and the Russo-Finnish Winter War* (London: Hammond, Hammond & Company, 1966), 29.

52. See Mannerheim, 191.

53. See Roberts, 46.

54. See MastersWork Media.

55. See Roger R. Reese, "Lessons of the Winter War: A Study in the Military Effectiveness of the Red Army, 1939–1940," *The Journal of Military History,* Vol. 72, No. 3 (Jul. 2008), 827.

56. See Kul kov, xvi.

57. See Greger Falk, *F19 — En Krönika: Den Svenska Frivilliga Flygflottiljen i Finland Under Vinterkriget, 1939–1940 (F19 — A Chronicle: The Swedish Volunteer Flight Squadron in Finland During the Winter War, 1939–1940)* (Stockholm, Sweden: Svensk Flyghistorisk Förening), 11–13.

58. See Isacson, 271–272.

59. See Lennart Ödeen, "Finland i Brännpunkten (Finland in Focus)," *Gefle Dagblad* (May 13, 2007).

60. See Clark, 26.

61. See Björkman, 43.

62. See Mannerheim, 192 & 248.

63. See Isacson, 64.

64. See Björkman, 42.

65. See MastersWork Media.

66. See Carl Nordling, *Stalin's Insistent Endeavors at Conquering Finland,* http://www.carlonordling.se/StalinFin.html.

67. See Nazi-Soviet Relations 1939–1941.

68. See Mannerheim, 331.

69. See Nazi-Soviet Relations 1939–1941.

70. See Öhquist, 69.

71. See Nazi-Soviet Relations 1939–1941.

72. See Documents on German Foreign Policy 1918–1945, Series D. Vol. VIII, No. 240 (Washington, DC: Department of State, publication 5436, 1954).

73. See Öhquist, 71–76.

74. The Versailles Treaty, signed in 1919, is perhaps one of the most controversial peace treaties ever signed and required that Germany accept full responsibility for World War I. The treaty also

stipulated that Germany yield control of several of its colonies and European territories, thereby giving Poland access to the Baltic Sea. The treaty, which was heavily protested by Germany, meant that many Germans became subjected to foreign rule.

75. See M. M. Borodin, editor-in-chief, "Report of Comrade V. M. Molotov, Chairman of the Council of People's Commissars and People's Commissar of Foreign Affairs, at Sitting of Supreme Soviet of USSR on Oct. 31, 1939," *Moscow News* (Nov. 6, 1939).

76. Ibid.

77. Ibid.

78. See Öhquist, 76.

79. See Nordling, *Stalin's Insistent Endeavors at Conquering Finland.*

80. See Öhquist, 76.

81. See Väinö Tanner, *The Winter War: Finland Against Russia 1939–40* (Stanford, CA: Stanford University Press, 1957), 48–49.

82. See A. K. Cajander, The address by Prime Minister A. K. Cajander on the 23rd of November 1939, at Helsinki Fair Hall, at a national defence celebration arranged by Finnish private enterprise owners, http://www.histdoc.net/history/cajander.html.

83. See Pravda, "A Buffoon Holding the Post of Prime Minister," *Pravda* (Nov. 26, 1939).

84. See Political Administration of Workers' and Peasants' Red Army (RKKA), *Propagandist and Agitator of the RKKA*, translated by Pauli Kruhse and Lahja Huovila, Moscow Nr. 22 (Nov. 1939).

85. See Edwards, 43.

86. See Björkman, 38.

87. See The Minister of Finland to the Secretary of State, Foreign Relations of the United States, Diplomatic Papers, 1939, Vol. I, General, Department of State, publication 6242, 1956.

88. See Björkman, 41–42.

89. See Öhquist, 77.

90. See Björkman, 42.

91. See Försvarsmakten (The National Defense, Sweden), http://www.mil.se.

92. Franklin D. Scott, *Sweden: The Nation's History* (Carbondale, IL: Southern Illinois University Press, 1988), 502.

93. See Försvarsmakten (The National Defense, Sweden). In 1941, the initial training period was again increased to a minimum of twelve months, with additional recurrent training occurring every sixth to twelfth year throughout a man's life. As a result, toward the end of the 1940s, Sweden once again had a well-trained force that stood ready to defend the country, including one of the best-developed air forces in Europe.

94. See Bengt Åhslund, "Det Militärpolitiska Läget vid Krigsutbrottet 1939 (The Military-Political Situation at the Outbreak of War 1939)," *Sveriges Militära Beredskap, 1939–1945 (Sweden's Military Preparedness, 1939–1945)*, edited by Carl-Axel Wangel (Stockholm, Sweden: Militärhistoriska Förlaget, 1982), 16.

95. See Försvarsmakten (The National Defense, Sweden).

96. See Skoglund, 32.

97. Scott, 503.

98. See Nils Palmstierna, "Mobiliseringen i September 1939 (The Mobilization in September 1939)," *Sveriges Militära Beredskap, 1939–1945 (Sweden's Military Preparedness, 1939–1945)*, edited by Carl-Axel Wangel (Stockholm, Sweden: Militärhistoriska Förlaget, 1982), 90.

99. See Thede Palm, "Förord (Introduction)," *Sveriges Militära Beredskap, 1939–1945 (Sweden's Military Preparedness, 1939–1945)*, edited by Carl-Axel Wangel (Stockholm, Sweden: Militärhistoriska Förlaget, 1982), 9.

100. See Beredskapsmuseet, *Per Albin Hansson*, http://www.beredskapsmuseet.com/peralbin.html.

101. See Carl-Axel Wangel, "Neutralitetsrätt — Regler och Tillämpning (Right to Neutrality — Rules and Application)," *Sveriges Militära Beredskap, 1939–1945 (Sweden's Military Preparedness, 1939–1945)*, edited by Carl-Axel Wangel (Stockholm, Sweden: Militärhistoriska Förlaget, 1982), 60.

102. See Palm, 11.

103. See Nils Palmstierna, "Krigsplanläggningen vid Krigsutbrottet (The Planned Defense at the Outbreak of War)," *Sveriges Militära Beredskap, 1939–1945 (Sweden's Military Preparedness, 1939–1945)*, edited by Carl-Axel Wangel (Stockholm, Sweden: Militärhistoriska Förlaget, 1982), 54–55.

104. See Åhslund, 15.

105. See Economic Expert, *Sweden During World War II*, http://www.economicexpert.com/a/Sweden:during:World:War:II.html.

106. See Carl-Axel Wangel, "Förstärkt Försvarsberedskap (Increased Defense Preparations)," *Sveriges Militära Beredskap, 1939–1945 (Sweden's Military Preparedness, 1939–1945)*, edited by Carl-Axel Wangel (Stockholm, Sweden: Militärhistoriska Förlaget, 1982), 73.

107. See Falk, 9.

108. See Arvid Cronenberg, "1936 Års Försvarsbeslut och Upprustningen 1936–1939 (The Decisions in Military Defense of 1936 and the Military Buildup of 1936–1939)," *Sveriges Militära Beredskap, 1939–1945 (Sweden's Military Preparedness, 1939–1945)*, edited by Carl-Axel Wangel (Stockholm, Sweden: Militärhistoriska Förlaget, 1982), 47–48.

109. See Svensk Utrikespolitik Under Andra Världskriget (Swedish Foreign Policy During the Second World War) (Stockholm, Sweden, 1946).

110. See Jan Nilsson, *Moder Svea och Kriget: Svensk Politik Under Andra Världskriget (Mother Sweden and the War: Swedish Politics During the Second World War)*, Artikelbiblioteket (1999),

http://web.comhem.se/akademin/artikelbiblioteket/artiklar/svepol.htm. The Scandinavian countries shared similar interests and languages with only small linguistic differences, and had been united through the Union of Kalmar from 1397 to 1523.

111. See Isacson, 223–224.

112. See Sarah Arildsson and Mikael Lidberg, *Vår Beredskap är God: En Studie Över den Militära Beredskapen i Övre Norrland, 1939–44 (We Are Well Prepared: A Study of the Military Preparedness in Upper Norrland, 1939–44)*, Luleå Tekniska Universitet, Sweden.

113. See Björkman, 7 & 10.

114. Ibid., 20, 68–70.

115. See Arildsson and Lidberg.

116. See Cronenberg, 28.

117. See Isacson, 24 & 43.

118. See Nilsson, *Svensk Diplomatrapportering Under Finska Vinterkriget Oktober 1939–Mars 1940 (Swedish Diplomacy Report During the Finnish Winter War October 1939–March 1940).* The casual observer might find it peculiar that Finland, a borderline country between the east and west with a language that differs vastly from Swedish, was of such emotional interest to Sweden. However, Sweden and Finland had been ruled as one country for more than six hundred years (1154–1809). The affiliation of Sweden and Finland before Finland was lost to Russia in the early nineteenth century had contributed to a Finnish population that was largely Swedish-speaking and largely Swedish or Scandinavian in its cultural norms. Business and other legal matters were generally conducted in Swedish. The joint capital, Stockholm, was located in Sweden, and Finns were part of the Parliament on equal terms with Swedes. Finland was not looked upon as a separate country; there was no definitive border that separated the Swedes from the Finns. See Björkman, 74. Moreover, during the Thirty Years' War, Finland had provided Sweden with one-third of the forces fighting in the historically great Swedish king Gustav II Adolf's army. The Swedes and the Finns therefore shared a military history. See Eloise Engle and Lauri Paananen, *The Winter War: The Soviet Attack on Finland 1939–1940* (Mechanicsburg, PA: Stackpole Books, 1973), xiii.

119. See Björkman, 74.

120. See Isacson, 190–191.

121. See NationMaster—Encyclopedia, *Gustav V of Sweden*, http://www.nationmaster.com/encyclopedia/Gustav-V-of-Sweden.

122. See Felicia Scholander, *Intervju Om Andra Världskriget med Lars Hallgren och Rut Scholander (Interview About the Second World War with Lars Hallgren and Rut Scholander)*, Levande Historia (Jan. 1, 2005), http://svefor.levandehistoria.se/1_0_1.php?id=4059.

123. See Karin Bülow Orrje, "En Svensk Tiger (A Swede Remains Silent)," *Värnpliktsnytt* (Nov. 25, 2008).

124. See Björkman, 18–19. Note that the Swedish kings of the twentieth century were ceremonial heads of state and generally did not get involved in politics. The government was run by the Prime Minister and democratically elected political parties.

125. See Vehviläinen, 24–25.

126. Sweden had strategic interests in the Åland Islands for the defense of Stockholm. The commander of Finland's armed forces, Carl Gustaf Mannerheim, had secretly worked with the Swedish military command on a plan for the defense of the islands. The islands had been the subject of dispute between Finland and Sweden for centuries; however, Sweden believed that the islands, inhabited mostly by a Swedish-speaking population, should rightfully belong to Sweden. Although the islands have achieved autonomy, they remain to this day a part of Finland. See Philip Marshall Brown, "The Aaland Islands Question," *American Journal of International Law*, Vol. 15, No. 2 (Apr. 1921), 268.

127. See Ericson, 215–221.

128. See Isacson, 217–218.

129. See Mannerheim, 177.

130. See Isacson, 213–216. There were also moral concerns regarding the defense of the Åland Islands. Although Finland desired help from Sweden, simultaneously it feared that Sweden would make a new attempt to annex the islands. Sweden, on the other hand, feared that if it failed to send Finland official military help, Finland might turn the predominantly Swedish island population into Finns. Given enough time, this would mean that Sweden would lose the close relationship it currently enjoyed with the islanders. See Johansson, 44–45.

131. See Björkman, 36.

132. Ibid., 17, 43 & 49.

133. See Carl-Axel Wangel, "Försvarsstabens Bedömningar Hösten 1939 (The Defense Establishment's Judgements in the Fall of 1939)," *Sveriges Militära Beredskap, 1939–1945 (Sweden's Military Preparedness, 1939–1945)*, edited by Carl-Axel Wangel (Stockholm, Sweden: Militärhistoriska Förlaget, 1982), 98.

134. See Tanner, 48.

135. See Memorandum of Conversation, by the Chief of the Division of European Affairs, Foreign Relations of the United States, Diplomatic Papers, 1939, Vol. I, General, Department of State, publication 6242, 1956.

136. See The Ambassador in the Soviet Union to the Secretary of State, Foreign Relations of the United States, Diplomatic Papers 1939, Vol. I, General, Department of State, publication 6242, 1956.

137. See Clark, 18–19.

138. The fact that Sweden was militarily weak because it had downsized its armed forces in the

years prior to the war contributed to the decision to continue supporting Germany with iron ore despite heavy protest from Britain and France.

139. See Edwards, 88.

140. See Clark, 19–20.

141. See W. H. Halsti, *Försvaret av Finland (The Defense of Finland)* (Stockholm, Sweden: P. A. Norsetdt & Söner, 1940), 86–87.

142. See Björkman, 17, 59–61. A Russian submarine with a crew of forty-six and four passengers, sunk in January 1940 by Swedish and Finnish mines, was rediscovered in February 2009 between the Swedish coast and the Åland Islands. See Per Nyberg, "Long-Lost World War II Sub Found off Swedish Coast," CNN, http://www.cnn.com/2009/WORLD/europe/06/09/sweden.ww2.sub/index.html.

143. See Gleb F. Chistov, Military Technician-Commissary 2nd Rank, 70th Automobile-Sanitary Platoon, 50th Rifle Corps, 7th Army, *The Mannerheim Line, 1920–39*, by Bair Irincheev, http://www.mannerheim-line.com/veterans/Chistove.htm.

144. See Göran Andolf, "Svenska Frivilligkåren (The Swedish Volunteer Corps)," *Svenska Frivilliga i Finland 1939–1940 (Swedish Volunteers in Finland 1939–1940)* (Stockholm, Sweden: Militärhistoriska Förlaget, 1989), 40.

145. See Nikita Chrusjtjov, "Vinterkriget Mot Finland (The Winter War Against Finland)," *Finska Vinterkriget, 1939–40 (The Finnish Winter War, 1939–40)*, http://www.marxistarkiv.se/europa/finland/finska_vinterkriget-artiklar.pdf. Otto Vilhelm Kuusinen became head of the Terijoki government, which was set up as a puppet government with the intention of ruling Finland after its capture.

146. See Björkman, 77.

147. Trotter, 20.

148. See People's Commissar for Foreign Affairs of the USSR, Note of M. Molotov, Commissar for Foreign Affairs, handed on November 26th, 1939 to M. Yrjö-Koskinen, Finnish Minister at Moscow (Nov. 26, 1939).

149. See A. S. Yrjö-Koskinen, Note of M. Yrjö-Koskinen, Finnish Minister at Moscow, handed on November 27th, 1939, to M. Molotov, Commissar for Foreign Affairs (Nov. 27, 1939).

150. See People's Commissar for Foreign Affairs of the USSR.

151. See V. M. Molotov, "Radio Speech of Comr. V. M. Molotov, Chairman of Council of People's Commissars of USSR, Nov. 29, 1939," *Moscow News* (Dec. 4, 1939).

152. See Björkman, 77.

153. See Edwards, 94.

154. See MastersWork Media.

155. See Nils Erik Villstrand, *Källkritik — Ett Förflutenhetsöppnande Sesam (Source Critique — An Examination of the Past)*, http://web.abo.fi/fak/hf/hist/kallkritik.pdf.

156. See Isacson, 67.

157. Reese, 844.

158. Khrushchev, 152.

159. Ibid.

160. See MastersWork Media.

161. Ibid.

162. See Mannerheim, 201.

163. See MastersWork Media.

164. See Albin Edlund, *Svenska Marinens Frivilliga i Finland, 1939–1944 (The Swedish Marine Volunteers in Finland, 1939–1944)* (Karlskrona, Sweden: Marinmusei Vänner och Axel Abrahamsons Tryckeri AB, 1995), 8.

165. See Mannerheim, 202.

166. See Öhquist, 96.

167. The Ambassador in the Soviet Union to the Secretary of State.

168. See Björkman, 83.

169. See Nordling, *Stalin's Insistent Endeavors at Conquering Finland.*

170. See Trotter, 21.

171. See Nordling, *Stalin's Insistent Endeavors at Conquering Finland.*

172. See MastersWork.

173. See Trotter, 39.

174. See Engle and Paananen, 5.

175. See Karsh, 84.

176. See Edwards, 28.

177. See Khrushchev, 208.

178. See Edlund, 8.

179. See Åhslund, 22.

180. See Lars Gyllenhaal and Lennart Westberg, *Svenskar i Krig, 1914–1945 (Swedes at War, 1914–1945)* (Lund, Sweden: Historiska Media, 2008), 233–234.

181. See Engle and Paananen, 59.

182. See Mannerheim, 175.

183. See Andolf, 41.

184. See Engle and Paananen, 26.

185. See The Ambassador in the Soviet Union to the Secretary of State.

186. See Andolf, 42.

187. See Järv, 49–51.

188. See Mannerheim, 202.

189. See Edwards, 115.

190. See Gyllenhaal and Westberg, 234.

191. See Ericson, 96.

192. See Kul kov, xvi.

193. See Andolf, 42.

194. See Falk, 14.

195. See Järv, 51.

196. See Mannerheim, 203.

197. See Öhquist, 92.

198. Nazi-Soviet relations 1939–1941.

199. See Documents on German Foreign Policy 1918–1945, Series D. Vol. VIII, No. 443 (Washington, DC: Department of State, publication 5436, 1954).

200. See Halsti, 36.

201. See Documents on German Foreign Policy 1918–1945, Series D. Vol. VIII, No. 426

(Washington, DC: Department of State, publication 5436, 1954).

202. See Halsti, 25–31.

203. Ibid., 37–38.

204. See Martin Gilbert, *The Second World War: A Complete History* (New York: Henry Holt, 1989), 31.

205. See Öhquist, 62.

206. See Isacson, 49–51.

207. See Öhquist, 12.

208. See Halsti, 41.

209. See Major George Fielding Eliot, "Russian Campaign Against Finland," *Life* (Jan. 15, 1940), 26.

210. See Halsti, 41.

211. See Öhquist, 11.

212. Ibid., 16–17.

213. See Isacson, 38.

214. See Öhquist, 17.

215. See MastersWork Media.

216. See Mannerheim, 204.

217. See Edwards, 97.

218. See MastersWork Media.

219. See Öhquist, 13.

220. Trotter, 40.

221. MastersWork Media.

222. See Documents on German Foreign Policy 1918–1945, Series D. Vol. VIII, No. 426.

223. See Engle and Paananen, 132.

224. See Öhquist, 67.

225. See Engle and Paananen, 132.

226. See Johansson, 80.

227. See Björkman, 13.

228. See Andolf, 47.

229. See Nicolas von Schmidt-Laussitz and Klaus-Jürgen von Schmidt-Laussitz, *För Finlands Frihet: Svenska Frivilligkåren, 1939–1940 (For the Liberation of Finland: The Swedish Volunteer Corps, 1939–1940)* (Hallstavik, Sweden: Svenskt Militärhistoriskt Bibliotek, 2008), 34.

230. See Lars Hammarén, *Sverige Under Andra Världskriget (Sweden During the Second World War)*, Lars Hammaréns Historiehemsida (2002), http://www.larshammaren.se/6_sv2vkr.html#kom2.

231. See Mannerheim, 204.

232. See Björkman, 87.

233. See Johansson, 403–404.

234. See Wangel, "Försvarsstabens Bedömningar Hösten 1939 (The Defense Establishment's Judgements in the Fall of 1939)," 100.

235. See Documents on German Foreign Policy 1918–1945, Series D. Vol. VIII, No. 426.

236. See Documents on German Foreign Policy 1918–1945, Series D. Vol. VIII, No. 443.

237. See Daniel Hjort, "Hans Ruin Kunde För Mycket (Hans Ruin Knew Too Much)," *Svenska Dagbladet* (Feb. 7, 2004).

238. See Björkman, 23.

Chapter 2

1. See MastersWork Media, *Fire and Ice: The Winter War of Finland and Russia*, produced and directed by Ben Strout, 2005.

2. See W. H. Halsti, *Försvaret av Finland (The Defense of Finland)* (Stockholm, Sweden: P. A. Norsetdt & Söner, 1940), 103–105.

3. See Major George Fielding Eliot, "Russian Campaign Against Finland," *Life* (Jan. 15, 1940), 26.

4. Ibid., 28.

5. See Halsti, 104–106.

6. See Jessica Eriksson, *F19: Frivilliga Flygande för Finlands Sak och Politiken Bakom (F19: Volunteer Pilots for Finland's Cause and the Politics Behind Their Missions)*, Luleå Tekniska Universitet, Sweden.

7. See Leif Björkman, *Det Svenska Vinterkriget, 1939–1940 (The Swedish Winter War, 1939–1940)* (Stockholm, Sweden: Hjalmarson & Högberg Bokförlag, 2007), 10.

8. See Magnus Dyrssen, *Diary*, Svenska Frivilligkåren (Swedish Volunteer Corps), Krigsarkivet (War Archives), Stockholm, Sweden.

9. See Jonas Sjöstedt, "Halvfascistiskt Finland (Half-Fascist Finland)," *Ny Tid* (May 16, 2007).

10. See Flamman, "Sveriges Värsta Terrordåd (Sweden's Worst Terror Act)," *Flamman* (Oct. 6, 2006).

11. See Anders Hagström, "Stalins Dyrköpta Vinterkrig (Stalin's Expensive Winter War)," *Finska Vinterkriget, 1939–40 (The Finnish Winter War, 1939–40)*, http://www.marxistarkiv.se/europa/finland/finska_vinterkriget-artiklar.pdf.

12. See Vasa Gymnasiet, *Om Motstånd och Kollaboration — Sverige Under 30- och 40-Talen: Tidningarna i Sverige Under Andra Världskriget (On Resistance and Collaboration — Sweden in the 30s and 40s: The Newspapers in Sweden During World War Two)*, Arboga, Sweden.

13. See Flamman.

14. See Vasa Gymnasiet.

15. See Sarah Arildsson and Mikael Lidberg, *Vår Beredskap är God: En Studie Över den Militära Beredskapen i Övre Norrland, 1939–44 (We Are Well Prepared: A Study of the Military Preparedness in Upper Norrland, 1939–44)*, Luleå Tekniska Universitet, Sweden.

16. See Björkman, 234–235.

17. See Flamman.

18. See Sjöstedt.

19. See Arildsson and Lidberg.

20. See Björkman, 102–104.

21. Ibid., 105.

22. See Harry Martinson, *Verklighet till Döds (Reality to Death)* (Stockholm, Sweden: P. A. Norstedt & Söner, 1940), 95.

23. See Erik Carlquist, *Solidaritet på Prov: Finlandshjälp Under Vinterkriget (A Test of Solidarity:*

Assistance for Finland During the Winter War) (Stockholm, Sweden: Allmänna Förlaget, 1971), 12.

24. See Albin Edlund, *Svenska Marinens Frivilliga i Finland, 1939–1944 (The Swedish Marine Volunteers in Finland, 1939–1944)* (Karlskrona, Sweden: Marinmusei Vänner och Axel Abrahamsons Tryckeri Ab, 1995), 16.

25. See Evgeni Nikolaevich Kulkov, *Stalin and the Soviet-Finnish War, 1939–40* (Portland, OR: Frank Cass Publishers, 2002), 31.

26. See Anna-Lena Laurén, "Mannerheim Blev Störste Finländaren (Mannerheim Became the Greatest Finn)," *Svenska Dagbladet* (Dec. 6, 2004). Mannerheim, who had become a symbol for Finland's independence, also led Finland through the Continuation War of 1941–44.

27. See The Winter War of 1939–1940: Telegrams from Each Day of the Winter War, based on Markku Onttonen's Documentary Series *Talvisodan Henki (The Spirit of the Winter War)*, http://www.mil.fi/perustietoa/talvisota_eng/index.html.

28. See MastersWork Media.

29. See Carl Gustaf Mannerheim, *Marskalkens Minnen (The Marshal's Memories)* (Helsingfors, Finland: Holger Schildts Förlag, 1954), 60.

30. See Olli Vehviläinen, *Finland in the Second World War: Between Germany and Russia* (New York: Palgrave Macmillan, 2002), 17–18.

31. See Orvar Nilsson, *När Finlands Sak Blev Min (When Finland's Cause Became Mine)* (Helsingfors, Finland: Schildts Förlags AB, 2002), 13–14.

32. See Alf W. Johansson, *Per Albin och Kriget: Samlingsregeringen och Utrikespolitiken Under Andra Världskriget (Per Albin and the War: The Coalition Government and Foreign Policy During the Second World War)* (Stockholm, Sweden: Tidens Förlag, 1984), 99.

33. See Jan Nilsson, *Svensk Diplomatrapportering Under Finska Vinterkriget Oktober 1939—Mars 1940 (Swedish Diplomacy Report During the Finnish Winter War October 1939—March 1940)*, Artikelbiblioteket, http://members.chello.se/akademin/artikelbiblioteket/artiklar/arngren.htm.

34. See Douglas Clark, *Three Days to Catastrophe: Britain and the Russo-Finnish Winter War* (London: Hammond, Hammond & Company, 1966), 61–63.

35. See Mannerheim, 198.

36. See Harald Öhquist, *Vinterkriget 1939–40 Ur Min Synvinkel (The Winter War 1939–40 from My View)* (Tammerfors, Finland: Tammerfors Handelstryckeri, 1949), 36–37.

37. See Tor Lange, "Vapenhjälpen till Finland (Weapons Export to Finland)," *Sveriges Militära Beredskap, 1939–1945 (Sweden's Military Preparedness, 1939–1945)*, edited by Carl-Axel Wangel (Stockholm, Sweden: Militärhistoriska Förlaget, 1982), 133.

38. Ibid., 135.

39. See William Trotter, *A Frozen Hell: The Russo-Finnish Winter War of 1939–40* (Chapel Hill, NC: Algonquin Books of Chapel Hill, 2000), 214.

40. See Öhquist, 100.

41. See Jan Nilsson.

42. See Nicolas von Schmidt-Laussitz and Klaus-Jürgen von Schmidt-Laussitz, *För Finlands Frihet: Svenska Frivilligkåren, 1939–1940 (For the Liberation of Finland: The Swedish Volunteer Corps, 1939–1940)* (Hallstavik, Sweden: Svenskt Militärhistoriskt Bibliotek, 2008), 66–67.

43. See Jan Linder, *När Finlands Sak Blev Svensk Folkrörelse (When Finland's Cause Became a Swedish Folk Movement)*, Försvarsfrämjandet, http://www.forsvarsframjandet.org/FMF-97-2/nar-finlands-sak.htm. Finland also equipped several of its divisions with materiel sent from Sweden in the Continuation War of 1941–44. See Trotter, 198.

44. See Trotter, 20. Bofors, founded in 1873, was once owned by Alfred Nobel, founder of the Nobel Prize. Nobel reorganized the company from an iron to a cannon manufacturer.

45. Robert Edwards, *The Winter War: Russia's Invasion of Finland, 1939–40* (New York: Pegasus Books, 2008), 113.

46. See Lange, 133.

47. See Hagström.

48. See Björkman, 39–40.

49. See Väinö Tanner, *The Winter War: Finland Against Russia 1939–40* (Stanford, CA: Stanford University Press, 1957), 133.

50. See Edwards, 132.

51. See Eloise Engle and Lauri Paananen, *The Winter War: The Soviet Attack on Finland 1939–1940* (Mechanicsburg, PA: Stackpole Books, 1973), 54.

52. See Öhquist, 114.

53. See Jan Nilsson.

54. See Claes-Göran Isacson, *Ärans Vinter: Finska Vinterkriget 1939–40 (A Winter of Honor: The Finnish Winter War 1939–40)* (Stockholm, Sweden: Norstedts Förlag, 2007), 225–226.

55. See Orvar Nilsson, 22.

56. See Isacson, 226.

57. See The Winter War of 1939–1940: Telegrams from Each Day of the Winter War.

58. See National Archive Exhibit of the Winter War, *Vinterkriget från Sommar till Sommar (The Winter War from Summer to Summer)*, Finland National Archive, http://www.narc.fi/naytt/naytxruo.htm.

59. See The Winter War of 1939–1940: Telegrams from Each Day of the Winter War.

60. See Greger Falk, *F19—En Krönika: Den Svenska Frivilliga Flygflottiljen i Finland Under Vinterkriget, 1939–1940 (F19—A Chronicle: The Swedish Volunteer Flight Squadron in Finland Dur-*

ing the Winter War, 1939–1940) (Stockholm, Sweden: Svensk Flyghistorisk Förening), 17.

61. See Björkman, 92.
62. See Fredrik Vahlquist, "Vinterkriget — När Finlands Sak var Vår (The Winter War — When Finland's Cause was Ours)," *Svenska Dagbladet* (Dec. 6, 2004).
63. See Carlquist, 111–112.
64. See Isacson, 33 & 38.
65. See MastersWork Media.
66. See The Winter War of 1939–1940: Telegrams from Each Day of the Winter War.
67. See Orvar Nilsson, 23–24.
68. See Isacson, 238.
69. See Öhquist, 42.
70. See von Schmidt-Laussitz, 36.
71. See Carlquist, 144.
72. See von Schmidt-Laussitz, 40.
73. See Johansson, 121.
74. See Carl-Johan Gardell, review of "Det Svenska Vinterkriget, 1939–40 (The Swedish Winter War, 1939–40)," by Leif Björkman, *Svenska Dagbladet* (Nov. 26, 2007).
75. See Vinterkriget, *Finska Vinterkrigets Historik (The History of the Finnish Winter War)*, http://www.geocities.com/Eureka/Park/5121/historik.html.
76. See Bertil Nelsson, *En Intervju med Orvar Nilsson (An Interview with Orvar Nilsson)*, Swedish Military History Library, http://www.smb.nu/pos/00/10_orvar_nilsson.asp. Orvar Nilsson participated in the war from the beginning of January until the war's end in March 1940. He was one of Sweden's most decorated soldiers and also participated in conjunction with Swedish volunteers in the battles of Tali-Ihantala in the summer of 1944, as part of the Continuation War. The battle, considered the largest in the history of the Nordic countries, ended with a decisive Finnish victory against the Soviet forces. Orvar Nilsson also fought in several other foreign wars, among them Korea.
77. See Göran Andolf, "Svenska Frivilligkåren (The Swedish Volunteer Corps)," *Svenska Frivilliga i Finland 1939–1940 (Swedish Volunteers in Finland 1939–1940)* (Stockholm, Sweden: Militärhistoriska Förlaget, 1989), 53.
78. See Krigsarkivet (War Archives), *Newspaper Clipping*, Mar. 22, 1940, Finlandskommitten, 1939–1940, Vol. 3–5, 7, och 44d.
79. See The Hague, *Convention (V) Respecting the Rights and Duties of Neutral Powers and Persons in Case of War on Land* (Oct. 18, 1907), http://www.icrc.org/IHL.NSF/FULL/200?OpenDocument.
80. See Björkman, 89–90, 121.
81. See Edlund, 10 & 21.
82. See Lars Gyllenhaal and Lennart Westberg, *Svenskar i Krig, 1914–1945 (Swedes at War, 1914–1945)* (Lund, Sweden: Historiska Media, 2008), 241–242.
83. See von Schmidt-Laussitz, 340
84. See Öhquist, 114.
85. See Falk, 18–19.
86. See Andolf, 53.
87. See Orvar Nilsson, 25.
88. See von Schmidt-Laussitz, 42.
89. See Vahlquist.
90. See Isacson, 230.
91. See Falk, 19.
92. See Tanner, 160.
93. See von Schmidt-Laussitz, 42.
94. See Andolf, 50.
95. See Linda Edvardsson, *Finlands Sak och Vår: Svenska Frivilliga i Finska Vinterkriget (Finland's Cause and Ours: Swedish Volunteers in the Finnish Winter War)*, Finska Vinterkriget, http://www.algonet.se/~bog/vinterkriget/finlandssak.htm.
96. See Krigsarkivet (War Archives), *Propaganda Letter*, Finlandskommitten, 1939–1940, Vol. 3–5, 7, och 44d.
97. See Krigsarkivet (War Archives), *Vilhelm Moberg — Letter to the Farmers, Dec. 12, 1939*, Finlandskommitten, 1939–1940, Vol. 3–5, 7, och 44d.
98. See Edvardsson.
99. See Gyllenhaal and Westberg, 236.
100. See Eriksson.
101. See Andolf, 62.
102. See Krigsarkivet (War Archives), *Rusthåll-Brev (Letter from the Committee for Finland)*, Finlandskommitten, 1939–1940, Vol. 3–5, 7, och 44d.
103. See Edvardsson, originally published in *I Rikets Tjänst: Händelser och Människor Från Min Bana (In Service of the Kingdom: Events and People in My Life)*, by Carl August Ehrensvärd (Stockholm, Sweden: P.A. Norstedt & Söner, 1965), 139.
104. See Nelsson, *En Intervju med Orvar Nilsson (An Interview with Orvar Nilsson)*.
105. See Edvardsson, originally published in *Till Bröders Hjälp: Gotländska Frivilliga i Finland, 1939–1940 (To the Aid of Our Brothers: The Gotland Volunteers in Finland)*, by Kjell Olsson (Visby, Sweden: Ödins Förlag, AB, 1997), 127.
106. See Ragnar Naess, *Marschen till Märkäjärvi (The March to Märkäjärvi)* (Solna, Sweden: Leandoer & Ekholm Förlag, originally published 1940), 40.
107. Ibid., 16 & 19.
108. See Gyllenhaal and Westberg, 236.
109. See Falk, 30.
110. See Trotter, 190.
111. See Isacson, 229.
112. See Falk, 31.
113. See The Winter War of 1939–1940: Telegrams from Each Day of the Winter War.
114. See Isacson, 229.
115. See The Winter War of 1939–1940: Telegrams from Each Day of the Winter War.
116. See Anders Umgård, *De Flög för Nordens Frihet (They Flew for Nordic Independence)*, Institution of History at Uppsala University, Sweden.

117. See Andolf, 57–58.
118. See Falk, 25–26, 30.
119. See Trotter, 190. The swastika, or hooked cross symbol, is several thousand years old and has been found on artifacts, not only from the Nordic countries but from several ancient cultures such as China, Japan, and India. The swastika, although later associated with Hitler and Nazi Germany, represented favorable circumstances; it was a sign of good luck and first appeared on the Finnish warplanes in 1918 when a Swedish nobleman named Eric von Rosen gifted an airplane bearing the hooked cross symbol in blue on a white background to the "white" side of Finland in their strife for independence. When Finland developed its air force later the same year, the swastika was adopted as the country's national symbol and remained in use until 1945. See Air Force Museum in Sweden, Pamphlet, *F19—Flygande Frivilliga för Finlands Sak (F19—Flying Volunteers for Finland's Cause).* Hitler adopted the swastika along with several other runes from Old Norse culture (for example, the Odal rune, which signified the ancestral home and kinship) as symbols of his white supremacy ideals.
120. See Umgård.
121. See Eriksson.
122. See Linder.
123. See Umgård.
124. See Isacson, 236.
125. See Svenskt Militärhistoriskt Bibliotek, *Svenskar på Östfronten (Swedes on the Eastern Front)*, http://www.smb.nu/index.php/component/content/article/1241.
126. See Martinson, 94.
127. See Isacson, 226.
128. See The Winter War of 1939–1940: Telegrams from Each Day of the Winter War.
129. See Andolf, 79.
130. See Björkman, 92.
131. See Vinterkriget, *Identitetskort (Identity Card)*, http://www.geocities.com/Eureka/Park/5121/idkort.html.
132. See von Schmidt-Laussitz, 68.
133. See Isacson, 237.
134. See von Schmidt-Laussitz, 68.
135. See Andolf, 68.
136. See Dyrssen.
137. See Andolf, 68.
138. See von Schmidt-Laussitz, 45.
139. See Mannerheim, 235.
140. See von Schmidt-Laussitz, 45.
141. See Tanner, 133.
142. See Dyrssen.
143. Ibid.
144. See Krigsarkivet (War Archives), *Utrustning (Equipment)*, Svenska Frivilligkåren, 1939–1940, Vol. 5a-5b.
145. See Dyrssen.
146. See Isacson, 237–238.
147. See Dyrssen.
148. See Naess, 22.
149. See von Schmidt-Laussitz, 71.
150. Ibid., 71 & 75.
151. See Naess, 56.
152. See von Schmidt-Laussitz 75.
153. See Naess, 25–26.
154. See von Schmidt-Laussitz, 74.
155. See Andolf, 83.
156. See Naess, 115–117.
157. See Falk, 204.
158. Ibid., 32.
159. See Isacson, 252.
160. See Öhquist, 248.
161. See Linder.
162. See Johansson, 121.
163. See Debatt Passagen, *Några Telegram Om Finska Vinterkriget (Some Telegrams from the Finnish Winter War)*, http://debatt.passagen.se.
164. See Tanner, 158.
165. See The Hague.
166. See Tanner, 158.
167. Ibid.
168. See Jan Nilsson.
169. See von Schmidt-Laussitz 40.
170. See Isacson, 230.
171. See Dyrssen.
172. See Lars Ericson, *Svenska Frivilliga: Militära Uppdrag i Utlandet Under 1800- och 1900-talen (Swedish Volunteers: Foreign Military Missions During the 1800s and 1900s)* (Lund, Sweden: Historiska Media, 1996), 99.
173. See Isacson, 227.
174. See Svenska Frivilliga, *Preludium (Prelude)*, http://www.svenskafrivilliga.com/sfk1.html. *Jäger*, which translates as "hunter," can be compared to a Special Forces unit used for scouting and sabotage behind enemy lines. The Finnish *jäger* troops came to play an important role in the Winter War as well as the Continuation War. Through their work to prepare Finland's defensive forces for armed conflict, they laid the base for the highly effective military establishment that the country has today. See Isacson, 30.
175. Trotter, 257.
176. See Isacson, 227.
177. See Harry Järv, *Oavgjort i Två Krig: Finland—Sovietunionen 1939–1944 (Undecided in Two Wars: Finland—the Soviet Union 1939–1940)* (Avesta, Sweden: Samfundet Sverige-Finland, 2001), 57.
178. See Falk, 15.
179. See Svenska Frivilliga, *Marschen till Märkäjärvi (The March to Märkäjärvi)*, http://www.svenskafrivilliga.com/sfk2a.html.
180. See Isacson, 238–240.
181. See Svenska Frivilliga, *Marschen till Märkäjärvi (The March to Märkäjärvi)*.
182. See Svenskt Militärhistoriskt Bibliotek, excerpt from *För Finlands Frihet: Svenska Frivilligkåren, 1939–1940 (For the Liberation of Finland: The Swedish Volunteer Corps, 1939–1940)*, by

Klaus-Jürgen von Schmidt-Laussitz and Nicolas von Schmidt-Laussitz, 91–92, http://www.smb.nu/index.php/component/content/article/1241.

183. See Dyrssen.

184. See Isacson, 238–240.

185. See Svenska Frivilliga, *Marschen till Märkäjärvi (The March to Märkäjärvi).*

186. See Krigsarkivet (War Archives), *Utrustning (Equipment).*

187. Nelsson, *En Intervju med Orvar Nilsson (An Interview with Orvar Nilsson).*

188. See Nelsson, *Frivillig i Finland (Volunteer in Finland)*, Svenskt Militärhistoriskt Bibliotek, http://www.smb.nu/pos/03/04_frivillig_i_finland.asp.

189. See von Schmidt-Laussitz, 87.

190. Ibid., 92.

191. See Svenskt Militärhistoriskt Bibliotek, excerpt from *För Finlands Frihet: Svenska Frivilligkåren, 1939–1940 (For the Liberation of Finland: The Swedish Volunteer Corps, 1939–1940).*

192. See Andolf, 104.

193. See Edvardsson.

194. See Nelsson, *En Intervju med Orvar Nilsson (An Interview with Orvar Nilsson).*

Chapter 3

1. See William Trotter, *A Frozen Hell: The Russo-Finnish Winter War of 1939–40* (Chapel Hill, NC: Algonquin Books of Chapel Hill, 2000), 146.

2. See Swedish Military History Library, *Den Stora Urladdningen (The Great Discharge)*, http://www.smb.nu/pos/06/01_europa_i_krig.asp.

3. See Linda Edvardsson, *Finlands Sak och Vår: Svenska Frivilliga i Finska Vinterkriget (Finland's Cause and Ours: Swedish Volunteers in the Finnish Winter War)*, Finska Vinterkriget, http://www.algonet.se/~bog/vinterkriget/finlandssak.htm.

4. See Ragnar Naess, *Marschen till Märkäjärvi (The March to Märkäjärvi)* (Solna, Sweden: Leandoer & Ekholm Förlag, originally published 1940), 53.

5. See National Archive Exhibit of the Winter War, *Vinterkriget från Sommar till Sommar (The Winter War from Summer to Summer)*, Finland National Archive, http://www.narc.fi/naytt/naytxruo.htm.

6. See Claes-Göran Isacson, *Ärans Vinter: Finska Vinterkriget 1939–40 (A Winter of Honor: The Finnish Winter War 1939–40)* (Stockholm, Sweden: Norstedts Förlag, 2007), 32–33. The *Lotta* organization, named after Lotta Svärd, was founded in 1920 and was (is) a women's auxiliary organization operational also in Sweden.

7. See Naess, 53.

8. See Douglas Clark, *Three Days to Catastrophe: Britain and the Russo-Finnish Winter War* (London: Hammond, Hammond & Company, 1966), 61.

9. See Harald Öhquist, *Vinterkriget 1939–40 Ur Min Synvinkel (The Winter War 1939–40 from My View)* (Tammerfors, Finland, Tammerfors Handelstryckeri, 1949), 19.

10. See Eloise Engle and Lauri Paananen, *The Winter War: The Soviet Attack on Finland 1939–1940* (Mechanicsburg, PA: Stackpole Books, 1973), xi & 5.

11. See Carl Gustaf Mannerheim, *Marskalkens Minnen (The Marshal's Memories)* (Helsingfors, Finland: Holger Schildts Förlag, 1954), 66.

12. See MastersWork Media, *Fire and Ice: The Winter War of Finland and Russia*, produced and directed by Ben Strout, 2005.

13. See Mannerheim, 242.

14. See Patrik Berghäll, *Finska Fjällpatrull Medlemmar Minns (Memories from the Members of the Finnish Mountain Patrol)*, Åbo (Oct. 27. 2004).

15. See Engle and Paananen, 45.

16. See Berghäll.

17. See Jorma Sarvanto, *Sex Fiendebombplan inom Fyra Minuter (Six Enemy Aircraft within Four Minutes)*, Arvet Efter Veteranerna — Ett Självständigt Fosterland 2002, http://www.veteraanienperinto.fi/svenska/Kertomukset/sotilas/sotilas/talvisota/luutnantti_sarvannon_taistelulen.htm.

18. See Naess, 28.

19. See Isacson, 40.

20. See Öhquist, 43.

21. See Isacson, 41–42.

22. See Mannerheim, 235.

23. See Öhquist, 45.

24. See Björn Nilsson, *Finska Armens Förberedelser och Taktik Under Finska Vinterkriget 1939–1940 (The Finnish Army's Preparations and Tactics During the Finnish Winter War 1939–1940)*, Finska Vinterkriget, http://www.algonet.se/~bog/vinterkriget/finsktaktik.htm.

25. See Engle and Paananen, 67.

26. See Nilsson.

27. See Engle and Paananen, 67.

28. See Öhquist, 48.

29. See Mannerheim, 205.

30. See Öhquist, 357.

31. Ibid., 361–363.

32. Ibid., 129–130.

33. See Carl Nordling, *Sacrificing Men or Machines? The Soviet Over-Sea Invasion of Finland in 1940*, http://www.carlonordling.se/winter_war.html.

34. See MastersWork Media.

35. See Öhquist, 154.

36. See Mannerheim,.

37. See John Hughes-Wilson, "Snow and Slaughter at Suomussalmi," *Military History* (Jan./Feb. 2006), 49.

38. See MastersWork Media.

39. Trotter, 73.
40. See Isacson, 35.
41. See Öhquist, 114.
42. "Motti" is a Finnish term that means "measure," or a cubic meter of firewood. It can also be translated as "wood that has been cut but not yet split." It describes the Finnish tactic of dividing the enemy units into smaller isolated cells, which the numerically inferior and disadvantaged Finnish forces could encircle and defeat. See Swedish Military History Library.
43. See Greger Falk, *F19—En Krönika: Den Svenska Frivilliga Flygflottiljen i Finland Under Vinterkriget, 1939–1940 (F19—A Chronicle: The Swedish Volunteer Flight Squadron in Finland During the Winter War, 1939–1940)* (Stockholm, Sweden: Svensk Flyghistorisk Förening), 30.
44. See Trotter, 223.
45. Ibid., 181.
46. See National Archive Exhibit of the Winter War.
47. See Engle and Paananen, 28.
48. Trotter, 72.
49. See Engle and Paananen, 36 & 40.
50. See Valde Hämäläinen, Finnish AT Gun Platoon Leader, Battle of Summa, *Personal Diary*, Fire and Ice, http://www.wfyi.org/FireandIce/educational_resources/diaries_Hamalainen.htm.
51. Ibid.
52. See Evgeni Nikolaevich Kulkov, *Stalin and the Soviet-Finnish War, 1939–40* (Portland, OR: Frank Cass Publishers, 2002), 68.
53. See MastersWork Media.
54. See Nilsson.
55. See MastersWork Media.
56. See Trotter, 74.
57. See Mannerheim, 212, 219 & 227.
58. See Engle and Paananen, 39.
59. Ibid., 36.
60. See Öhquist, 269 & 272.
61. Hughes-Wilson, 50.
62. See Trotter, 81 & 175.
63. See Mannerheim, 210.
64. See Isacson, 40.
65. See Göran Andolf, "Svenska Frivilligkåren (The Swedish Volunteer Corps)," *Svenska Frivilliga i Finland 1939–1940 (Swedish Volunteers in Finland 1939–1940)* (Stockholm, Sweden: Militärhistoriska Förlaget, 1989), 43.
66. See Robert Edwards, *The Winter War: Russia's Invasion of Finland, 1939–40* (New York: Pegasus Books, 2008), 109.
67. See MastersWork Media.
68. See Mannerheim, 213.
69. See Dagens Nyheter, "Rysk Massattack med Tanks på Karelska Näset (Russian Massattack with Tanks on the Karelian Isthmus)," *Dagens Nyheter* (Dec. 21, 1939).
70. See Dagens Nyheter, "800 Ryssar Stupade i Slag vid Kemi Älv (800 Russians Fallen in Battle at Kemi River)," *Dagens Nyheter* (Dec. 21, 1939).
71. See Dagens Nyheter, "Ägläjärvi Blev Nytt Segernam: Två Tusen Ryssar Stupade (Ägläjärvi Became New Victory Name: Two Thousand Russians Fallen)," *Dagens Nyheter* (Dec. 24, 1939).
72. See Mannerheim, 215–216 & 224.
73. Öhquist, 148–152.
74. Ibid., 162–164.
75. See Krigsarkivet (War Archives), *Den Svenske Folksocialisten,* Newspaper Clipping (Feb. 3, 1940), Finlandskommitten, 1939–1940, Vol. 3–5, 7, och 44d.
76. See Öhquist, 166 &176.
77. Ibid., 61–177.
78. See MastersWork Media.
79. See Öhquist, 183.
80. Ibid., 252–271.
81. See Jan Linder, *När Finlands Sak Blev Svensk Folkrörelse (When Finland's Cause Became a Swedish Folk Movement)*, Försvarsfrämjandet, http://www.forsvarsframjandet.org/FMF-97-2/nar-finlands-sak.htm.
82. See Öhquist, 216–220 & 311.
83. Hughes-Wilson, 47–48.
84. See Öhquist, 62.
85. See Veteraanien Perinto, *Luftstridskrafterna: Vinterkriget (The Air Force: The Winter War)*, Arvet Efter Veteranerna — Ett Självständigt Fosterland 2002, http://www.veteraanienperinto.fi/svenska/t_pankki/a_lajit/lentajan_maailmanennatys.htm.
86. See Viktor M. Iskrov, Colonel of the Guards, Lieutenant, Forward Observation Platoon Leader, 68th Independent Mortar Battery, *The Mannerheim Line, 1920–39*, by Bair Irincheev, http://www.mannerheim-line.com/veterans/iskrove.htm.
87. See Falk, 148.
88. See Albin Edlund, *Svenska Marinens Frivilliga i Finland, 1939–1944 (The Swedish Marine Volunteers in Finland, 1939–1944)* (Karlskrona, Sweden: Marinmusei Vänner och Axel Abrahamsons Tryckeri AB, 1995), 36.
89. See Lars Ericson, *Svenska Frivilliga: Militära Uppdrag i Utlandet Under 1800- och 1900-talen (Swedish Volunteers: Foreign Military Missions During the 1800s and 1900s)* (Lund, Sweden: Historiska Media, 1996), 102–103.
90. See The Winter War of 1939–1940: Telegrams from Each Day of the Winter War, based on Markku Onttonen's Documentary Series *Talvisodan Henki (The Spirit of the Winter War)*, http://www.mil.fi/perustietoa/talvisota_eng/index.html.
91. See Veteraanien Perinto.
92. See The Winter War of 1939–1940: Telegrams from Each Day of the Winter War.
93. See Roger R. Reese, "Lessons of the Winter War: A Study in the Military Effectiveness of the Red Army, 1939–1940," *The Journal of Military History*, Vol. 72, No. 3 (Jul., 2008), 828.
94. See Kulkov, 1–3.

95. See Engle and Paananen 64.
96. See Trotter, 34.
97. See W. H. Halsti, *Försvaret av Finland (The Defense of Finland)* (Stockholm, Sweden: P. A. Norsetdt & Söner, 1940), 19.
98. See Toivo M. Kattonen, Machine Gunner, 1st Machine Gun Company, 99th Detached Volunteer Ski Battalion, *The Mannerheim Line, 1920–39*, by Bair Irincheev, http://www.mannerheim-line.com/veterans/Toivo.htm.
99. See Ivan S. Chetyrbok, Senior Sergeant, 3rd Battalion, 85th Rifle Regiment, 100th Rifle Division, *The Mannerheim Line, 1920–39*, by Bair Irincheev, http://www.mannerheim-line.com/veterans/chetyrboke.htm.
100. See Trotter, 176.
101. See Ivan S. Chetyrbok, Senior Sergeant, 3rd Battalion, 85th Rifle Regiment, 100th Rifle Division, *Personal Diary*, Fire and Ice, http://www.wfyi.org/FireandIce/educational_resources/diaries_Chetyrbok.htm.
102. See Capt. Sipovich, 100th Rifle Division, Battle of Summa, *Personal Diary*, Fire and Ice, http://www.wfyi.org/FireandIce/educational_resources/diaries_Sipovich.htm.
103. See Isacson, 286.
104. See Sipovich.
105. See Engle and Paananen, 45.
106. See Isacson, 293–294.
107. See Chetyrbok, The Mannerheim Line.
108. See Chetyrbok, Personal Diary.
109. See Kul kov, 22.
110. See Engle and Paananen, 45.
111. See Georgi V. Prusakov, Medic, 100th Independent Volunteer Ski Battalion, *The Mannerheim Line, 1920–39*, by Bair Irincheev, http://www.mannerheim-line.com/veterans/Prusakov.htm.
112. See Kattonen.
113. See Nikolai Alexeevich Ponomarenko, Colonel (Retired), Lieutenant During the Winter War, Chief of Forward Observers, 4th Artillery Battalion, 168 Super Heavy Artillery Regiment, *The Mannerheim Line, 1920–39*, by Bair Irincheev, http://www.mannerheim-line.com/veterans/ponomarenko.htm.
114. See Nicolas von Schmidt-Laussitz and Klaus-Jürgen von Schmidt-Laussitz, *För Finlands Frihet: Svenska Frivilligkåren, 1939–1940 (For the Liberation of Finland: The Swedish Volunteer Corps, 1939–1940)* (Hallstavik, Sweden: Svenskt Militärhistoriskt Bibliotek, 2008), 151.
115. See Öhquist, 110.
116. See Vasily F. Davidenko, Lieutenant of Artillery, Forward Observer Platoon Leader, 7th Rifle Regiment, 24th Samara — Ulyanovsk "Iron" Rifle Division, *The Mannerheim Line, 1920–39*, by Bair Irincheev, http://www.mannerheim-line.com/veterans/davidenkoe.htm.
117. See Kul kov, 52 & 88.
118. MastersWork Media.
119. See Arnd Bernaerts, *Climate Change & Naval War: A Scientific Assessment* (Victoria, BC, Canada: Trafford Publishing, 2005), 137.
120. See Chetyrbok, *Personal Diary*.
121. See Harry Martinson, *Verklighet till Döds (Reality to Death)* (Stockholm, Sweden: P. A. Norstedt & Söner, 1940), 146.
122. MastersWork Media.
123. See Kattonen.
124. See Nikita Khrushchev, *Khrushchev Remembers*, translated by Strobe Talbott (Boston, MA: Little, Brown, 1970), 153.
125. See Isacson, 121.
126. See Iskrov.
127. See Engle and Paananen, 103.
128. See Chetyrbok, *Personal Diary*.
129. See Isacson, 292.
130. See Kattonen.
131. See Isacson, 277–279.
132. See Kulkov, 46.
133. See Dmitri A. Krutskih, Lieutenant, Engineer Platoon Leader, 16th Independent Engineer Battalion, 54th Rifle Division, *The Mannerheim Line, 1920–39*, interview by Artem Drabkin, translation by Bair Irincheev, http://www.mannerheim-line.com/veterans/krutskih.htm.
134. See Ponomarenko.
135. See Berghäll.
136. See Kulkov, 18 & 32.
137. Ibid., 5–9.
138. Ibid., 9.
139. Ibid., 9 & 14.
140. See Chetyrbok, *Personal Diary*.
141. See Kulkov, 55.
142. See Engle and Paananen, 70.
143. See Isacson, 294–298.
144. See Hughes-Wilson, 47.
145. See Reese, 830.
146. See Alf W. Johansson, *Per Albin och Kriget: Samlingsregeringen och Utrikespolitiken Under Andra Världskriget (Per Albin and the War: The Coalition Government and Foreign Policy During the Second World War)* (Stockholm, Sweden: Tidens Förlag, 1984), 122.
147. Trotter, 257.
148. See Svenskt Militärhistoriskt Bibliotek, excerpt from *För Finlands Frihet: Svenska Frivilligkåren, 1939–1940 (For the Liberation of Finland: The Swedish Volunteer Corps, 1939–1940)*, by Klaus-Jürgen von Schmidt-Laussitz and Nicolas von Schmidt-Laussitz, 93 & 97, http://www.smb.nu/index.php/component/content/article/1241.
149. See Andolf, 109.
150. Ibid., 104 & 116.
151. See Magnus Dyrssen, *Diary*, Svenska Frivilligkåren (Swedish Volunteer Corps), Krigsarkivet (War Archives), Stockholm, Sweden.
152. See Andolf, 116.
153. See Isacson, 245.

154. See von Schmidt-Laussitz, 113.

155. See Flames of War, *Svenska Frivilliga Kåren (The Swedish Volunteer Corps)*, Battlefront, http://www.battlefront.co.nz/Article.asp?ArticleID=153.

156. See Svenska Frivilliga, *Den Grafströmska Raiden (The Grafström Raid)*, http://www.svenskafrivilliga.com/sfk3.html.

157. Ibid.

158. See von Schmidt-Laussitz, 116.

159. See Öhquist, 244.

160. Ibid., 28.

161. Ibid., 317.

162. See Andolf, 119–126.

163. See von Schmidt-Laussitz, 101.

164. See Ebbe Lindblom, "Harry Martinson och Författarnas Vinterkrig (Harry Martinson and the Winter War of the Authors)," *Svenska Frivilliga i Finland 1939–1940 (Swedish Volunteers in Finland 1939–1940)* (Stockholm, Sweden: Militärhistoriska Förlaget, 1989), 216.

165. See von Schmidt-Laussitz, 122.

166. See Svenska Frivilliga, *Jervants Patrull (Jervant's Patrol)*, http://www.svenskafrivilliga.com/sfk4.html.

167. See Andolf, 130.

168. See von Schmidt-Laussitz, 127–129.

169. See Orvar Nilsson, *När Finlands Sak Blev Min (When Finland's Cause Became Mine)* (Helsingfors, Finland: Schildts Förlags Ab, 2002), 46.

170. See von Schmidt-Laussitz, 130.

171. Ibid., 130–132.

172. See Svenska Frivilliga, *Ryskt Anfall Väntas i Söder (Russian Attack Expected from the South)*, http://www.svenskafrivilliga.com/sfk6a.html.

173. See von Schmidt-Laussitz, 164.

174. See Krigsarkivet (War Archives), *Utrustning (Equipment)*, Svenska Frivilligkåren, 1939–1940, Vol. 5a–5b.

175. See Naess, 103–104.

176. See Andolf, 164.

177. See von Schmidt-Laussitz, 68–71.

178. See Naess, 99.

179. See von Schmidt-Laussitz, 105.

180. Dyrssen.

181. See Orvar Nilsson, 42.

182. Ibid., 42.

183. See Martinson, 174.

184. See Naess, 102.

185. See Orvar Nilsson, 42.

186. See von Schmidt-Laussitz, 164.

187. See Andolf, 92.

188. Ibid., 165.

189. See von Schmidt-Laussitz, 164.

190. See Andolf, 165.

191. See Isacson, 303.

192. See Martinson, 196.

193. See Veteraanien Perinto. The "F" in F19 denotes "flyg flottilj" or flight squadron, and the number 19 the order in which it was developed; thus the 19th flight squadron. It is also speculated that the number 19 was General Linder's favorite number, which he used as a talisman in order to provide psychological protection to the members of the squadron. See Falk, 52. Many of the twenty-two flight squadrons in Sweden are no longer operative, including, of course, F19, whose sole purpose was to assist Finland in its time of need. F19 operated a mere 120 days of which 100 were spent in Finland. Combat missions were flown from January 12 to March 13, 1940. See Falk, 8. Many of the flight squadrons have become inoperative just within the last decade, as Sweden no longer considers the country at risk and has downsized its armed forces.

194. See Clark, 127.

195. See Silvervingar, *Beredskapstid, 1939–1945 (Military Preparedness, 1939–1945)*, http://www.silvervingar.se/Beredskapstid.html.

196. See Lars Gyllenhaal, *Luftstrid Över Lappland (Air Fights Above Lapland)*, Svenskt Militärhistoriskt Bibliotek, http://www.smb.nu/index.php/militara-artiklar/finlands-krig/1199-i-luftstrid-oever-lappland.

197. See Håkans Flygsida, *J8 Gloster Gladiator in the Swedish Air Force*, http://surfcity.kund.dalnet.se/gladiator_sweden.htm. The Gloster Gladiator was the last airplane in the Royal Air Force that flew as a single-seat fighter biplane. England exported it to several countries. Sweden was considered a relatively large purchaser and bought fifty-five such airplanes. The Gladiators were stationed at Barkarby airport just north of Stockholm. Some were reassigned to southern Sweden at the start of World War II. Others were sent to Finland. See Lars Henriksson, *J8 — Gloster Gladiator (1937–1947)*, http://www.avrosys.nu/aircraft/jakt/108J8.htm.

198. See Henriksson.

199. See Lars Gyllenhaal. Sweden had contributed with five airplanes to the defense of the "whites," who lacked both aircraft and pilots, during Finland's War of Independence in 1918. The airplanes, which had been donated through the collection of money from individuals, had been transported to Finland secretly via the land route, while escaping border police and customs officials. The task succeeded mainly because of the support of the local citizenry and certain military chiefs. See Falk, 4.

200. See Gyllenhaal.

201. See Björn Bjuggren, *Svenska Flygare i Österled (Swedish Pilots in the East)* (Stockholm, Sweden: Albert Bonniers Förlag), 82–83.

202. See Falk, 8.

203. See Leif Björkman, *Det Svenska Vinterkriget, 1939–1940 (The Swedish Winter War, 1939–1940)* (Stockholm, Sweden: Hjalmarson & Högberg Bokförlag, 2007), 118.

204. See Isacson, 250–251.

205. See Jessica Eriksson, *F19: Frivilliga Flygande för Finlands Sak och Politiken Bakom (F19:*

Volunteer Pilots for Finland's Cause and the Politics Behind Their Missions), Luleå Tekniska Universitet, Sweden.

206. See Falk, 6–8.
207. Ibid., 53–54.
208. See Björkman, 122.
209. See Falk, 32–33.
210. See Jessica Eriksson. The author who is a pilot can testify that taking off and landing small aircraft on frozen lakes in Sweden and Finland works quite well. The ice sheet is thick and smooth enough to facilitate safe takeoffs and landings, and is often covered only by a few inches of snow. It is a myth, however, that Sweden and Finland are extremely cold. Being surrounded by water, the temperature in the winter normally ranges from a few degrees below to a few degrees above the freezing point, although larger variations can be seen further north. The winter of 1939–40 was an exception.
211. See Falk, 38–39, 43 & 69.
212. Ibid., 35, 43 & 60.
213. In March 1940, the Swedish government bought 216 airplanes from Italy which did not arrive in Finland in time to take part in the war, since the war ended shortly thereafter. See Jessica Eriksson.
214. See Falk, 42–49.
215. See Bjuggren, 50–52.
216. See Rune Eriksson, "En Personlig Krönika (A Personal Chronicle)," *Finsk-Ryska Vinterkriget, 1939–40 (The Finnish-Russo Winter War, 1939–40)*, compiled by Ulf Söderback (Aug. 17, 1997), http://www.geocities.com/eureka/park/5121/fvkrig.doc.
217. See Falk, 141.
218. See Krigsarkivet (War Archives), *Analysis*, Svenska Frivilligkåren, Kriget 1939–1940.
219. See Falk, 156.
220. See Bjuggren, 85.
221. See Falk, 145 & 159–162.
222. Ibid., 73–81 &152.
223. Ibid., 82–85 & 108.
224. See Björkman, 123.
225. See Ericson, 100–101.
226. See Falk, 86 & 91.
227. See Bjuggren, 38.
228. See Falk, 92.
229. See Ericson, 100–101.
230. See von Schmidt-Laussitz, 52.
231. See Björkman, 124–125.
232. See Gyllenhaal.
233. See Bjuggren, 61–62.
234. See Falk, 101–102.
235. See Bjuggren, 69.
236. See Falk, 142.
237. See Kulkov, 84–85.
238. See Falk, 148.
239. Ibid., 154–155.
240. See Mannerheim, 247.
241. See Bjuggren, 112.
242. See Krigsarkivet (War Archives), *Analysis*.
243. See Bjuggren, 112.
244. See Krigsarkivet (War Archives), *Analysis*.
245. See Mannerheim, 247.
246. See Falk, 153.
247. Ibid., 118.
248. See Bjuggren, 72.
249. See Mannerheim, 247–248.
250. See Andolf, 180.
251. See Falk, 62–63 & 126–127.
252. See Bjuggren, 108.
253. See Falk, 117.
254. Ibid., 57.
255. See Krigsarkivet (War Archives), *Analysis*.
256. See Falk, 88–89.
257. Ibid., 203.
258. See Krigsarkivet (War Archives), *Daily Log*, Svenska Frivilligkåren, Kriget 1939–1940.
259. See Edlund, 11–12.
260. See Ericson, 102–103.
261. See Krigsarkivet (War Archives), *Anmälan till Åbo, Mar. 1, 1940 (Application to Åbo, Mar. 1, 1940)*, Luftvärnsdivisionen i Åbo, 1939–1940, Vol. 1.
262. See Edlund, 54.
263. See Ericson, 102–103.
264. See Edlund, 22–30.
265. See Krigsarkivet (War Archives), *Instruktion för Signalisterna i Åbo, Mar. 8, 1940 (Instruction for the Telephone Operators in Åbo, Mar. 8, 1940)*, Luftvärnsdivisionen i Åbo, 1939–1940, Vol. 1.
266. See Krigsarkivet (War Archives), *Åbo Permissionsordning, Mar. 6, 1940 (Åbo Policy for Leave, Mar. 6, 1940)*, Luftvärnsdivisionen i Åbo, 1939–1940, Vol. 1.
267. See Krigsarkivet (War Archives), *Telegram från Stockholm till Åbo, Feb. 26, 1940 (Telegram from Stockholm to Åbo, Feb. 26, 1940)*, Luftvärnsdivisionen i Åbo, 1939–1940, Vol. 1.
268. See Krigsarkivet (War Archives), *Luftvärnsdivisionen Åbo Krigsdagbok (Anti-Aircraft Artillery in Åbo, Daily Log)*, Luftvärnsdivisionen i Åbo, 1939–1940, Vol. 1.
269. See Edlund, 29–35.

Chapter 4

1. See Carl Gustaf Mannerheim, *Marskalkens Minnen (The Marshal's Memories)* (Helsingfors, Finland: Holger Schildts Förlag, 1954), 253–254.
2. See Krigsarkivet (War Archive), *Newspaper Clipping, Feb. 3, 1940*, Finlandskommitten, 1939–1940, Vol. 3–5, 7, och 44d.
3. See Göran Andolf, "Svenska Frivilligkåren (The Swedish Volunteer Corps)," *Svenska Frivilliga i Finland 1939–1940 (Swedish Volunteers*

in Finland 1939–1940) (Stockholm, Sweden: Militärhistoriska Förlaget, 1989), 60.

4. See The Winter War of 1939–1940: Telegrams from Each Day of the Winter War, based on Markku Onttonen's Documentary Series *Talvisodan Henki (The Spirit of the Winter War)*, http://www.mil.fi/perustietoa/talvisota_eng/index.html.

5. See Leif Björkman, *Det Svenska Vinterkriget, 1939–1940 (The Swedish Winter War, 1939–1940)* (Stockholm, Sweden: Hjalmarson & Högberg Bokförlag, 2007), 181.

6. See Väinö Tanner, *The Winter War: Finland Against Russia 1939–40* (Stanford, CA: Stanford University Press, 1957), 126.

7. See Harry Järv, *Oavgjort i Två Krig: Finland — Sovietunionen 1939–1944 (Undecided in Two Wars: Finland — the Soviet Union 1939–1940)* (Avesta, Sweden: Samfundet Sverige-Finland, 2001), 59–60. It was unlikely that Stalin was in the dark with respect to Germany. The greater war in Europe had developed to the degree that it was conceivable that the Soviet Union would soon get dragged into the conflict. It was thus crucial that the war in Finland ended and all efforts be focused on preparing for coming hostilities with Germany. See Geoffrey Roberts, *Stalin's Wars from World War to Cold War, 1939–1953* (New Haven, CT: Yale University Press, 2006), 50.

8. Although the Soviet Union might have been in position to overrun Finland and occupy Helsinki in March 1940, Stalin worried about giving Hitler the impression that the Soviet Union was unable to defeat Finland, a little midget neighbor, and therefore had to find a way to peace. See MastersWork Media, *Fire and Ice: The Winter War of Finland and Russia*, produced and directed by Ben Strout, 2005. A Russian ambassador had told British politician Sir Stafford Cripps that Stalin's aim was not to annex any parts of Finland, but to find a mutually agreeable solution to the problem as soon as "the Finns had a government which really represented the interests of the people." It is prudent to remember that Stalin had established the Kuusinen puppet government without the support of the Finns. See Douglas Clark, *Three Days to Catastrophe: Britain and the Russo-Finnish Winter War* (London: Hammond, Hammond & Company, 1966), 107.

9. See Documents on German Foreign Policy 1918–1945, Series D. Vol. VIII, No. 471 (Washington, DC: Department of State, publication 5436, 1954).

10. See Economic Expert, *Anglo-German Naval Agreement*, http://www.economicexpert.com/a/Anglo:German:Naval:Agreement.htm.

11. See Documents on German Foreign Policy 1918–1945, Series D. Volume VIII, No. 513 (Washington, DC: Department of State, publication 5436, 1954).

12. See Svensk Utrikespolitik Under Andra Världskriget (Swedish Foreign Policy During the Second World War) (Stockholm, Sweden, 1946).

13. See Olli Vehviläinen, *Finland in the Second World War: Between Germany and Russia* (New York: Palgrave Macmillan, 2002), 60.

14. See Claes-Göran Isacson, *Ärans Vinter: Finska Vinterkriget 1939–40 (A Winter of Honor: The Finnish Winter War 1939–40)* (Stockholm, Sweden: Norstedts Förlag, 2007), 103–106.

15. See Greger Falk, *F19 — En Krönika: Den Svenska Frivilliga Flygflottiljen i Finland Under Vinterkriget, 1939–1940 (F19 — A Chronicle: The Swedish Volunteer Flight Squadron in Finland During the Winter War, 1939–1940)* (Stockholm, Sweden: Svensk Flyghistorisk Förening), 151.

16. See Väinö Tanner, *The Winter War.*

17. See Mannerheim, 262.

18. See Jan Nilsson, *Svensk Diplomatrapportering Under Finska Vinterkriget Oktober 1939–Mars 1940 (Swedish Diplomacy Report During the Finnish Winter War October 1939–March 1940)*, Artikelbiblioteket, http://members.chello.se/akademin/artikelbiblioteket/artiklar/arngren.htm.

19. See Mannerheim, 262. Finland remained a corridor open for invasion after the war, which prompted Russia to seek a defensive agreement with Finland. During the Cold War years between 1948 and 1992, Finland and the Soviet Union entered into an Agreement of Friendship, Cooperation, and Mutual Assistance, also known as the YYA Treaty. The purpose of the treaty was to deter Western powers from attacking the Soviet Union through Finnish territory. The Finns were obligated to resist attacks and ask for Soviet assistance if needed, and in return would be free to maintain political independence and adopt a policy of neutrality.

20. See Falk, 124–125.

21. See Time, "Darkening Up Here," *Time Magazine* (Mar. 4, 1940).

22. See Björn Bjuggren, *Svenska Flygare i Österled (Swedish Pilots in the East)* (Stockholm, Sweden: Albert Bonniers Förlag), 56.

23. See Time.

24. See Alf W. Johansson, *Per Albin och Kriget: Samlingsregeringen och Utrikespolitiken Under Andra Världskriget (Per Albin and the War: The Coalition Government and Foreign Policy During the Second World War)* (Stockholm, Sweden: Tidens Förlag, 1984), 21–25.

25. See Björkman, 207.

26. See Time.

27. See Robert Edwards, *The Winter War: Russia's Invasion of Finland, 1939–40* (New York: Pegasus Books, 2008), 146.

28. See Winston S. Churchill, *The Gathering Storm* (New York: Houghton Mifflin, 1948), 361.

29. Ibid., 489.

30. See Lars Ericson, *Svenska Frivilliga: Militära Uppdrag i Utlandet Under 1800- och 1900-*

talen (Swedish Volunteers: Foreign Military Missions During the 1800s and 1900s) (Lund, Sweden: Historiska Media, 1996), 54–57.

31. See John Simkin, *Britain and the Spanish Civil War*, Spartacus Educational, http://www.spartacus.schoolnet.co.uk/SPbritain.htm.

32. See Mannerheim, 152.

33. See James L. Stokesbury, *A Short History of World War II* (New York: HarperCollins, 1980), 83.

34. See Churchill, 481.

35. See. Stokesbury, 83.

36. See Clark, 70.

37. See Björkman, 173.

38. See Clark, 116 & 211.

39. See Björkman, 173.

40. See The Hague, *Convention (V) Respecting the Rights and Duties of Neutral Powers and Persons in Case of War on Land* (Oct. 18, 1907), http://www.icrc.org/IHL.NSF/FULL/200?OpenDocument.

41. See Björkman, 115.

42. See Falk, 165. The main purpose of the German occupation of Norway in April 1940 was to secure the port city of Narvik on the west coast of northern Norway. Britain considered a blockade of the port; however, this would have had little effect as long as iron ore could still be shipped from the Swedish city of Luleå in the far north by the Gulf of Bothnia. See Sarah Arildsson and Mikael Lidberg, *Vår Beredskap är God: En Studie Över den Militära Beredskapen i Övre Norrland, 1939–44 (We Are Well Prepared: A Study of the Military Preparedness in Upper Norrland, 1939–44)*, Luleå Tekniska Universitet, Sweden.

43. See Roberts, 51–52.

44. See Harald Öhquist, *Vinterkriget 1939–40 Ur Min Synvinkel (The Winter War 1939–40 from My View)* (Tammerfors, Finland: Tammerfors Handelstryckeri, 1949), 225–226.

45. See Edwards, 145.

46. Ibid., 208.

47. See Churchill, 490–491.

48. See Mannerheim, 255.

49. See Öhquist, 296 & 304.

50. See Isacson, 191–192.

51. See Mitchell G. Bard, *The Complete Idiot's Guide to World War II* (Indianapolis, IN: Alpha Books, 2004), 69.

52. See Isacson, 192.

53. See Clark, 179 & 186.

54. See Edwards, 271.

55. See Isacson, 192. Mannerheim was of the opposite opinion, however, and reasoned that if Sweden became a battleground for the Great Powers, England and France would benefit because Sweden would have to join the war on the side of the Allies against Germany. See Clark, 161.

56. See Nils Palmstierna, "Försvaret av Övre Norrland 1 September 1939–March 1940 (The Defense of Upper Norrland September 1, 1939–March 1940)," *Sveriges Militära Beredskap, 1939–1945 (Sweden's Military Preparedness, 1939–1945)*, edited by Carl-Axel Wangel (Stockholm, Sweden: Militärhistoriska Förlaget, 1982), 121.

57. See Edlund, 18.

58. See Falk, 166.

59. See Björkman, 178 & 209.

60. See Johansson, 58–59 & 126.

61. See Leif Björkman, *Det Svenska Vinterkriget, 1939–1940 (The Swedish Winter War, 1939–1940)* (Stockholm, Sweden: Hjalmarson & Högberg Bokförlag, 2007), 186–193.

62. See Tanner, 183.

63. See Johansson, 128–129.

64. Magnus Dyrssen, *Diary*, Svenska Frivilligkåren (Swedish Volunteer Corps), Krigsarkivet (War Archives), Stockholm, Sweden.

65. Ibid.

66. See Tanner, 184 & 189.

67. Ibid., 197 & 200.

68. Ibid., 170–171 & 183.

69. Ibid., 171.

70. See Clark, 155.

71. See Jason Edward Lavery, *The History of Finland* (Westport, CT: Greenwood Press, 2006), 120.

72. See Mannerheim, 69.

73. See Clark, 155.

74. William Trotter, *A Frozen Hell: The Russo-Finnish Winter War of 1939–40* (Chapel Hill, NC: Algonquin Books of Chapel Hill, 2000), 251.

75. See The Ambassador in the Soviet Union to the Secretary of State, Foreign Relations of the United States, Diplomatic Papers, 1940, Vol. I, General, Department of State, Historical Division, Bureau of Public Affairs, 1959.

76. See Mannerheim, 263.

77. See Björkman, 198.

78. See Andolf, 61.

79. See Eloise Engle and Lauri Paananen, *The Winter War: The Soviet Attack on Finland 1939–1940* (Mechanicsburg, PA: Stackpole Books, 1973), 132–133.

80. See Björkman, 200.

81. Ibid., 202.

82. See Edwards, 140.

83. See Björkman, 204–205.

84. See Edwards, 269.

85. See The Ambassador in the Soviet Union to the Secretary of State.

86. See Björkman, 203–205.

87. See Clark, 121, 164 & 176–177.

88. See Tanner, 202.

89. See Clark, 164.

90. See Björkman, 114 & 224–226.

91. See The Winter War of 1939–1940: Telegrams from Each Day of the Winter War.

92. See Carl O. Nordling, *Sacrificing Men or Machines? The Soviet Over-Sea Invasion of Finland in 1940*, http://www.carlonordling.se/winter_war.html.

93. See MastersWork Media.
94. See Nordling.
95. Ibid.
96. See Andolf, 46.
97. See Öhquist, 327.
98. See Järv, 60–61.
99. Wilhelm Odelberg, "Moskvafreden — Ett Mellanspel (The Moscow Peace — An Interlude)," *Svenska Frivilliga i Finland 1939–1940 (Swedish Volunteers in Finland 1939–1940)* (Stockholm, Sweden: Militärhistoriska Förlaget, 1989), 235.
100. See Edwards, *The Winter War: Russia's Invasion of Finland, 1939–40* (New York: Pegasus Books, 2008), 266–267.
101. See Mannerheim, 265–266.
102. See Nicolas von Schmidt-Laussitz and Klaus-Jürgen von Schmidt-Laussitz, *För Finlands Frihet: Svenska Frivilligkåren, 1939–1940 (For the Liberation of Finland: The Swedish Volunteer Corps, 1939–1940)* (Hallstavik, Sweden: Svenskt Militärhistoriskt Bibliotek, 2008), 138–139.
103. See Öhquist, 340.
104. See Andolf, 46.
105. See Jan Linder, *När Finlands Sak Blev Svensk Folkrörelse (When Finland's Cause Became a Swedish Folk Movement)*, Försvarsfrämjandet, http://www.forsvarsframjandet.org/FMF-97–2/nar-finlands-sak.htm.
106. See Orvar Nilsson, *När Finlands Sak Blev Min (When Finland's Cause Became Mine)* (Helsingfors, Finland: Schildts Förlags Ab, 2002), 47–49.
107. See Falk, 163.
108. See von Schmidt-Laussitz, 142–143 & 151.
109. See Falk, 166.
110. See Linda Edvardsson, *Finlands Sak och Vår: Svenska Frivilliga i Finska Vinterkriget (Finland's Cause and Ours: Swedish Volunteers in the Finnish Winter War)*, Finska Vinterkriget, http://www.algonet.se/~bog/vinterkriget/finlandssak.htm, originally published in *Finland och Andra Världskriget (Finland and the Second World War)* (Ekenäs, Sweden: Ekenäs Tryckeri, AB:s Förlag, 1958), 149–150, by Leonard Lundin.
111. See The Winter War of 1939–1940: Telegrams from Each Day of the Winter War.
112. See Den Frivillige, "Finlands Sak Var Inte Vår (Finland's Cause Was Not Ours)," *Den Frivillige*, No. 8 (Mar. 14, 1940), from Nicolas von Schmidt-Laussitz and Klaus-Jürgen von Schmidt-Laussitz, *För Finlands Frihet: Svenska Frivilligkåren, 1939–1940 (For the Liberation of Finland: The Swedish Volunteer Corps, 1939–1940)* (Hallstavik, Sweden: Svenskt Militärhistoriskt Bibliotek, 2008), 144.
113. See Öhquist, 337.
114. See Edwards, 256.
115. See Isacson, 206–207.
116. See Den Frivillige, 144.
117. See von Schmidt-Laussitz, 146.
118. See Björkman, 230.
119. See Öhquist, 337–338.
120. See Trotter, 263.
121. See Edvardsson, originally published in *Vinterkrigets Diplomati 1939–1940 (The Diplomacy of the Winter War 1939–1940)*, by Max Jakobson (Stockholm, Sweden: P.A. Norstedt & Söners Förlag, 1967), 166.
122. See Catherine Merridale, *Ivan's War: Life and Death in the Red Army, 1939–1945* (New York: Picador, 2006), 19.
123. See Trotter, 263. Note that sources differ as to the exact number of Soviet casualties.
124. See Isacson, 208.
125. See Finlandsfrivilliga. *Svenska Finlandsfrivilligas Minnesförening—The Association for Swedish Volunteers in Finland*, http://www.finlandsfrivilliga.se/historik.html.
126. See Edlund, 43.
127. See Edvardsson, originally published in *Finlandsaktivismen i Svensk Press. En Studie av Ledarmaterialet i de Svenska Dagstidningarna Under Vinterkriget 1939–1940 (Finnish Activists in Swedish Press. A Study of Leadership in the Swedish Newspapers During the Winter War 1939–1940)*, by Yngve Mohlin (Umeå Universitet, Sweden: Rapport, 1984), 52.
128. See Orvar Nilsson, 52.
129. See Rune Eriksson, "En Personlig Krönika (A Personal Chronicle)," *Finsk-Ryska Vinterkriget, 1939–40 (The Finnish-Russo Winter War, 1939–40)*, compiled by Ulf Söderback (Aug. 17, 1997), http://www.geocities.com/eureka/park/5121/fvkrig.doc.
130. See von Schmidt-Laussitz, 144.
131. See Bjuggren, 122.
132. See Johansson, 135–136.
133. See Edlund, 45.
134. See Johansson, 138.
135. See Documents on German Foreign Policy 1918–1945, Series D. Vol. VIII, No. 672 (Washington, DC: Department of State, publication 5436, 1954).
136. See Nikita Khrushchev, *Khrushchev Remembers*, translated by Strobe Talbott (Boston, MA: Little, Brown, 1970), 157.
137. In early spring of 1943, as the German troops were taking a beating in Russia, in a pathetic attempt to save face, Hermann Göring suggested that the enormous Russian losses during the early days of the Winter War had roots in a Soviet attempt to trick the world. If Europe, and particularly Germany, came to believe that the Red Army lacked the ability to fight well, they would underestimate the real strength of Stalin's forces. See Öhquist, 347.
138. See Jan Nilsson.
139. Author's translation of audio recording of Carl Gustaf Mannerheim's speech to the Swedish troops. The speech reprinted here has

been shortened from its original version, but retains its full meaning.

140. See Anders Umgård, *De Flög för Nordens Frihet (They Flew for Nordic Independence)*, Institution of History at Uppsala University.

141. See Falk, 180.

142. See von Schmidt-Laussitz, 167.

143. Ibid., 146–154.

144. Ibid., 169–170.

Chapter 5

1. John Hughes-Wilson, "Snow and Slaughter at Suomussalmi," *Military History* (Jan./Feb. 2006), 50.

2. See W. H. Halsti, *Försvaret av Finland (The Defense of Finland)* (Stockholm, Sweden: P. A. Norsetdt & Söner, 1940), 76.

3. See Halsti, 53 & 57.

4. See Harald Öhquist, *Vinterkriget 1939–40 Ur Min Synvinkel (The Winter War 1939–40 from My View)* (Tammerfors, Finland: Tammerfors Handelstryckeri, 1949), 28.

5. See Eloise Engle and Lauri Paananen, *The Winter War: The Soviet Attack on Finland 1939–1940* (Mechanicsburg, PA: Stackpole Books, 1973), 36.

6. See William Trotter, *A Frozen Hell: The Russo-Finnish Winter War of 1939–40* (Chapel Hill, NC: Algonquin Books of Chapel Hill, 2000), 69.

7. See Halsti, 72 & 98.

8. Ibid., 66.

9. See Öhquist, 30, 102 & 129.

10. See Winston S. Churchill, *The Gathering Storm* (New York: Houghton Mifflin, 1948), 488–489.

11. See Öhquist, 25–27.

12. See Carl Gustaf Mannerheim, *Marskalkens Minnen (The Marshal's Memories)* (Helsingfors, Finland: Holger Schildts Förlag, 1954), 175.

13. See Öhquist, 23 & 29.

14. Ibid., 353–354.

15. Ibid., 30.

16. Ibid., 351–355.

17. Ibid., 350.

18. See Claes-Göran Isacson, *Ärans Vinter: Finska Vinterkriget 1939–40 (A Winter of Honor: The Finnish Winter War 1939–40)* (Stockholm, Sweden: Norstedts Förlag, 2007), 121 & 171.

19. See Halsti, 17.

20. See Öhquist, 22.

21. See Mannerheim, 386.

22. See Öhquist, 365.

23. See Lennart Westberg, *Marschen till Märkäjärvi (The March to Märkäjärvi)* (Solna, Sweden: Leandoer & Ekholm Förlag, originally published 1940), 8. The Finnish peace proved short lived, however. In Operation Barbarossa, or Germany's invasion of the Soviet Union in 1941, Finland entered the conflict on the side of Germany in what came to be known as the Continuation War, which is beyond the scope of this book.

24. See Engle and Paananen, 33.

25. See Öhquist, 345.

26. See Engle and Paananen, 3.

27. See Nikita Khrushchev, *Khrushchev Remembers*, translated by Strobe Talbott (Boston, MA: Little, Brown, 1970), 150–152.

28. See Carl Nordling, *Stalin's Insistent Endeavors at Conquering Finland*, http://www.carlonordling.se/StalinFin.html.

29. See Evgeni Nikolaevich Kul kov, *Stalin and the Soviet-Finnish War, 1939–40* (Portland, OR: Frank Cass Publishers, 2002), 1.

30. See Öhquist, 177.

31. Ibid., 50.

32. See Kul kov, 6.

33. See Mannerheim, 243.

34. See Kul kov, 4

35. See Harry Järv, *Oavgjort i Två Krig: Finland—Sovietunionen 1939–1944 (Undecided in Two Wars: Finland—the Soviet Union 1939–1940)* (Avesta, Sweden: Samfundet Sverige-Finland, 2001), 54–55.

36. See Halsti, 15–16.

37. See Svenskt Militärhistoriskt Bibliotek, excerpt from *För Finlands Frihet: Svenska Frivilligkåren, 1939–1940 (For the Liberation of Finland: The Swedish Volunteer Corps, 1939–1940)*, by Klaus-Jürgen von Schmidt-Laussitz and Nicolas von Schmidt-Laussitz, 97–99, http://www.smb.nu/index.php/component/content/article/1241.

38. See MastersWork Media, *Fire and Ice: The Winter War of Finland and Russia*, produced and directed by Ben Strout, 2005.

39. The Ambassador in the Soviet Union to the Secretary of State, Foreign Relations of the United States Diplomatic Papers, 1939, Vol. I, General, Department of State, Publ. 6242, 1956.

40. See Robert Edwards, *The Winter War: Russia's Invasion of Finland, 1939–40* (New York: Pegasus Books, 2008), 92.

41. See Halsti, 98.

42. See Kulkov, 42.

43. See MastersWork Media.

44. See Kulkov, 42.

45. See Khrushchev, 124.

46. See Ivan S. Chetyrbok, Senior Sergeant, 3rd Battalion, 85th Rifle Regiment, 100th Rifle Division, *The Mannerheim Line, 1920–39*, by Bair Irincheev, http://www.mannerheim-line.com/veterans/chetyrboke.htm.

47. See Kulkov, 120.

48. Ibid., 87–88 & 112–113.

49. Ibid., 40.

50. Ibid, 15, 20 & 42.

51. See Öhquist, 39.

52. See Krigsarkivet (War Archives), *Analysis*, Svenska Frivilligkåren, Kriget 1939–1940.

53. See Kulkov, 83.

54. See Krigsarkivet.

55. See Veteraanien Perinto, *Luftstridskrafterna: Vinterkriget (The Air Force: The Winter War)*, Arvet Efter Veteranerna — Ett Självständigt Fosterland 2002, http://www.veteraanienperinto.fi/svenska/t_pankki/a_lajit/lentajan_maailmanennatys.htm.

56. See Öhquist, 39.

57. See Kulkov, 12–19.

58. See Major George Fielding Eliot, "Russian Campaign Against Finland," *Life* (Jan. 15, 1940), 26.

59. See Halsti, 16.

60. See Kulkov, 67.

61. See Öhquist, 168.

62. See Kulkov, 38.

63. Ibid., 33.

64. See Khrushchev, 153.

65. See Järv, 53.

66. See Kulkov, 1.

67. See Järv, 61.

68. See Kulkov, 113–115.

69. See Öhquist, 349.

70. See Kulkov, 47 & 80.

71. Ibid., 33 & 45.

72. See Khrushchev, 155.

73. Chetyrbok.

74. See Geoffrey Roberts, *Stalin's Wars from World War to Cold War, 1939–1953* (New Haven, CT: Yale University Press, 2006), 46–47.

75. Ibid., 53.

76. See Halsti, 57.

77. See Douglas Clark, *Three Days to Catastrophe: Britain and the Russo-Finnish Winter War* (London: Hammond, Hammond & Company, 1966), 32.

78. See Roger R. Reese, "Lessons of the Winter War: A Study in the Military Effectiveness of the Red Army, 1939–1940," *The Journal of Military History*, Vol. 72, No. 3 (Jul. 2008), 825–831.

79. See Nordling.

80. See Reese, 848–849.

81. See Khrushchev, 152.

82. Viktor M. Iskrov, Colonel of the Guards, Lieutenant, Forward Observation Platoon Leader, 68th Independent Mortar Battery, *The Mannerheim Line, 1920–39*, by Bair Irincheev, http://www.mannerheim-line.com/veterans/iskrove.htm.

83. Dmitri A. Krutskih, Lieutenant, Engineer Platoon Leader, 16th Independent Engineer Battalion, 54th Rifle Division, *The Mannerheim Line, 1920–39*, interview by Artem Drabkin, translation by Bair Irincheev, http://www.mannerheim-line.com/veterans/krutskih.htm.

84. See Alf W. Johansson, *Per Albin och Kriget: Samlingsregeringen och Utrikespolitiken Under Andra Världskriget (Per Albin and the War: The Coalition Government and Foreign Policy During the Second World War)* (Stockholm, Sweden: Tidens Förlag, 1984), 130.

85. See Krister Wahlbäck, *Finlandsfrågan i Svensk Politik 1937–1940 (The Finland Question in Swedish Politics 1937–1940)* (Stockholm, Sweden: P. A. Norstedt & Söners Förlag, 1964), 395.

86. See Leif Björkman, *Det Svenska Vinterkriget, 1939–1940 (The Swedish Winter War, 1939–1940)* (Stockholm, Sweden: Hjalmarson & Högberg Bokförlag, 2007), 113.

87. See Lars Ericson Wolke, "Sverige Under Andra Världskriget (Sweden During the Second World War)," *Populär Historia* (Apr., 2004).

88. See Björkman, 6. Sweden was the only Scandinavian country that managed to avoid direct military confrontation in World War II. The idea that the Winter War was Sweden's war, and it was crucial that Finland succeed against Russia, can be traced to an event that took place twenty years earlier: In 1918, Swedish king Gustav V Adolf invited Mannerheim to Stockholm to receive honors for his "services to Sweden during [Finland's] War of Independence." See Mannerheim, 113.

89. See Johansson, 59.

90. See Harry Martinson, *Verklighet till Döds (Reality to Death)* (Stockholm, Sweden: P. A. Norstedt & Söner, 1940), 100.

91. See Erik Carlquist, *Solidaritet på Prov: Finlandshjälp Under Vinterkriget (A Test of Solidarity: Assistance for Finland During the Winter War)* (Stockholm, Sweden: Allmänna Förlaget, 1971), 272.

92. See Flames of War, *Svenska Frivilliga Kåren (The Swedish Volunteer Corps)*, Battlefront, http://www.battlefront.co.nz/Article.asp?ArticleID=153.

93. See Lars Gyllenhaal and Lennart Westberg, *Svenskar i Krig, 1914–1945 (Swedes at War, 1914–1945)* (Lund, Sweden: Historiska Media, 2008), 240.

94. See Göran Andolf, "Svenska Frivilligkåren (The Swedish Volunteer Corps)," *Svenska Frivilliga i Finland 1939–1940 (Swedish Volunteers in Finland 1939–1940)* (Stockholm, Sweden: Militärhistoriska Förlaget, 1989), 181.

95. See Krigsarkivet.

96. See Björkman, 129–133.

97. Ibid., 133–136.

98. Ibid., 141–144.

99. Ibid., 136–144.

100. See Jessica Eriksson, *F19: Frivilliga Flygande för Finlands Sak och Politiken Bakom (F19: Volunteer Pilots for Finland's Cause and the Politics Behind Their Missions)*, Luleå Tekniska Universitet, Sweden.

101. See Björkman, 246–252.

102. See Gyllenhaal and Westberg, 241.

103. See Nicolas von Schmidt-Laussitz and

Klaus-Jürgen von Schmidt-Laussitz, *För Finlands Frihet: Svenska Frivilligkåren, 1939–1940 (For the Liberation of Finland: The Swedish Volunteer Corps, 1939–1940)* (Hallstavik, Sweden: Svenskt Militärhistoriskt Bibliotek, 2008), 171.

104. See Mannerheim, 272.

105. See Lars Ericson, *Svenska Frivilliga: Militära Uppdrag i Utlandet Under 1800- och 1900-talen (Swedish Volunteers: Foreign Military Missions During the 1800s and 1900s)* (Lund, Sweden: Historiska Media, 1996), 111–112.

106. See Gyllenhaal and Westberg, 244–245.

107. See Erik Helmerson, "Finlands Sak Var Hans: Orvar Nilsson Upplevde Kriget i Verkligheten" (Finland's Cause Was His: Orvar Nilsson Experienced the Real War), *TT Spektra* (2008).

108. See Efraim Karsh, *Neutrality and Small States* (New York: Routledge, 1988), 84–86.

109. See Kul kov, xv–xvi.

110. See Karsh, 86.

111. See Clark, 44.

112. See Edwards, 103.

113. See Clark, 45 & 49.

114. See Völkischer Beobachter, "Kampfblatt der national-sozialistischen Bewegung Großdeutschlands (The combat newspaper of the national-socialist movement in Greater Germany)," translated by Pauli Kruhse (Mar. 14, 1940), http://www.histdoc.net/history/VB1940-03-14.html.

115. See Clark, 201.

116. See Edwards, 259.

117. See Encyclopædia Britannica, *Anglo-German Naval Agreement*, http://www.britannica.com/EBchecked/topic/25048/Anglo-German-Naval-Agreement.

118. See Izidors Vizulis, *The Molotov-Ribbentrop Pact of 1939: The Baltic Case* (New York: Praeger Publishers, 1990), 4.

119. See Karsh, 23–25.

120. Ibid., 4.

121. See Carl-Axel Wangel, "Neutralitetsrätt — Regler och Tillämpning (Right to Neutrality — Rules and Application)," *Sveriges Militära Beredskap, 1939–1945 (Sweden's Military Preparedness, 1939–1945)*, edited by Carl-Axel Wangel (Stockholm, Sweden: Militärhistoriska Förlaget, 1982), 62–65.

122. See Karsh, 54.

123. See Ericson, 190–192.

124. See Björkman, 218.

125. Churchill, 489.

126. See Clark, 8.

127. A revealing example of Sweden's continued strife for impartiality is the fact that, by 1950, Sweden had the fourth largest air force in the world. Sweden made its first military flight in 1912, and established its first flight squadron in the summer of that year. SAAB — Svenska Aeroplan Aktie Bolaget (Swedish Airplane Incorporated) — was in the 1980s involved in the development of the modern fighter airplane JAS 39 Gripen, which had replaced most of the older fighters by 2006. The decision that Sweden, a small and sparsely populated country, should develop its own fighter airplane rather than buying, for example, from the United States, has been viewed as overly ambitious and has been criticized by the Swedish population on economic grounds. In order to maintain neutrality in war, however, Sweden had to develop its internal resources and garner the military strength to resist offensive action by enemy forces. The manufacture of military equipment demonstrates to the world that Sweden takes its neutrality seriously.

128. See Olof Palme, *Att Vilja Gå Vidare (The Desire to Progress)* (Stockholm, Sweden: Kungliga Boktryckeriet Norstedt & Söner, 1974), 203.

129. See Christian Leitz, *Nazi Germany and Neutral Europe During the Second World War* (Manchester, UK: Manchester University Press, 2000), 50.

130. In contemporary times, Sweden has sent several hundred peacekeeping troops to Afghanistan as part of the NATO-led International Security Assistance Force (ISAF).

Bibliography

Åhslund, Bengt. "Det Militärpolitiska Läget vid Krigsutbrottet 1939 (The Military-Political Situation at the Outbreak of War 1939)." *Sveriges Militära Beredskap, 1939–1945 (Sweden's Military Preparedness, 1939–1945)*. Edited by Carl-Axel Wangel. Stockholm, Sweden: Militärhistoriska Förlaget, 1982.

Air Force Museum in Sweden. Pamphlet. *F19—Flygande Frivilliga för Finlands Sak (F19—Flying Volunteers for Finland's Cause)*.

The Ambassador in the Soviet Union to the Secretary of State. Foreign Relations of the United States. Diplomatic Papers 1939, Vol. I, General, Department of State, Publication 6242, 1956.

_____. Diplomatic Papers, 1940, Vol. I, General, Department of State, Historical Division, Bureau of Public Affairs, 1959.

Andolf, Göran. "Svenska Frivilligkåren (The Swedish Volunteer Corps)." *Svenska Frivilliga i Finland 1939–1940 (Swedish Volunteers in Finland 1939–1940)*. Stockholm, Sweden: Militärhistoriska Förlaget, 1989.

Arildsson, Sarah, and Lidberg, Mikael. *Vår Beredskap är God: En Studie Över den Militära Beredskapen i Övre Norrland, 1939–44 (We Are Well Prepared: A Study of the Military Preparedness in Upper Norrland, 1939–44)*. Luleå Tekniska Universitet, Sweden.

Army Museum. Stockholm, Sweden, 2000.

Bard, Mitchell G. *The Complete Idiot's Guide to World War II*. Indianapolis, IN: Alpha Books, 2004.

Beredskapsmuseet. *Per Albin Hansson*. http://www.beredskapsmuseet.com/peralbin.html.

Berghäll, Patrik. *Finska Fjällpatrull Medlemmar Minns (Memories from the Members of the Finnish Mountain Patrol)*. Åbo (Oct. 27, 2004).

Bernaerts, Arnd. *Climate Change & Naval War: A Scientific Assessment*. Victoria, BC, Canada: Trafford Publishing, 2005.

Björkman, Leif. *Det Svenska Vinterkriget, 1939–1940 (The Swedish Winter War, 1939–1940)*. Stockholm, Sweden: Hjalmarson & Högberg Bokförlag, 2007.

Bjuggren, Björn. *Svenska Flygare i Österled (Swedish Pilots in the East)*. Stockholm, Sweden: Albert Bonniers Förlag.

Borodin, M. M., editor-in-chief. "Report of Comrade V. M. Molotov, Chairman of the Council of People's Commissars and People's Commissar of Foreign Affairs, at Sitting of Supreme Soviet of USSR on Oct. 31, 1939." *Moscow News* (Nov. 6, 1939).

Brown, Philip Marshall. "The Aaland Islands Question." *American Journal of International Law*, Vol. 15, No. 2 (Apr. 1921).

Bülow Orrje, Karin. "En Svensk Tiger (A Swede Remains Silent)." *Värnpliktsnytt* (Nov. 25, 2008).

Cajander, A. K. The address by Prime Minister A. K. Cajander on the 23rd of November 1939, at Helsinki Fair Hall, at a national defence celebration arranged by Finnish private enterprise owners. http://www.histdoc.net/history/cajander.html.

Carlquist, Erik. *Solidaritet på Prov: Finlandshjälp Under Vinterkriget (A Test of Solidarity: Assistance for Finland During the Winter War)*. Stockholm, Sweden: Allmänna Förlaget, 1971.

Chetyrbok, Ivan S., Senior Sergeant, 3rd Battalion, 85th Rifle Regiment, 100th Rifle Division. *Personal Diary*. Fire and Ice. http:

//www.wfyi.org/FireandIce/educational_resources/diaries_Chetyrbok.htm.
Chistov, Gleb F., Military Technician-Commissary 2nd Rank, 70th Automobile-Sanitary Platoon, 50th Rifle Corps, 7th Army. *The Mannerheim Line, 1920–39*, by Bair Irincheev. http://www.mannerheim-line.com/veterans/Chistove.htm.
Chrusjtjov, Nikita. "Vinterkriget Mot Finland (The Winter War Against Finland)." *Finska Vinterkriget, 1939–40 (The Finnish Winter War, 1939–40).* http://www.marxistarkiv.se/europa/finland/finska_vinterkriget-artiklar.pdf.
Churchill, Winston S. *The Gathering Storm.* New York: Houghton Mifflin, 1948.
Clark, Douglas. *Three Days to Catastrophe: Britain and the Russo-Finnish Winter War.* London: Hammond, Hammond & Company, 1966.
Cronenberg, Arvid. "1936 Års Försvarsbeslut och Upprustningen 1936–1939 (The Decisions in Military Defense of 1936 and the Military Buildup of 1936–1939)." *Sveriges Militära Beredskap, 1939–1945 (Sweden's Military Preparedness, 1939–1945).* Edited by Carl-Axel Wangel. Stockholm, Sweden: Militärhistoriska Förlaget, 1982.
Dagens Nyheter. "800 Ryssar Stupade i Slag vid Kemi Älv (800 Russians Fallen in Battle at Kemi River)." *Dagens Nyheter* (Dec. 21, 1939).
_____. "Rysk Massattack med Tanks på Karelska Näset (Russian Massattack with Tanks on the Karelian Isthmus)." *Dagens Nyheter* (Dec. 21, 1939).
_____. "Ägläjärvi Blev Nytt Segernam: Två Tusen Ryssar Stupade (Ägläjärvi Became New Victory Name: Two Thousand Russians Fallen)." *Dagens Nyheter* (Dec. 24, 1939).
Davidenko, Vasily F., Lieutenant of Artillery, Forward Observer Platoon Leader, 7th Rifle Regiment, 24th Samara — Ulyanovsk "Iron" Rifle Division. *The Mannerheim Line, 1920–39*, by Bair Irincheev. http://www.mannerheim-line.com/veterans/davidenkoe.htm.
Debatt Passagen. *Några Telegram Om Finska Vinterkriget (Some Telegrams from the Finnish Winter War).* http://debatt.passagen.se.
Documents on German Foreign Policy 1918–1945. Series D. Vol. VIII, No. 240. Washington, DC: Department of State, publication 5436, 1954.
_____. Series D. Vol. VIII, No. 426. Washington, DC: Department of State, publication 5436, 1954.
_____. Series D. Vol. VIII, No. 443. Washington, DC: Department of State, publication 5436, 1954.
_____. Series D. Vol. VIII, No. 471. Washington, DC: Department of State, publication 5436, 1954.
_____. Series D. Vol. VIII, No. 513. Washington, DC: Department of State, publication 5436, 1954.
_____. Series D. Vol. VIII, No. 672. Washington, DC: Department of State, publication 5436, 1954.
Dyrssen, Magnus. *Diary.* Svenska Frivilligkåren (Swedish Volunteer Corps). Krigsarkivet (War Archives). Stockholm, Sweden.
Economic Expert. *Anglo-German Naval Agreement.* http://www.economicexpert.com/a/Anglo:German:Naval:Agreement.htm.
_____. *Sweden During World War II.* http://www.economicexpert.com/a/Sweden:during:World:War:II.html.
Edlund, Albin. *Svenska Marinens Frivilliga i Finland, 1939–1944 (The Swedish Marine Volunteers in Finland, 1939–1944).* Karlskrona, Sweden: Marinmusei Vänner och Axel Abrahamsons Tryckeri AB, 1995.
Edvardsson, Linda. *Finlands Sak och Vår: Svenska Frivilliga i Finska Vinterkriget (Finland's Cause and Ours: Swedish Volunteers in the Finnish Winter War).* Finska Vinterkriget. http://www.algonet.se/~bog/vinterkriget/finlandssak.htm.
Edwards, Robert. *The Winter War: Russia's Invasion of Finland, 1939–40.* New York: Pegasus Books, 2008.
Eliot, George Fielding, Major. "Russian Campaign Against Finland." *Life* (Jan. 15, 1940).
Encyclopædia Britannica. *Anglo-German Naval Agreement.* http://www.britannica.com/EBchecked/topic/25048/Anglo-German-Naval-Agreement.
Engle, Eloise, and Paananen, Lauri. *The Winter War: The Soviet Attack on Finland 1939–1940.* Mechanicsburg, PA: Stackpole Books, 1973.
Ericson, Lars. *Svenska Frivilliga: Militära Uppdrag i Utlandet Under 1800- och 1900-talen (Swedish Volunteers: Foreign Military Missions During the 1800s and 1900s).* Lund, Sweden: Historiska Media, 1996.
Ericson Wolke, Lars. "Sverige Under Andra

Världskriget (Sweden During the Second World War)." *Populär Historia* (Apr. 2004).

Eriksson, Jessica. *F19: Frivilliga Flygande för Finlands Sak och Politiken Bakom (F19: Volunteer Pilots for Finland's Cause and the Politics Behind Their Missions).* Luleå Tekniska Universitet, Sweden.

Eriksson, Rune. "En Personlig Krönika (A Personal Chronicle)." *Finsk-Ryska Vinterkriget, 1939–40 (The Finnish-Russo Winter War, 1939–40).*Compiled by Ulf Söderback (Aug. 17, 1997). http://www.geocities.com/eureka/park/5121/fvkrig.doc.

Falk, Greger. *F19—En Krönika: Den Svenska Frivilliga Flygflottiljen i Finland Under Vinterkriget, 1939–1940 (F19—A Chronicle: The Swedish Volunteer Flight Squadron in Finland During the Winter War, 1939–1940).* Stockholm, Sweden: Svensk Flyghistorisk Förening.

Finlandsfrivilliga. *Svenska Finlandsfrivilligas Minnesförening (The Association for Swedish Volunteers in Finland).* http://www.finlandsfrivilliga.se/historik.html.

Flames of War. *Svenska Frivilliga Kåren (The Swedish Volunteer Corps).* Battlefront. http://www.battlefront.co.nz/Article.asp?ArticleID=153.

Flamman. "Sveriges Värsta Terrordåd (Sweden's Worst Terror Act)." *Flamman* (Oct. 6, 2006).

Försvarsmakten (The National Defense, Sweden). http://www.mil.se.

Den Frivillige. "Finlands Sak Var Inte Vår (Finland's Cause Was Not Ours)." *Den Frivillige,* No. 8 (Mar. 14, 1940). From Nicolas von Schmidt-Laussitz and Klaus-Jürgen von Schmidt-Laussitz, *För Finlands Frihet: Svenska Frivilligkåren, 1939–1940 (For the Liberation of Finland: The Swedish Volunteer Corps, 1939–1940).* Hallstavik, Sweden: Svenskt Militärhistoriskt Bibliotek, 2008.

Gardell, Carl-Johan. Review of "Det Svenska Vinterkriget, 1939–40 (The Swedish Winter War, 1939–40)," by Leif Björkman. *Svenska Dagbladet* (Nov. 26, 2007).

Gilbert, Martin. *The Second World War: A Complete History.* New York: Henry Holt, 1989.

Gyllenhaal, Lars. *Luftstrid Över Lappland (Air Fights Above Lapland).* Svenskt Militärhistoriskt Bibliotek. http://www.smb.nu/index.php/militara-artiklar/finlandskrig/1199-i-luftstrid-oever-lappland.

_____, and Westberg, Lennart. *Svenskar i Krig, 1914–1945 (Swedes at War, 1914–1945).* Lund, Sweden: Historiska Media, 2008.

Hagström, Anders. "Stalins Dyrköpta Vinterkrig (Stalin's Expensive Winter War)." *Finska Vinterkriget, 1939–40 (The Finnish Winter War, 1939–40).* http://www.marxistarkiv.se/europa/finland/finska_vinterkriget-artiklar.pdf.

The Hague. *Convention (V) Respecting the Rights and Duties of Neutral Powers and Persons in Case of War on Land* (Oct. 18, 1907). http://www.icrc.org/IHL.NSF/FULL/200?OpenDocument.

Håkans Flygsida. *J8 Gloster Gladiator in the Swedish Air Force.* http://surfcity.kund.dalnet.se/gladiator_sweden.htm.

Halsti, W. H. *Försvaret av Finland (The Defense of Finland).* Stockholm, Sweden: P. A. Norsetdt & Söner, 1940.

Hämäläinen, Valde., Finnish AT Gun Platoon Leader, Battle of Summa. *Personal Diary.* Fire and Ice. http://www.wfyi.org/FireandIce/educational_resources/diaries_Hamalainen.htm.

Hammarén, Lars. *Sverige Under Andra Världskriget (Sweden During the Second World War).* Lars Hammaréns Historiehemsida (2002). http://www.larshammaren.se/6_sv2vkr.html#kom2.

Helmerson, Erik. "Finlands Sak Var Hans: Orvar Nilsson Upplevde Kriget i Verkligheten (Finland's Cause Was His: Orvar Nilsson Experienced the Real War)." *TT Spektra* (2008).

Henriksson, Lars. *J8—Gloster Gladiator (1937–1947).* http://www.avrosys.nu/aircraft/jakt/108J8.htm.

Hjort, Daniel. "Hans Ruin Kunde För Mycket (Hans Ruin Knew Too Much)." *Svenska Dagbladet* (Feb. 7, 2004).

Hughes-Wilson, John. "Snow and Slaughter at Suomussalmi." *Military History* (Jan./Feb. 2006).

Irincheev, Bair. *The Mannerheim Line, 1920–39,* by http://www.mannerheim-line.com/veterans/chetyrboke.htm.

Isacson, Claes-Göran. *Ärans Vinter: Finska Vinterkriget 1939–40 (A Winter of Honor: The Finnish Winter War 1939–40).* Stockholm, Sweden: Norstedts Förlag, 2007.

Iskrov, Viktor M., Colonel of the Guards, Lieutenant, Forward Observation Platoon Leader, 68th Independent Mortar Battery.

The Mannerheim Line, 1920–39, by Bair Irincheev. http://www.mannerheim-line.com/veterans/iskrove.htm.

Järv, Harry. *Oavgjort i Två Krig: Finland—Sovietunionen 1939–1944 (Undecided in Two Wars: Finland—the Soviet Union 1939–1944)*. Avesta, Sweden: Samfundet Sverige-Finland, 2006.

Johansson, Alf W. *Per Albin och Kriget: Samlingsregeringen och Utrikespolitiken Under Andra Världskriget (Per Albin and the War: The Coalition Government and Foreign Policy During the Second World War)*. Stockholm, Sweden: Tidens Förlag, 1984.

Karsh, Efraim. *Neutrality and Small States*. New York: Routledge, 1988.

Kattonen, Toivo M., Machine Gunner, 1st Machine Gun Company, 99th Detached Volunteer Ski Battalion. *The Mannerheim Line, 1920–39*, by Bair Irincheev. http://www.mannerheim-line.com/veterans/Toivo.htm.

Keyes, Gene. "Stalin's Finland Fiasco: The Kusinen Government Reconsidered." First published in *Crossroads: An International Socio-Political Journal*, No. 17 (1985).

Khrushchev, Nikita. *Khrushchev Remembers*. Translated by Strobe Talbott. Boston, MA: Little, Brown, 1970.

Krigsarkivet (War Archives). *Analysis*. Svenska Frivilligkåren, Kriget 1939–1940.

_____. *Anmälan till Åbo, Mar. 1, 1940 (Application to Åbo, Mar. 1, 1940)*. Luftvärnsdivisionen i Åbo, 1939–1940, Vol. 1.

_____. *Daily Log*. Svenska Frivilligkåren, Kriget 1939–1940.

_____. *Instruktion för Signalisterna i Åbo, Mar. 8, 1940 (Instruction for the Telephone Operators in Åbo, Mar. 8, 1940)*. Luftvärnsdivisionen i Åbo, 1939–1940, Vol. 1.

_____. *Luftvärnsdivisionen Åbo Krigsdagbok (Anti-Aircraft Artillery in Åbo, Daily Log)*. Luftvärnsdivisionen i Åbo, 1939–1940, Vol. 1.

_____. *Newspaper Clipping, Feb. 3, 1940*. Finlandskommitten, 1939–1940, Vol. 3–5, 7, och 44d.

_____. *Newspaper Clipping, Mar. 22, 1940*. Finlandskommitten, 1939–1940, Vol. 3–5, 7, och 44d.

_____. *Propaganda Letter*. Finlandskommitten, 1939–1940, Vol. 3–5, 7, och 44d.

_____. *Rusthåll-Brev (Letter from the Committee for Finland)*. Finlandskommitten, 1939–1940, Vol. 3–5, 7, och 44d.

_____. *Den Svenske Folksocialisten*. Newspaper Clipping (Feb. 3, 1940). Finlandskommitten, 1939–1940, Vol. 3–5, 7, och 44d.

_____. *Telegram från Stockholm till Åbo, Feb. 26, 1940 (Telegram from Stockholm to Åbo, Feb. 26, 1940)*. Luftvärnsdivisionen i Åbo, 1939–1940, Vol. 1.

_____. *Utrustning (Equipment)*. Svenska Frivilligkåren, 1939–1940, Vol. 5a-5b.

_____. *Vilhelm Moberg—Letter to the Farmers, Dec. 12, 1939*. Finlandskommitten, 1939–1940, Vol. 3–5, 7, och 44d.

_____. *Åbo Permissionsordning, Mar. 6, 1940 (Åbo Policy for Leave, Mar. 6, 1940)*. Luftvärnsdivisionen i Åbo, 1939–1940, Vol. 1.

Krutskih, Dmitri A., Lieutenant, Engineer Platoon Leader, 16th Independent Engineer Battalion, 54th Rifle Division. *The Mannerheim Line, 1920–39*. Interview by Artem Drabkin. Translation by Bair Irincheev. http://www.mannerheim-line.com/veterans/krutskih.htm.

Kulkov, Evgeni Nikolaevich. *Stalin and the Soviet-Finnish War, 1939–40*. Portland, OR: Frank Cass Publishers, 2002.

Lange, Tor. "Vapenhjälpen till Finland (Weapons Export to Finland)." *Sveriges Militära Beredskap, 1939–1945 (Sweden's Military Preparedness, 1939–1945)*. Edited by Carl-Axel Wangel. Stockholm, Sweden: Militärhistoriska Förlaget, 1982.

Laurén, Anna-Lena. "Mannerheim Blev Störste Finländaren (Mannerheim Became the Greatest Finn)." *Svenska Dagbladet* (Dec. 6, 2004).

Lavery, Jason Edward. *The History of Finland*. Westport, CT: Greenwood Press, 2006.

Leitz, Christian. *Nazi Germany and Neutral Europe During the Second World War*. Manchester, UK: Manchester University Press, 2000.

Lindblom, Ebbe. "Harry Martinson och Författarnas Vinterkrig (Harry Martinson and the Winter War of the Authors)." *Svenska Frivilliga i Finland 1939–1940 (Swedish Volunteers in Finland 1939–1940)*. Stockholm, Sweden: Militärhistoriska Förlaget, 1989.

Linder, Jan. *När Finlands Sak Blev Svensk Folkrörelse (When Finland's Cause Became a Swedish Folk Movement)*. Försvarsfrämjandet. http://www.forsvarsframjandet.org/FMF-97–2/nar-finlands-sak.htm.

Mannerheim, Carl Gustaf. *Marskalkens Minnen (The Marshal's Memories)*. Helsingfors, Finland: Holger Schildts Förlag, 1954.

Martinson, Harry. *Verklighet till Döds (Reality to Death)*. Stockholm, Sweden: P. A. Norstedt & Söner, 1940.

MastersWork Media. *Fire and Ice: The Winter War of Finland and Russia*. Produced and directed by Ben Strout, 2005.

Memorandum of Conversation, by the Chief of the Division of European Affairs. Foreign Relations of the United States. Diplomatic Papers, 1939, Vol. I, General, Department of State, Publication 6242, 1956.

Merridale, Catherine. *Ivan's War: Life and Death in the Red Army, 1939–1945*. New York: Picador, 2006.

The Minister of Finland to the Secretary of State. Foreign Relations of the United States. Diplomatic Papers, 1939, Vol. I, General, Department of State, Publication 6242, 1956.

Molotov, V. M. "Radio Speech of Comr. V. M. Molotov, Chairman of Council of People's Commissars of USSR, Nov. 29, 1939." *Moscow News* (Dec. 4, 1939).

Naess, Ragnar. *Marschen till Märkäjärvi (The March to Märkäjärvi)*. Solna, Sweden: Leandoer & Ekholm Förlag, originally published 1940.

National Archive Exhibit of the Winter War. *Vinterkriget från Sommar till Sommar (The Winter War from Summer to Summer)*. Finland National Archive. http://www.narc.fi/naytt/naytxruo.htm.

NationMaster — Encyclopedia. *Gustav V of Sweden*. http://www.nationmaster.com/encyclopedia/Gustav-V-of-Sweden.

Nazi-Soviet Relations 1939–1941. Documents from the Archives of the German Foreign Office. Washington, DC, 1948.

Nelsson, Bertil. *Frivillig i Finland (Volunteer in Finland)*. Svenskt Militärhistoriskt Bibliotek. http://www.smb.nu/pos/03/04_frivillig_i_finland.asp.

_____. *En Intervju med Orvar Nilsson (An Interview with Orvar Nilsson)*. Swedish Military History Library. http://www.smb.nu/pos/00/10_orvar_nilsson.asp.

Nilsson, Björn. *Finska Armens Förberedelser och Taktik Under Finska Vinterkriget 1939–1940 (The Finnish Army's Preparations and Tactics During the Finnish Winter War 1939–1940)*. Finska Vinterkriget. http://www.algonet.se/~bog/vinterkriget/finsktaktik.htm.

Nilsson, Jan. *Moder Svea och Kriget: Svensk Politik Under Andra Världskriget (Mother Sweden and the War: Swedish Politics During the Second World War)*. Artikelbiblioteket. http://web.comhem.se/akademin/artikelbiblioteket/artiklar/svepol.htm.

_____. *Svensk Diplomatrapportering Under Finska Vinterkriget Oktober 1939–Mars 1940 (Swedish Diplomacy Report During the Finnish Winter War October 1939–March 1940)*. Artikelbiblioteket. http://members.chello.se/akademin/artikelbiblioteket/artiklar/arngren.htm.

Nilsson, Orvar. *När Finlands Sak Blev Min (When Finland's Cause Became Mine)*. Helsingfors, Finland: Schildts FörlagsAb, 2002.

Nordling, Carl. *The Molotov-Ribbentrop Pact Provoked the Outbreak of World War II*. http://www.carlonordling.se/ww2/stalinevoke.html.

_____. *Sacrificing Men or Machines? The Soviet Over-Sea Invasion of Finland in 1940*. http://www.carlonordling.se/winter_war.html.

_____. *Stalin's Insistent Endeavors at Conquering Finland*. http://www.carlonordling.se/StalinFin.html.

_____. *Stalin's Speech to the Politburo on 19 August 1939*. Reconstructed from Renderings in Novyi Mir, Moscow, and Revue de Droit International, Geneva. http://www.carlonordling.se/ww2/stalin_speech_complete.html.

Nyberg, Per. "Long-Lost World War II Sub Found off Swedish Coast." *CNN*. http://www.cnn.com/2009/WORLD/europe/06/09/sweden.ww2.sub/index.html.

Ödeen, Lennart. "Finland i Brännpunkten (Finland in Focus)." *Gefle Dagblad* (May 13, 2007).

Odelberg, Wilhelm. "Moskvafreden — Ett Mellanspel (The Moscow Peace — An Interlude)." *Svenska Frivilliga i Finland 1939–1940 (Swedish Volunteers in Finland 1939–1940)*. Stockholm, Sweden: Militärhistoriska Förlaget, 1989.

Öhquist, Harald. *Vinterkriget 1939–40 Ur Min Synvinkel (The Winter War 1939–40 from My View)*. Tammerfors, Finland: Tammerfors Handelstryckeri, 1949.

Palm, Thede. "Förord (Introduction)." *Sveriges Militära Beredskap, 1939–1945 (Sweden's Military Preparedness, 1939–1945)*. Edited by Carl-Axel Wangel. Stockholm, Sweden: Militärhistoriska Förlaget, 1982.

Palme, Olof. *Att Vilja Gå Vidare (The Desire to Progress)*. Stockholm, Sweden: Kungliga Boktryckeriet Norstedt & Söner, 1974.

Palmstierna, Nils. "Försvaret av Övre Norrland 1 September 1939–March 1940 (The Defense of Upper Norrland September 1, 1939–March 1940)." *Sveriges Militära Beredskap, 1939–1945 (Sweden's Military Preparedness, 1939–1945)*. Edited by Carl-Axel Wangel. Stockholm, Sweden: Militärhistoriska Förlaget, 1982.

_____. "Krigsplanläggningen vid Krigsutbrottet (The Planned Defense at the Outbreak of War)." *Sveriges Militära Beredskap, 1939–1945 (Sweden's Military Preparedness, 1939–1945)*. Edited by Carl-Axel Wangel. Stockholm, Sweden: Militärhistoriska Förlaget, 1982.

_____. "Mobiliseringen i September 1939 (The Mobilization in September 1939)." *Sveriges Militära Beredskap, 1939–1945 (Sweden's Military Preparedness, 1939–1945)*. Edited by Carl-Axel Wangel. Stockholm, Sweden: Militärhistoriska Förlaget, 1982.

People's Commissar for Foreign Affairs of the USSR. Note of V. M. Molotov, Commissar for Foreign Affairs, handed on November 26th, 1939 to M. Yrjö-Koskinen, Finnish Minister at Moscow (Nov. 26, 1939).

Political Administration of Workers' and Peasants' Red Army (RKKA). *Propagandist and Agitator of the RKKA*. Translated by Pauli Kruhse and Lahja Huovila. Moscow, Nr. 22 (Nov. 1939).

Ponomarenko, Nikolai Alexeevich, Colonel (Retired), Lieutenant During the Winter War, Chief of Forward Observers, 4th Artillery Battalion, 168 Super Heavy Artillery Regiment. *The Mannerheim Line, 1920–39*, by Bair Irincheev. http://www.mannerheim-line.com/veterans/ponomarenko.htm.

Pravda. "A Buffoon Holding the Post of Prime Minister." *Pravda* (Nov. 26, 1939).

Prusakov, Georgi V., Medic., 100th Independent Volunteer Ski Battalion. *The Mannerheim Line, 1920–39*, by Bair Irincheev. http://www.mannerheim-line.com/veterans/Prusakov.htm.

Reese, Roger R. "Lessons of the Winter War: A Study in the Military Effectiveness of the Red Army, 1939–1940." *The Journal of Military History*, Vol. 72, No. 3 (Jul. 2008).

Roberts, Geoffrey. *Stalin's Wars from World War to Cold War, 1939–1953*. New Haven, CT: Yale University Press, 2006.

Sarvanto, Jorma. *Sex Fiendebombplan inom Fyra Minuter (Six Enemy Aircraft within Four Minutes)*. Arvet Efter Veteranerna — Ett Självständigt Fosterland 2002. http://www.veteraanienperinto.fi/svenska/Kertomukset/sotilas/sotilas/talvisota/luutnantti_sarvannon_taistelulen.htm.

Schmidt-Laussitz, Nicholas von. *Svenska Frivilliga (Swedish Volunteers)*. Svenska Frivilliga. http://www.svenskafrivilliga.com.

_____, and Schmidt-Laussitz, Klaus-Jürgen von. *För Finlands Frihet: Svenska Frivilligkåren, 1939–1940 (For the Liberation of Finland: The Swedish Volunteer Corps, 1939–1940)*. Hallstavik, Sweden: Svenskt Militärhistoriskt Bibliotek, 2008.

Scholander, Felicia. *Intervju Om Andra Världskriget med Lars Hallgren och Rut Scholander (Interview About the Second World War with Lars Hallgren and Rut Scholander)*. Levande Historia (Jan. 1, 2005). http://svefor.levandehistoria.se/1_0_1.php?id=4059.

Scott, Franklin D. *Sweden: The Nation's History*. Carbondale, IL: Southern Illinois University Press, 1988.

Silvervingar. *Beredskapstid, 1939–1945 (Military Preparedness, 1939–1945)*. http://www.silvervingar.se/Beredskapstid.html.

Simkin, John. *Britain and the Spanish Civil War*. Spartacus Educational. http://www.spartacus.schoolnet.co.uk/SPbritain.htm.

Sipovich, Capt., 100th Rifle Division, Battle of Summa. *Personal Diary*. Fire and Ice. http://www.wfyi.org/FireandIce/educational_resources/diaries_Sipovich.htm.

Sjöstedt, Jonas. "Halvfascistiskt Finland (Half-Fascist Finland)." *Ny Tid* (May 16, 2007).

Skoglund, Claes. "Sverige — Finland från Vikingatågen till Andra Världskriget (Sweden — Finland from the Vikings to the Second World War)." *Svenska Frivilliga i Finland 1939–1944 (Swedish Volunteers in Finland 1939–1944)*. Stockholm, Sweden: Militärhistoriska Förlaget, 1989.

Stokesbury, James L. *A Short History of World War II*. New York: HarperCollins, 1980.

Svensk Utrikespolitik Under Andra Världskriget (Swedish Foreign Policy During the Second World War). Stockholm, Sweden, 1946.

Svenska Frivilliga. *Den Grafströmska Raiden*

(The Grafström Raid). http://www.svenskafrivilliga.com/sfk3.html.

_____. *Jervants Patrull (Jervant's Patrol).* http://www.svenskafrivilliga.com/sfk4.html.

_____. *Marschen till Märkäjärvi (The March to Märkäjärvi).* http://www.svenskafrivilliga.com/sfk2a.html.

_____. *Preludium (Prelude).* http://www.svenskafrivilliga.com/sfk1.html.

_____. *Ryskt Anfall Väntas i Söder (Russian Attack Expected from the South).* http://www.svenskafrivilliga.com/sfk6a.html.

Svenskt Militärhistoriskt Bibliotek. Excerpt from *För Finlands Frihet: Svenska Frivilligkåren, 1939–1940 (For the Liberation of Finland: The Swedish Volunteer Corps, 1939–1940),* by Klaus-Jürgen von Schmidt-Laussitz and Nicolas von Schmidt-Laussitz. http://www.smb.nu/index.php/component/content/article/1241.

_____. *Svenskar på Östfronten (Swedes on the Eastern Front).* http://www.smb.nu/index.php/component/content/article/1241.

Swedish Military History Library. *Den Stora Urladdningen (The Great Discharge).* http://www.smb.nu/pos/06/01_europa_i_krig.asp.

Tanner, Väinö. *The Winter War: Finland Against Russia 1939–40.* Stanford, CA: Stanford University Press, 1957.

Time. "Darkening Up Here." *Time Magazine* (Mar. 4, 1940).

Treaty of Non-Aggression and Pacific Settlement of Disputes between the Soviet Union and Finland, concluded on January 21, 1932. Translation published in *The Major International Treaties 1914–1973,* by J.A.S. Grenville. London, UK: 1974.

Trotter, William. *A Frozen Hell: The Russo-Finnish Winter War of 1939–40.* Chapel Hill, NC: Algonquin Books of Chapel Hill, 2000.

Umgård, Anders. *De Flög för Nordens Frihet (They Flew for Nordic Independence).* Institution of History at Uppsala University, Sweden.

Vahlquist, Fredrik. "Vinterkriget — När Finlands Sak var Vår (The Winter War — When Finland's Cause Was Ours)." *Svenska Dagbladet* (Dec. 6, 2004).

Vasa Gymnasiet. *Om Motstånd och Kollaboration — Sverige Under 30- och 40-Talen: Tidningarna i Sverige Under Andra Världskriget (On Resistance and Collaboration — Sweden in the 30s and 40s: The Newspapers in Sweden During World War Two).* Arboga, Sweden.

Vehviläinen, Olli. *Finland in the Second World War: Between Germany and Russia.* New York: Palgrave Macmillan, 2002.

Veteraanien Perinto. *Luftstridskrafterna: Vinterkriget (The Air Force: The Winter War).* Arvet Efter Veteranerna — Ett Självständigt Fosterland 2002. http://www.veteraanienperinto.fi/svenska/t_pankki/a_lajit/lentajan_maailmanennatys.htm.

Villstrand, Nils Erik. *Källkritik — Ett Förflutenhetsöppnande Sesam (Source Critique — An Examination of the Past).* http://web.abo.fi/fak/hf/hist/kallkritik.pdf.

Vinterkriget. *Finska Vinterkrigets Historik (The History of the Finnish Winter War).* http://www.geocities.com/Eureka/Park/5121/historik.html.

_____. *Identitetskort (Identity Card).* http://www.geocities.com/Eureka/Park/5121/idkort.html.

Vizulis, Izidors. *The Molotov-Ribbentrop Pact of 1939: The Baltic Case.* New York: Praeger Publishers, 1990.

Völkischer Beobachter. "Kampfblatt der national-sozialistischen Bewegung Großdeutschlands (The combat newspaper of the national-socialist movement in Greater Germany)." Translated by Pauli Kruhse (Mar. 14, 1940). http://www.histdoc.net/history/VB1940-03-14.html.

Wahlbäck, Krister. *Finlandsfrågan i Svensk Politik 1937–1940 (The Finland Question in Swedish Politics 1937–1940).* Stockholm, Sweden: P. A. Norstedt & Söners Förlag, 1964.

Wangel, Carl-Axel. "Förstärkt Försvarsberedskap (Increased Defense Preparations)." *Sveriges Militära Beredskap, 1939–1945 (Sweden's Military Preparedness, 1939–1945).* Edited by Carl-Axel Wangel. Stockholm, Sweden: Militärhistoriska Förlaget, 1982.

_____. "Försvarsstabens Bedömningar Hösten 1939 (The Defense Establishment's Judgements in the Fall of 1939)." *Sveriges Militära Beredskap, 1939–1945 (Sweden's Military Preparedness, 1939–1945).* Edited by Carl-Axel Wangel. Stockholm, Sweden: Militärhistoriska Förlaget, 1982.

_____. "Neutralitetsrätt — Regler och Tillämpning (Right to Neutrality — Rules and Application)." *Sveriges Militära Beredskap, 1939–1945 (Sweden's Military Preparedness,*

1939–1945). Edited by Carl-Axel Wangel. Stockholm, Sweden: Militärhistoriska Förlaget, 1982.

Westberg, Lennart. *Marschen till Märkäjärvi (The March to Märkäjärvi)*. Solna, Sweden: Leandoer & Ekholm Förlag, originally published 1940.

The Winter War of 1939–1940: Telegrams from Each Day of the Winter War. Based on Markku Onttonen's Documentary Series *Talvisodan Henki (The Spirit of the Winter War)*. http://www.mil.fi/perustietoa/talvisota_eng/index.html.

Yrjö-Koskinen, A. S. Note of M. Yrjö-Koskinen, Finnish Minister at Moscow, handed on November 27th, 1939, to M. Molotov, Commissar for Foreign Affairs (Nov. 27, 1939).

Index

Numbers in ***bold italics*** indicate pages with photographs.